LATENT VARIABLE MODELING WITH R

This book demonstrates how to conduct latent variable modeling (LVM) in R by highlighting the features of each model, their specialized uses, examples, sample code and output, and an interpretation of the results. Each chapter features a detailed example including the analysis of the data using R, the relevant theory, the assumptions underlying the model, and other statistical details to help readers better understand the models and interpret the results. Every R command necessary for conducting the analyses is described along with the resulting output which provides readers with a template to follow when they apply the methods to their own data. The basic information pertinent to each model, the newest developments in these areas, and the relevant R code to use them are reviewed. Each chapter also features an introduction, summary, and suggested readings. A glossary of the text's boldfaced key terms and key R commands serve as helpful resources. The book is accompanied by a website with exercises, an answer key, and the in-text example data sets.

Latent Variable Modeling with R:

- Provides some examples that use messy data providing a more realistic situation readers will encounter with their own data.
- Reviews a wide range of LVMs including factor analysis, structural equation modeling, item response theory, and mixture models and advanced topics such as fitting nonlinear structural equation models, nonparametric item response theory models, and mixture regression models.
- Demonstrates how data simulation can help researchers better understand statistical methods and assist in selecting the necessary sample size prior to collecting data.
- www.routledge.com/9780415832458 provides exercises that apply the models along with annotated R output answer keys and the data that corresponds to the in-text examples so readers can replicate the results and check their work.

Intended for use in graduate or advanced undergraduate courses in latent variable modeling, factor analysis, structural equation modeling, item response theory, measurement, or multivariate statistics taught in psychology, education, human development, and social and health sciences, researchers in these fields also appreciate this book's practical approach. The book provides sufficient conceptual background information to serve as a standalone text. Familiarity with basic statistical concepts is assumed but basic knowledge of R is *not*.

Brian F. French is a Professor of Measurement, Statistics, and Research Methods at Washington State University. **W. Holmes Finch** is the George and Frances Ball Distinguished Professor of Educational Psychology and Professor of Statistics and Psychometrics at Ball State University.

LATENT VARIABLE MODELING WITH R

W. Holmes Finch, Jr.
Brian F. French

Routledge
Taylor & Francis Group

NEW YORK AND LONDON

First published 2015
by Routledge
711 Third Avenue, New York, NY 10017

and by Routledge
27 Church Road, Hove, East Sussex BN3 2FA

Routledge is an imprint of the Taylor & Francis Group, an informa business

© 2015 Taylor & Francis

Library of Congress Cataloging in Publication Data
Finch, W. Holmes (William Holmes)
   Latent variable modeling with R / authored by W. Holmes Finch, Jr. and Brian F. French.
      pages   cm
   Includes bibliographical references and index.
   1. Latent variables.   2. Latent structure analysis.   3. R (Computer program language)
   I. French, Brian F.   II. Title.
   QA278.6.F56 2015
   519.5'35–dc23
   2014049475

ISBN: 978-0-415-83244-1 (hbk)
ISBN: 978-0-415-83245-8 (pbk)
ISBN: 978-1-315-86979-7 (ebk)

Typeset in Times New Roman
by Out of House Publishing

Printed and bound in the United States of America by Edwards Brothers Malloy
on sustainably sourced paper.

HF: To Maria, my referent indicator.

BF: To Sarah, Elise, and Evan, the three paths that fit my life model well.

CONTENTS

Preface   xi
Acknowledgments   xv
About the authors   xvii

Chapter 1:   **Introduction to basic data handling in R**   **1**
                 Introduction   1
                 The R console and R scripts   1
                 R libraries   2
                 Reading data into R   3
                 Missing data   5
                 Types of data   6
                 R Commander and RStudio   7
                 Summary   8
                 Further reading   8
                 References   8

Chapter 2:   **Exploratory factor analysis**   **9**
                 Introduction   9
                 Exploratory factor analysis   10
                 Factor extraction   13
                 Factor rotation   13
                 Statistical methods for determining the optimal number of
                 factors   14
                 Fitting EFA models using `factanal`   17
                 Fitting EFA models using `fa`   27
                 Principal components analysis   33
                 Summary   34
                 Further reading   35
                 References   35

Chapter 3:	**Confirmatory factor analysis**	**37**
	Introduction	37
	Model parameter estimation	39
	Assessing model fit	40
	Fitting CFA models in R using `lavaan`	45
	Summary	56
	Further reading	56
	References	56
Chapter 4:	**Foundations of structural equation modeling**	**59**
	Introduction	59
	The importance of substantive theory in SEM	60
	Fitting the measurement model in R	62
	Fitting the structural model in R	65
	Fitting alternative SEMs	71
	Summary	81
	Further reading	82
	References	82
Chapter 5:	**SEM for multiple groups, the MIMIC model, and latent means comparisons**	**83**
	Introduction	83
	Multiple groups SEM	83
	Steps in assessing model invariance	85
	Multiple groups CFA with `lavaan`	87
	Comparison of latent means	95
	Multiple indicators multiple causes (MIMIC) model	101
	Summary	109
	Further reading	110
	References	110
Chapter 6:	**Further topics in SEM**	**112**
	Introduction	112
	Nonrecursive SEM	112
	Interactions in latent variable models	117
	Structural equation model trees	124
	Summary	131
	Further reading	132
	References	132
Chapter 7:	**Growth curve modeling**	**134**
	Introduction	134
	Growth curve models	135

Fitting linear growth curve models in R — 136
Fitting nonlinear growth curve models in R — 141
Including covariates in growth curve models — 143
Assessing change over time in multiple variables
simultaneously — 145
Summary — 150
Further reading — 150
References — 150

Chapter 8:   Mixture models   151
Introduction — 151
Latent class models — 151
Fitting a basic LCA in R — 154
Fitting an LCA model with covariates in R — 164
Fitting mixture regression models in R — 169
Summary — 175
Further reading — 176
References — 176

Chapter 9:   Item response theory for dichotomous and polytomous items   177
Introduction — 177
Classical test theory in R — 178
Dichotomous IRT — 180
Polytomous item response theory models — 217
Summary — 231
Further reading — 231
References — 231

Chapter 10:   Further topics in item response theory   233
Introduction — 233
Assessing unidimensionality — 233
Assessing local independence — 238
Fitting multidimensional models in R — 241
Bifactor model — 245
Differential item functioning — 247
Mokken scaling and nonparametric IRT modeling — 265
Kernel smoothing IRT — 272
Summary — 275
Further reading — 276
References — 276

Chapter 11:   Data simulation for latent variable modeling in R   279
Introduction — 279
Simulations for SEM — 280

Simulations for IRT   289
Simulations for LCA   295
Summary   297
Further reading   298
References   298

Appendix A: Key R commands   299
Glossary   310
Index   317

PREFACE

The purpose of this text is to provide an introduction to the use of R for latent variable modeling. The rise in popularity of the R software package over the last few years has brought with it a plethora of new functions for carrying out an ever increasing array of statistical analyses. Among these are functions to fit latent variable models in different contexts. Our purpose in writing this book was to provide applied examples of a variety of R functions to assist students, faculty, and researchers with engaging in latent variable modeling with R. This book is meant to be easily pulled off the shelf, opened to a specific topic of interest, and serve as a template for conducting the analysis. In addition, while not the focus of the book, we have also included basic explanations of the various models that are demonstrated, in order to provide context for the methods that we cover. We hope that this book will serve as a ready reference, allowing for quick access to R code for fitting latent variable models, and explanation of the resulting output produced by these R functions. We purposefully have attempted to encompass a very wide range of latent variable models so that the text can serve as something of a "one-stop shop" for individuals working in this area of statistics. At the same time, we recognize that a single book cannot cover every possible aspect of such a broad area as latent variable modeling.

CONTENT OVERVIEW

The book is organized into 11 chapters, each of which (except for the first) focuses on one particular latent variable model, or modeling paradigm. After the introductory chapter, which is designed as a brief primer on using R, Chapter 2 includes discussion of the exploratory factor analysis (EFA) model. We first differentiate EFA from confirmatory factor analysis (CFA), and then introduce major topics in the conduct of EFA including factor extraction, factor rotation, and methods for determining the number of factors. After this conceptual discussion, we include examples of using EFA in R, and finish the chapter with a discussion of principal components analysis. The focus of Chapter 3 is CFA. We provide technical discussion of model parameter estimation and model fit statistics before turning our attention to fitting CFA models using the `lavaan` package in R. Chapter 3 is a continuation of Chapter 2, building upon ideas in factor analysis, and rounding out the topic with the confirmatory factor model. Chapter 4 extends upon Chapter 3 by introducing the topic of structural equation modeling (SEM). Here we see how structural models can be used to link the factors that we learned about in the previous two chapters. Chapter 5 is designed to show the reader how to address the question of whether a CFA or SEM solution holds across multiple groups in the population. Thus, the models described in Chapters 3 and 4 are assessed in terms of their equivalence across two or more groups of individuals. These assessments can take the form of multiple groups CFA/SEM for invariance testing, as well as comparison of latent means on the factor of interest. The chapter finishes with a discussion of the multiple indicators multiple causes (MIMIC) model, which can be used for group mean comparison, as well as estimation of the relationship between observed covariates and a latent variable. Chapter 6 extends our coverage of topics in SEM, in particular describing nonrecursive models, and showing how the two-stage least squares estimation method can be used to fit this model. We also describe how moderated SEMs can be fit in R, through the inclusion of interaction terms for the latent variables. Chapter 6 finishes with a discussion of an extremely recent (as of this writing) development in SEM involving recursive partitioning algorithms as applied to latent variable models in the form of SEM trees. Chapter 7, which focuses on growth curve modeling, completes the set of chapters devoted to what we consider traditional SEM-related topics.

Chapter 8 is dedicated to mixture modeling using R, with sections covering latent class analysis (LCA), LCA with covariates, and mixture regression models. In each case, we provide the basic technical and conceptual underpinnings of mixture models, followed by a discussion of how these models are fit using R. Chapters 9 and 10 are dedicated to the important topic of item response theory (IRT), and approaches for modeling item response data. Chapter 9 includes descriptions of the primary parametric IRT models for dichotomous and polytomous data, as well as discussion of assessing model fit and comparing the fit of two models. Chapter 10 extends upon this foundation by describing assessment of the unidimensionality assumption underlying standard IRT models, using exploratory factor analysis for item responses, and investigation of local independence using Yen's Q_3 statistic. We then devote the bulk of the chapter to differential item functioning (DIF), which is an essential aspect of scale validation. Chapter 10 ends with demonstrations of two nonparametric approaches to dealing with item responses when samples are small, and/or assumptions underlying standard parametric IRT models can be assumed to hold. The book concludes with Chapter 11, which discusses data simulation for latent variable models using R. We show how data simulation can serve as a tool for statisticians to better understand the workings of a statistical method, and as a way to assist researchers in deciding on the necessary sample size prior to collecting data for a study involving latent variables (e.g. power analysis). The chapter includes a mixture of independently developed R code for this purpose, along with already available libraries for the simulation of latent models in R. We would encourage the reader to take the content of Chapter 11 and use it to simulate data that can then be analyzed using methods from some of the other chapters. Indeed, for most of the models described in Chapters 2 through 10, Chapter 11 provides the building blocks upon which simulated data could be developed and tested.

LEARNING TOOLS AND WEBSITE

We hope that you find reading this book as enjoyable and rewarding as we found writing it. We have attempted to provide you, the reader, with clear examples of R code and detailed descriptions of the resulting output so that when you apply the methods yourself, you will have a template to follow. We have included other items to facilitate learning such as a glossary of terms with bold key words in the chapters, recommended reading on each topic, and a set of key commands for each chapter in the appendix. In addition, we have made exercises and the associated answer key available online in order to provide students and others with opportunities for practicing with the code presented here. The example datasets used in the book are also available so that the reader can replicate the results. These supplementary materials are available at www.routledge.com/9780415832458.

ACKNOWLEDGMENTS

Writing a book is a major undertaking that could not be done without the help and support of a number of folks. In particular, we would like to thank Debra Riegert at Routledge/ /Taylor & Francis, who has worked with us from the conception of this project through to its completion. Without Debra's assistance, this book would not have come into existence. We would also like to thank our colleagues at Washington State and Ball State, respectively. They have been a source of interesting research problems that have forced us to continue expanding our statistical horizons by learning more. We are also grateful to the reviewers commissioned by Routledge/ /Taylor & Francis, who provided us with many excellent suggestions and recommendations at the beginning of this process: Natalie D. Eggum, Arizona State University; Brian Lawton, George Mason University; Patrick S. Malone, University of South Carolina; D. Betsy McCoach, University of Connecticut; and Ke-Hai Yuan, University of Notre Dame. Through their encouragement to include a wide variety of topics, they are in part responsible for what we hope you agree is the relatively broad scope of our book. Finally, we would like to thank the production staff at Routledge/ /Taylor & Francis, whose expertise made this book possible.

ABOUT THE AUTHORS

W. Holmes Finch, Jr. is the George and Frances Ball Distinguished Professor of Educational Psychology at Ball State University where he has been since 2003. He received his PhD from the University of South Carolina in 2002. Holmes teaches courses in factor analysis, structural equation modeling, categorical data analysis, regression, multivariate statistics, and measurement to graduate students in psychology and education. His research interests are in the areas of latent variable modeling, multilevel models, methods of prediction and classification, and nonparametric multivariate statistics. Holmes has published two books and over 100 peer-reviewed manuscripts, and made over 150 presentations at conferences. He has also served as the chair of the Educational Statisticians SIG and the Multiple Linear Regression SIG, both part of the American Educational Research Association.

Brian F. French is a Professor of Educational Psychology with an emphasis on measurement in the Department of Educational Leadership, Sports Studies, and Educational Counseling Psychology at Washington State University. Dr. French teaches measurement and quantitative methods courses on topics ranging from introduction to educational and psychological measurement to multilevel modeling and factor analysis. His research focuses on methods mainly related to test score validity, particularly the use of various statistical models to investigate measurement invariance. His work involves both application and empirical evaluation of methods.

Chapter 1

INTRODUCTION TO BASIC DATA HANDLING IN R

INTRODUCTION

The purpose of this chapter is to provide a simple introduction to using R for those readers not familiar with how R works or its environment. In addition, readers familiar with R but who would like a brief review of basic issues regarding data handling, variable creation, and so forth may find this chapter helpful. R is open source software, meaning that anyone is able to write functions and add to the software. The process for doing this is governed by a nonprofit organization housed in Vienna, Austria. More information can be found at http://cran.r-project.org/. In addition, R is freely available to users on a wide variety of computing platforms, most notably Windows, Macintosh OS, and Unix/Linux. Thus, R offers researchers a potentially valuable tool for conducting statistical analyses ranging from the most basic to complex, cutting-edge analyses employing sophisticated statistical models. The downside of the open source environment is that functions do change frequently, occasionally rendering commands that worked at one time inoperable. Nonetheless, we believe, and hope you will as well, that R is an extremely rich and fertile field on which to conduct data analysis for both statisticians and researchers in other fields using statistics to inform their work.

THE R CONSOLE AND R SCRIPTS

When working with R, commands are entered at the red > prompt on the screen, after which you will press the return key to execute a given command. In Figure 1.1 we can see an image of the basic R console. If we type in a command and would like to do it again, we can simply use the up and down arrow keys to cycle through all previous commands and find the one that we would like.

▪ **Figure 1.1:** R console

Using the console in this fashion can be very slow and laborious if we have many commands to implement simultaneously. In addition, the commands are not saved in a convenient location. Therefore, we may find it easier when programming in R to type our commands into the script editor that is a part of R itself, or into a simple word processing package such as Notepad in Windows or TextEdit in Mac OS. Regardless of platform, we can open the script editor using the menu sequence FILE>NEW SCRIPT, at which point an empty script window will open. We can then type commands in this window that we would submit to R. To submit the developed code to run in R, we simply select the portion that we would like to run and then click the submit icon (▣) in the menu. The code is automatically submitted to the R console. As an example, consider the basic script below in which we create a variable called `test.me` consisting of eight numbers, and then request its mean.

```
test.me<-c(5,4,7,4,9,6,10,1)
mean(test.me)
```

To execute these commands, we highlight the code in R and then click the submit icon displayed above. The R console then appears as in Figure 1.2.

R LIBRARIES

The R software consists of a main base package, containing many of the basic R functions that we will want to use. In addition, there are also a number of additional **libraries** which can be downloaded from the primary R website and installed on your local machine. We will use these for a number of our analyses in this book. In order to install these additional packages, we would simply use the following menu command sequence: PACKAGES>INSTALL PACKAGES. We may be asked to select a "mirror", which is simply a computer from which we

■ **Figure 1.2:** Simple command execution in the R console

download the package of interest. Generally speaking, any of the mirrors will be fine. Next, we see the window shown in Figure 1.3.

We would then scroll through the list and select the package that we wish to download. After clicking OK, the package will automatically download to our computer and be installed in the form of a library. Once a library is installed, we can access it simply by typing the `library` command. For example, the command `library(lavaan)` would install the `lavaan` library that we will use to conduct many of the structural equation modeling (SEM) or latent variable analyses in the following chapters. Once the library has been loaded, we then have access to the various functions contained therein. If help is required for a specific function, we type `help` with the name of the function between `()`. For example, if we would like help with the `cfa` function in `lavaan`, we simply type `help(cfa)`, and the help documentation will appear in our web browser.

READING DATA INTO R

In most situations, we will want to load our data into R in the form of a file from SPSS, Excel, or some other external format (e.g. .txt, .dat), rather than by entering individual data points as in the example above. One way to read in text files using R is with the `read.table` command. If the data file has variable names in the first row, we would use the `header=T` statement to indicate that the top row of values in the file contains variable names. For example, in Windows, if we wish to open a text file in the c:\ directory called test.txt which has the variable names in the first row, we could use the following command:

```
test <- read.table(c:\test.txt, header=T).
```

It is also possible in R to find the file with the familiar operating system dialogue box through the use of `file.choose`. This function opens a dialogue search window, thereby allowing us to browse until we find the file that we want. This is similar to searching or browsing for other files on our computers or uploading files

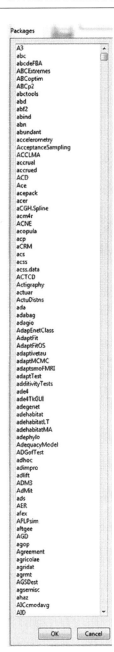

■ Figure 1.3: Package list to download from R

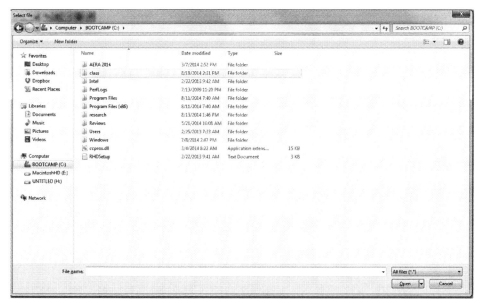

■ **Figure 1.4:** Dialogue box opened by `file.choose`

to websites. Thus an alternative approach for reading the test.txt file, using `file.choose`, would be:

```
test <- read.table(file.choose(), header=T)
```

This command opens the dialogue box shown in Figure 1.4.

Finally, through the `foreign` library, R provides the user with read commands for specific file types, such as comma delimited (`read.csv`), Excel (`read.xlsx`), and SPSS (`read.spss`) files, among others. The reader is encouraged to look at the help functions for these commands to learn more about the specifics of their use.

MISSING DATA

Missing data are common in research endeavors, and can prove to be problematic for some R functions. At the very least, the researcher using R must be cognizant of the presence of missing data in a file, and the need to properly handle it in R. Perhaps the most common method for dealing with missing data is simply to delete individual entries from the dataset which are missing values to be used in a given analysis. This can be done using the `na.omit` function in R. Missing data in R should be coded as "NA". The `na.omit` function removes all cases with the

"NA" code in a dataset. As an example, if we want a "clean" dataset including no observations with missing data, we could use the following command to create it:

```
test.nomiss<-na.omit(test)
```

We do want to point out that such listwise deletion is not often the optimal method for dealing with missing data, and that there exist in R a number of functions designed specifically for this purpose. These are, however, beyond the purview of this book to discuss. In addition, the reader should be aware that different R functions deal with missing data in different ways, so that it is of key importance to learn how a particular function will handle missing observations before using it. Again, we point the reader to the help function in R for a given package.

TYPES OF DATA

Each function in R is designed to handle data of specific types, and will not work properly if the data are of another type. Typically (though by no means always) data are either numeric or factor. One shorthand way to think of these is that numeric variables are treated as continuous, while factor variables are treated as categorical. There are greater complexities associated with these types than this simple heuristic would imply, but it serves as a good starting point for our consideration of data types. When data are read into R, numbers will be assumed to be numeric and characters (e.g. letters) will be treated as factors. Generally speaking, this works well for the latter but not always for the former. As an example, if we have a variable indicating the gender of a subject, with males coded as 1 and females as 2, we may want to convert this numeric variable to a factor for use with various statistical analyses. If we leave the data as is, gender will be treated as numeric. This conversion is carried out easily using the `as.factor` function, as follows:

```
gender.factor<-as.factor(gender)
```

The variable `gender.factor` would then be treated as a categorical, or factor, variable. We can also convert a variable to numeric if for some reason it is not. For example, if the variable `age` was read in as a list, rather than numeric, we can use the `as.numeric` function as follows:

```
age.numeric<- as.numeric(age)
```

A final point to note here is that, as with missing data, different functions have different requirements and conventions when it comes to the types of variables that they expect to see. Therefore, it is important to read the documentation for a particular function in order to determine whether a factor is required or not.

R COMMANDER AND RSTUDIO

R software programmers have developed graphical user interfaces (GUIs) for the purpose of making interaction with R somewhat easier. In particular, both **R Commander** and RStudio have automated much of the reading in of external data files, as well as some basic statistical analyses through their menu options. The interested reader is encouraged to learn more about these tools.

R Commander is installed in the same manner as any library in R and then called through the command `library(Rcmdr)`. Readers may find it particularly helpful when it comes to reading in data from external files, and for having a menu option to conduct some basic analyses and use basic graphical tools. After loading R Commander, the window shown in Figure 1.5 will appear.

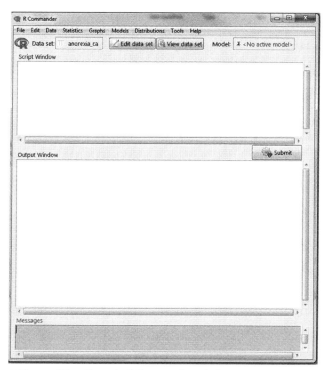

■ **Figure 1.5:** Example R Commander window

R program commands can be written in the Script Window, and output will appear in the Output Window. Errors and other messages to the user will appear in the Messages window. R Commander may prove to be a useful tool, making the transition to R for new users a little easier.

RStudio is an integrated development environment (IDE) providing a more sophisticated set of options for the user compared to R Commander. It can be obtained from the third-party website http://www.rstudio.com/. RStudio is, like R, an open source and freely available program for Macintosh OS, Windows, and Linux. The RStudio interface includes a syntax window, a list of available objects in the workspace, a help window, the files and folders in a selected directory, plots, and packages. This interface is more complex than R Commander, making it perhaps less ideal for users new to R. However, it does present the user with a number of useful tools available all in one location, and may be particularly helpful for the researcher already familiar with the R environment.

SUMMARY

The purpose of this chapter is to introduce the reader new to R to some basic ideas about how to navigate within the new program framework. It is by no means a comprehensive review of this topic, nor is it intended to be the only resource the reader new to R may need for this purpose. However, there are a number of quite useful references available for those wanting to learn more about how to use R and basic statistical analysis with R (e.g., Crawley, 2013; Field, Miles, & Field, 2012). Nonetheless, we hope that what is provided here is sufficient to get you started as we move forward into the conduct of latent variable analyses with R.

FURTHER READING

Crawley, M.J. (2013). *The R Book*. Chichester, West Sussex, UK: John Wiley & Sons, Ltd.

Field, A., Miles, J., & Field, Z. (2012). *Discovering Statistics using R*. Los Angeles: Sage.

Spector, P. (2008). *Data Manipulation with R*. New York: Springer.

REFERENCES

Crawley, M.J. (2013). *The R Book* (2nd ed.).Hoboken, NJ: Wiley.

Field, A., Miles, J., & Field, Z. (2012). *Discovering Statistics using R*. Thousand Oaks, CA: Sage.

Chapter 2

EXPLORATORY FACTOR ANALYSIS

INTRODUCTION

Factor analysis is certainly one of the most widely used statistical techniques in the social and behavioral sciences. Researchers use this latent variable modeling approach to gain insights into a wide variety of constructs, including intelligence, personality, academic achievement and aptitude, mental illness, social phobias, and anxiety, to name a few. Factor analysis can best be understood as a latent variable modeling paradigm in which a set of observed variables are the indicators of a latent variable. In this schema, the latent variable (e.g. intelligence) is of primary interest, but cannot be directly observed. However, it is theorized that the latent variable has a direct influence on each of the observed indicators (e.g. items on a scale, subscales in a battery of measures), so that they can in turn be used to gain insights into the latent variable. This idea is at the core of educational and psychological measurement of abilities.

Factor analysis is typically described as consisting of two broad types: exploratory (EFA) and confirmatory (CFA). We will learn about each of these, and in particular how to conduct each of these analyses using R. We handle EFA in this chapter and provide information in general about CFA; the technical details and R code for CFA are covered in Chapter 3. The two types of factor analysis are differentiated by the degree of a priori structure that is assumed and then specified by the researcher. For example, in the context of EFA, the researcher does not impose a specific latent structure on the observed indicators, but rather allows the optimal number of factors to be determined based on several statistical and interpretability criteria (e.g. Bandalos & Finney, 2010). This does not mean that the researcher has no preconceptions about the number or nature of the number of factors or the underlying latent structure. Indeed, it is generally best if some prior notions of the latent structure are used to assist in reaching the ultimate goal of the analysis: interpretability. However, the researcher does not explicitly link an indicator with a factor, but rather relies on the factor algorithm and set criteria to identify the optimal structure. In contrast to EFA, with CFA the researcher explicitly links the indicators with the factors to which they theoretically belong. This model specification or proposed model is then examined for model–data fit. This issue is discussed in detail later in the chapter. As is generally recommended, multiple factor models based in substantive theories are compared to one another based on a variety of statistical and theoretical criteria. The model that provides both the best statistical fit and the strongest theoretical interpretation is then selected as optimal. In this chapter, we only deal with the statistical components of this process, as the theoretical issues lie within the realm of the area of research.

Given the differences in how EFA and CFA are conceived statistically, we can consider when each is most appropriate for use. When the researcher has a definite theory regarding the latent variables and their relationships to the observed indicators, then CFA is the most appropriate technique to use. It allows for multiple models to be compared with one another, and accommodates the definition of specific structure in the data. On the other hand, use of CFA also requires the researcher to have a strong theory that has been vetted in the literature and that has already received some empirical support, either in the form of EFA or CFA in prior research. Without such theoretical and empirical evidence, CFA may not be appropriate. Conversely, when the theory is not as strong, and/or relatively little empirical evidence exists regarding the construct, EFA may be most appropriate. EFA places a relatively small burden on the researcher regarding the expected nature of the latent constructs and their relationships with the observed indicators. At the same time, the researcher can have some general notions regarding the nature of the latent structure, including how many factors are expected and which variables should be associated with which of these factors. However, no a priori determination of these relationships is required. In the following pages, we will explore the modeling of indicators in the EFA framework using R. We also will learn how to interpret the results from such an analysis.

EXPLORATORY FACTOR ANALYSIS

To begin, let us consider an example in which a researcher has collected data on achievement goal orientation using the 12-item Likert achievement goal scale (AGS). Each item has seven options ranging from "not at all like me" to "very true of me". The items appear below.

AGS1 = My goal is to completely master the material presented in my classes. (MAP)

AGS2 = I want to avoid learning less than it is possible to learn. (MAV)

AGS3 = It is important for me to do better than other students. (PAP)

AGS4 = I want to avoid performing poorly compared to others. (PAV)

AGS5 = I want to learn as much as possible. (MAP)

AGS6 = It is important for me to avoid an incomplete understanding of the course material. (MAV)

AGS7 = It is important for me to understand the content of my courses as thoroughly as possible. (MAP)

AGS8 = My goal is to avoid performing worse than other students. (PAV)

AGS9 = I want to do well compared to other students. (PAP)

AGS10 = It is important for me to avoid doing poorly compared to other students. (PAV)

AGS11 = My goal is to perform better than the other students. (PAP)

AGS12 = My goal is to avoid learning less than I possibly could. (MAV)

The researcher would like to investigate the latent structure of achievement goal orientation, using the responses to these 12 items from 430 college students. The theory underlying the AGS states that there exist four distinct latent traits: mastery approach (MAP), mastery avoidant (MAV), performance approach (PAP), and performance avoidant (PAV). Very briefly, mastery goal orientation means that an individual is interested in new material to be learned for its own sake, while performance goal orientation means that an individual is interested in new material to be learned based on how it will make them appear to others. Thus, learners with high MAP scores will be interested in gaining mastery over new material because they want to learn as much as possible about the subject. Conversely, those with high MAV scores will want to avoid not learning about new things; i.e. won't want to miss an opportunity to learn. In contrast, students with high PAP scores will want to learn new material in order to appear smart to their parents, friends, and teachers, whereas those with high PAV scores will want to learn new material in order to avoid looking less than smart to the important people in their lives. In parentheses at the end of each item is the latent trait to which the item theoretically belongs.

Although the designers of the AGS presumed that their four-factor structure was appropriate, this may not be the case. Indeed, other researchers have proposed that in actuality achievement goal orientation consists of three latent variables: mastery (MAV and MAP together), PAP, and PAV, while still others suggest that perhaps only two latent variables actually exist: mastery (MAV and MAP together) and performance (PAP and PAV together). If there is little empirical evidence in this area clearly supporting one theory over another, then the researcher may select EFA, rather than CFA, to begin to understand the underlying latent structure. In this case, there are definite ideas about the possible latent structure underlying achievement goal orientation, but there is not definitive empirical evidence supporting any one of them.

The factor model underlying the four latent variable structure is:

$$y = \Lambda\eta + \varepsilon, \tag{2.1}$$

where

y = Observed indicator variables

η = Factors, i.e. MAV, MAP, PAP, PAV

Λ = Factor pattern coefficients (i.e. loadings) linking observed indicators with factors

ε = Unique variances for the indicators, i.e. variance in the observed variables that is not associated with the factors.

In this model, we assume that ε for a given indicator variable is independent of the ε for all other indicators, and independent of η. In addition, each indicator will have a **factor loading** associated with each factor. These loadings reflect the relationships between the factors and the indicators, with larger values being indicative of a closer association between a latent and observed variable. In general, loadings range between -1 and 1, much like correlation coefficients, though in some specific instances this will not be the case. The factor model in (2.1) can be used to predict the correlation (or covariance) matrix of the indicator variables as expressed in (2.2):

$$\Sigma = \Lambda\Psi\Lambda' + \Theta, \tag{2.2}$$

where

Σ = Model-predicted correlation matrix of the indicators

Ψ = Correlation matrix for the factors

Θ = Diagonal matrix of unique error variances.

EFA consists of two primary steps: (1) factor extraction, and (2) factor rotation. These steps are carried out by the software simultaneously, but the researcher must make decisions regarding the method to use for each. Factor extraction involves the initial estimation of model parameters, in particular the loadings, given the data at hand. There are potentially as many factors as there are observed indicators in the data. Thus, for 12 items there are 12 possible factors that could be extracted. However, given that the goal of EFA is to identify a latent structure present in the data whereby a small number of latent variables account for values of the observed indicators, in practice a small number of factors will actually be retained. Below, we will discuss methods for determining the number of factors to retain.

FACTOR EXTRACTION

A number of factor extraction methods are available, with the most popular probably being maximum likelihood (ML) and principal axis factoring (PAF). Other EFA extraction methods that are available, though used less frequently than ML and PAF, are generalized least squares, unweighted least squares, weighted least squares, alpha factoring, and image factoring, to name a few. Whichever method is used, the algorithm seeks to find estimates of factor loadings that will yield Σ as close as possible to the observed correlation matrix, S, among the indicators. Indeed, ML extraction uses the proximity of Σ and S to form a test statistic for evaluating the quality of a factor solution, which we will discuss below. Though ML has the advantage of providing a direct assessment of model fit, it also rests on an assumption of multivariate normality of the observed indicators. When this assumption is violated, model parameter estimates may not be accurate, and in some cases the algorithm will not be able to find a solution (Brown, 2015; Fabrigar & Wegener, 2011). PAF does not rely on distributional assumptions about the indicators, and thus may be particularly attractive to use when the data are not normally distributed. However, it does not provide a statistical test of model fit.

FACTOR ROTATION

An important aspect of EFA that must be understood is that when there exist more than one factor, the model identified in the extraction step is indeterminate in nature. This means that there are an infinite number of factor loading combinations that will yield the same mathematical fit to the data; i.e. the same Σ. This leads to the question of how we determine which factor loading solution is optimal for our purposes? This determination is made using **factor rotation**, which refers to the transformation of the initial set of factor loadings so as to simplify interpretation of the results by seeking a simple structure solution. Thurstone (1947) defined **simple structure** as occurring when two conditions are met. First, each latent variable or factor has associated with it a subset of the indicator variables with which it is highly associated (i.e. large loadings). Second, each indicator is highly associated with only one factor and has loadings near zero on the other factors. Rotation simply adjusts all of the loadings in order to approximate this goal of simple structure. Rotation does not alter the underlying fit of the model, so that the values of Σ for the unrotated and rotated solutions are exactly the same. Thought of differently, the variance in the observed indicators that is accounted for by the factor model does not change. Only the values of the loadings are changed in an attempt to achieve Thurstone's simple structure, in order to make interpretation of the results easier.

Factor rotation methods are generally described as being in one of two broad families, orthogonal and oblique. Orthogonal rotations constrain the correlations among factors to be zero, whereas oblique rotations allow the factors to be correlated. Within both broad rotational families there exist many varieties, differing based upon the criterion used to transform the data. As with methods of estimation, no one approach is always optimal, but perhaps the most popular orthogonal rotation method is VARIMAX, while among the oblique rotations PROMAX and OBLIMIN are popular. The decision as to whether to use an orthogonal or oblique rotation should be based on both theoretical and empirical grounds. If the researcher anticipates that the factors will be correlated, then she should begin the analysis using an oblique rotation such as PROMAX. If the resulting correlations are small (e.g. close to zero), then the model can be reestimated using an orthogonal rotation. On the other hand, if the researcher feels that the correlations among factors should be constrained to zero for some theoretical reason, then she may only use the orthogonal rotation from the beginning. However, it should be noted that if the factors are in fact correlated but an orthogonal rotation is used, the resulting factor loadings may be adversely affected, with the potential for a number of cross loadings (variables having relatively large loadings with more than one factor) to be present.

STATISTICAL METHODS FOR DETERMINING THE OPTIMAL NUMBER OF FACTORS

Several potential solutions (i.e. number of factors) are typically investigated and then compared with one another as there is general uncertainty regarding the number of factors present. How then does the researcher decide on the final solution? There are a number of approaches, some of which have been shown to work better than others, but none of which have been shown to be optimal in all cases. One of the earliest, and most popular, approaches for determining the number of factors is the eigenvalue greater than 1 criterion, also sometimes referred to as Kaiser's Little Jiffy, in honor of its progenitor (Fabrigar & Wegener, 2011; Kaiser, 1960; Pett, Lackey, & Sullivan, 2003). This method utilizes the eigenvalues that are associated with each of the factors, and retains those with values larger than 1. The rationale behind this method is based upon the fact that an eigenvalue reflects the variance associated with a factor. When the observed indicator variables are standardized, they each have a variance of 1. Thus, factors with eigenvalues larger than 1 account for more variance in the data than any one observed variable. However, while simple and somewhat intuitive, this method for determining the number of factors to retain has been found to frequently yield solutions that are too complex, i.e. it retains too many factors (Pett, Lackey, & Sullivan, 2003).

An approach for determining the optimal EFA solution that is related to the eigenvalue greater than 1 method is the Scree plot. This is simply a scatterplot with the eigenvalue on the y-axis and the factor number on the x-axis, and with the relationship between the two variables decreasing; i.e. earlier factors have larger eigenvalues than later ones. The researcher using this approach examines the plot, looking for the point where a line connecting the eigenvalues begins to flatten out in its rate of decline. A third descriptive approach for determining the number of factors to retain that relies on the eigenvalues involves an examination of the proportion of variation in the entire set of observed indicators that is accounted for by each factor, and by a set of factors as a whole. There are no hard and fast rules regarding what constitutes a sufficient amount of variance accounted for in the solution. However, as with the Scree plot, the researcher would examine the proportions and attempt to ascertain at what point including more factors in the solution does not yield an appreciable increase in the overall proportion of explained variance. An additional descriptive tool for determining the number of factors involves an examination of the residual correlation matrix for the observed indicators. Recall that the factor analysis algorithm seeks to identify model parameters (i.e. loadings) that will yield a predicted covariance (or correlation) matrix as similar to the actual such matrix as possible. Thus, one tool that might prove useful in ascertaining whether an EFA solution is a good fit to the data is the matrix of residual correlations (difference between the observed and model-predicted correlations) for the indicators. By convention, residuals larger than 0.05 are considered to be too large, so that a good solution is one which produces few residual correlations greater than 0.05 in absolute value.

While the four methods described above are descriptive in nature, there are also inferential methods for determining the number of factors to retain in an EFA. In particular, when ML is used for factor extraction, a chi-square test can be constructed comparing the relative fit of differing factor solutions. As noted above, results from ML extraction can be used to compare the relative proximity of Σ and S in the form of a chi-square goodness of fit test. The null hypothesis of this test is that Σ = S. Unfortunately, such a perfect fit is rarely achieved, even for sample models that are reasonably close to the population-generating model. Therefore, in many cases the null hypothesis will be rejected, leading the researcher to conclude that the model does not provide a good fit to the data, when in fact the proposed model does provide a reasonably good data model fit. Thus, this test is not particularly useful for assessing the fit of an individual model, and in fact when the sample size is large one could end up with too many factors (Kim & Muller, 1978).

A second inferential approach for factor retention decisions is parallel analysis, which was first described by Horn (1965). Parallel analysis consists of the following steps:

1. Fit an EFA to the original dataset and retain the eigenvalues for each factor.
2. Generate observed data with marginal characteristics identical to the observed data (i.e. same means and standard deviations), but with uncorrelated indicators, either by randomly sorting the values of the observed indicators or by simulating such data.
3. Fit an EFA to the generated data and retain the eigenvalues for each factor.
4. Repeat steps 2 and 3 many (e.g. 1000) times in order to develop distributions for each eigenvalue under the case where indicators are not related to one another.
5. Compare the observed eigenvalue for the first factor with the 95th percentile of the distribution of first factor eigenvalues from the generated data. If the observed value is greater than or equal to the 95th percentile value, conclude that at minimum one factor should be retained, and continue to step 6. If the observed value is less than the 95th percentile then stop and conclude that there exist no common factors.
6. Compare the observed eigenvalue for each successive factor with the 95th percentile for the corresponding eigenvalue distribution of the generated data. If the observed value is greater than or equal to the 95th percentile, retain that factor (e.g. the second factor, the third factor, etc.), and move to the next factor in line. This process stops when the observed eigenvalue is less than the 95th percentile of the generated data.

Parallel analysis in EFA, while by no means perfect, is frequently more accurate compared to other approaches that are commonly used (Fabrigar & Wegener, 2011). However, as noted above, no single approach, including parallel analysis, is always optimal. Therefore, we recommend that the researcher use several approaches for determining the number of factors in an attempt to build a case for a final number to retain. These criteria should be stated prior to the beginning of the analysis.

FITTING EFA MODELS USING FACTANAL

Now that we have discussed the basics of EFA, it is time to turn our attention to fitting the model using R. Remember that our example involves a 12-item scale designed to measure achievement motivation. The original developers of the scale hypothesized the presence of four factors (MAV, MAP, PAV, PAP), with later researchers suggesting that perhaps three (Mastery, PAV, PAP) or even two factors (Mastery, Performance) are more appropriate. One popular approach for fitting ML-based EFA uses the factanal command, which is part of the basic statistics library in R, and thus does not require the installation of a special library. The R code for fitting the initial four-factor EFA solution using factanal appears below.

```
attach(performance.data)
achievement.goal.efa.results4<-factanal(~ags1+ags2
  +ags3+ags4+ags5+ags6+ags7+ags8+ags9+ags10+ags11+
  ags12, factors=4, rotation="promax")
achievement.goal.efa.results4
```

In the first line we attach the data file of interest, performance.data, so that in subsequent commands we can reference its variables. We then name the R object that will contain the output for the EFA including four factors. This name can be anything we like, and should reflect the analysis that produced it. Within the parentheses we include the indicator variables following ~. We then indicate the number of factors to retain (four in this case), and the type of rotation that we would like to use. The default method of factor extraction in factanal is ML, and in this analysis we used promax rotation. By typing the name of the output object, achievement.goal.efa.results4, we can obtain the EFA output, which appears below.

```
Call:
factanal(x = ~ags1 + ags2 + ags3 + ags4 + ags5 + ags6 +
  ags7 + ags8 + ags9 + ags10 + ags11 + ags12, factors = 4,
  rotation = "promax")
Uniquenesses:
ags1 ags2 ags3 ags4 ags5 ags6 ags7 ags8 ags9 ags10 ags11 ags12
0.487 0.335 0.279 0.342 0.557 0.388 0.104 0.005 0.231 0.201
  0.300 0.306
```

```
Loadings:
        Factor1  Factor2  Factor3  Factor4
ags1             0.667
ags2                               0.844
ags3   0.864
ags4   0.793             0.104    -0.116
ags5             0.565   0.123
ags6             0.764
ags7             1.023  -0.120
ags8   0.756                       0.583
ags9   0.884
ags10  0.866                       0.143
ags11  0.799                       0.195
ags12                    0.833

                Factor1  Factor2  Factor3  Factor4
SS loadings     4.122    2.404    1.461    0.426
Proportion Var  0.344    0.200    0.122    0.036
Cumulative Var  0.344    0.544    0.666    0.701

Factor Correlations:
         Factor1  Factor2  Factor3   Factor4
Factor1  1.0000   0.0919  -0.08477   0.20174
Factor2  0.0919   1.0000   0.18936   0.66077
Factor3 -0.0848   0.1894   1.00000  -0.00277
Factor4  0.2017   0.660   -0.00277   1.00000

Test of the hypothesis that 4 factors are sufficient.
The chi square statistic is 77.4 on 24 degrees of freedom.
The p-value is 1.57e-07
```

The first portion of the EFA results includes the function call, reflecting what we asked R to do. A good habit to form is to check the call to be sure that R conducted the analysis in the manner that you intended. After the function call, R next presents the uniquenesses for each of the variables. These correspond to the unique variances in equations (2.1) and (2.2), and reflect the proportion of variance in the indicators that are not explained by the factors. Thus, for example, approximately 48.7% of the variance in item ags1 is not associated with the four retained factors. We can also use the uniqueness values to estimate the proportion of variance in each indicator associated with the factors themselves. This value, which is called the communality, is calculated as 1-uniqueness. In R the command to calculate the communalities is:

```
1-achievement.goal.efa.results4$uniquenesses
ags1    ags2    ags3    ags4    ags5    ags6    ags7    ags8    ags9
0.5134  0.6649  0.7214  0.6583  0.4425  0.6123  0.8956  0.9950  0.7693
ags10   ags11   ags12
0.7992  0.7001  0.6938
```

Thus, approximately 51% of the variance in ags1 is associated with the four factors, compared to 99.5% of the factor accounted for variance in ags8.

Following the uniquenesses, the output next contains the factor loadings. R leaves loadings with absolute values less than 0.1 blank in the output. From these results, we can see that items ags3, ags4, ags8, ags9, ags10, and ags11 were all associated with (loaded on) factor 1. Factor 2 was associated with items ags1, ags5, ags6, and ags7. Items ags2 and ags12 loaded on factor 3, and item ags8 loaded on factor 4. Note that this last result means that ags8 is cross loaded on two factors. An examination of these results suggests that they do not conform to the expected four-factor solution. For example, factor 1 includes six items representing a mix of PAP and PAV. Factor 2 includes four mastery items, three of which are associated with the theoretical MAP latent trait. Factor 3 is associated with two MAV items, and factor 4 includes the cross-loaded item that is associated with the theoretical PAV factor.

To ascertain the proportion of variance explained by each factor, we can refer to the table that includes the sum of squared loadings for each factor (SS loadings). These are the sum of the squared loadings for each factor, and represent the variance in the observed indicators associated with that factor. Larger values indicate greater variance accounted for. The next row in the table presents the proportion of variance accounted for by each factor across all of the possible factors that can be extracted. Thus, since there are 12 indicators there are 12 potential factors to be extracted. The values appearing in the second row of the table reflect the proportion of variance in the observed variables associated with each factor, out of the 12 total factors possible. Factor 1 accounts for 34.4% of the variance present in the items, with factor 2 associated with another 20%, factor 3 with 12.2%, and factor 4 with 3.6%. Together, the four factors accounted for 70.1% of the variance in the 12 items.

The factor correlations appear directly below the table containing proportion of variance explained by the factors. The relationships among these factors are fairly low, with the exception of factors 2 and 4, which were correlated at 0.66. Finally, the chi-square goodness of fit test is the last portion of the output from factanal. For this model, the chi-square was 77.4 with 24 degrees of freedom, and a p-value of 0.000000157. This value is well below our α of 0.05, leading us to reject the null hypothesis that the model adequately fits the data.

Based on the factor loadings, it does not appear that the four-factor solution proposed by the designers of the achievement motivation instrument matches with the data at hand. Therefore, we will want to investigate other solutions with perhaps fewer factors. In addition, however, we also need to examine the indices that provide us with information regarding the number of factors to retain based solely on statistical grounds. Recall that the determination of the adequacy of the EFA factor solution involves both conceptual and statistical considerations regarding which items group together to form interpretable factors. Some of these model fit assessments are a part of the standard output from `factanal`, including the proportion of variance accounted for by each factor and the factors as a whole, as well as the chi-square goodness of fit test. Based on these statistics, we would conclude that four factors does explain a large proportion of the variance in the items, but that the covariance matrix predicted by the four-factor model is not statistically equivalent to the observed covariance matrix among the items. However, it is important to remember that this test is highly influenced by the sample size. Thus, we turn to parallel analysis for additional information. This approach can be employed in R using a function within the `psych` library, which you need to install. Once this installation is complete, the commands for requesting a parallel analysis from R, and the resulting output, appear below.

```
library(psych)
fa.parallel(performance.data, fa="fa", fm="ml")
Parallel analysis suggests that the number of factors = 3 and
the number of components = 2
```

In this command, we must specify the dataset to be analyzed (`performance.data`), and we have the option of asking for parallel analysis results based on principal components analysis, factor analysis, or both. The default in R is both, but in this instance we request only those results from factor analysis since we are not performing a principal components analysis. Finally, we have the option of selecting the method for factor extraction to be used. The default is principal axis factoring, but given that the prior analysis was conducted using ML extraction, we will examine ML-extracted parallel analysis results. After completing the analysis, R responds with a message telling us for how many factors the observed eigenvalues were greater than those from the generated data. In this case the answer is three factors. The parallel analysis plot automatically resulting from this R function appears in Figure 2.1.

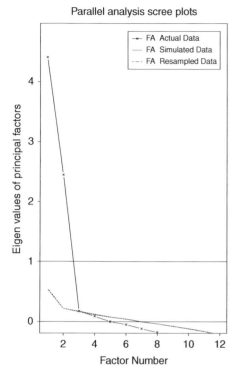

Parallel analysis scree plots

■ Figure 2.1: Parallel analysis results for EFA solution of performance data

The *x*-axis contains the factor number, and *y*-axis contains the eigenvalues. The solid line represents the eigenvalues from the observed data, and the dotted line represents eigenvalues from data that were generated by the computer (FA Simulated Data) to have characteristics (i.e. means and variances) like those of the real data, but with no correlations among the observed indicators (i.e. no underlying structure). The dashed line represents the eigenvalues for the data generated when scores from individuals in the original sample are mixed up with one another. Using this method, the computer might take the value of ags2 for person 1 and replace it with the ags2 value for person 97, and the ags2 value for person 97 might be replaced by the value for person 14, and so on. By mixing the variable values around among the individuals, the marginal statistics (means and standard deviations) remain equal to those in the original data, but the correlations among the variables are made to be essentially zero, given that the variables are now randomly ordered. Both approaches for generating the uncorrelated data worked very similarly here, as is evidenced by the nearly complete overlapping of the dashed and dotted lines. Examining this plot reveals precisely what R told us in the message, that three factors should be retained.

In addition to the ML goodness of fit chi-square test, the proportion of variance explained by each factor, and parallel analysis, recall that two other methods for ascertaining the number of factors to retain were Kaiser's Little Jiffy and the Scree plot. While we include these methods in the book for the sake of completeness, we do not recommend their use for determining the number of factors to extract, based upon prior research demonstrating problems associated with them. In order to obtain the eigenvalues with R we will use the following commands.

```
performance.eigenvalues<-eigen(cor(performance.
data, use="complete"))
performance.eigenvalues
$values
 [1] 4.7369260 3.3822029 0.9206686 0.5715372 0.4891213 0.4140819
 0.3413789 0.3162146 0.2605112
[10] 0.2229983 0.1953569 0.1490022
```

The subcommand use="complete" ensures that only complete data cases are used. Otherwise, the cor command will not yield results for us. This is precisely identical to the listwise deletion approach that is used by the factor analysis algorithm. We then type the name of the output file in order to see the eigenvalues. Based on the rule for using eigenvalues that was described previously, these results would suggest that we retain two factors, as only two have eigenvalues greater than 1. We can create a Scree plot of these eigenvalues using functions from the nFactors library in R. Specifically, the following command will create the Scree plot for us. In particular, note that the eigenvalues that we obtained from the correlation matrix are extracted from the performance.eigenvalues output object and then submitted to the functions nScree and plotnScree, with the option model="factors" to indicate that we are interested in results for a factor analysis and not a principal components analysis.

```
plotnScree(nScree(x=performance.eigenvalues$values,
model="factors"))
```

The resulting plot appears in Figure 2.2.

It appears that the line flattens at the fourth eigenvalue, suggesting that there are three factors present in the data. In addition to the standard descriptive approach for interpreting the Scree plot, the plotnScree function also provides the user with descriptive indicators regarding the number of factors to retain. The first of these, titled Eigenvalues (>mean), is simply the eigenvalue greater than 1 rule, as the mean of the eigenvalues will be 1 when the correlation matrix is used to obtain

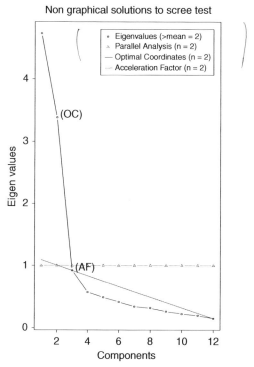

Non graphical solutions to scree test

■ **Figure 2.2:** Scree plot for performance data

the eigenvalues. In this example, the result matches with our own examination of the eigenvalues, suggesting that two factors should be retained. The second method used to indicate the number factors to retain is parallel analysis, which was already described above. The Optimal Coordinates approach to interpreting the Scree plot is described in Raîche *et al.* (2013). Briefly, this method examines individual regression lines linking the last eigenvalue to each of the other eigenvalues in an attempt to find where the Scree plot line bends. For each eigenvalue other than the last one, a predicted eigenvalue is obtained using regression. The last factor that should be retained corresponds to the one that has an eigenvalue greater than or equal to the one predicted by the regression equation. In this example, factor 2 is the last such eigenvalue, and thus only two factors would be retained based on this method. Finally, the Acceleration Factor approach (Yakovitz & Szidarovszky, 1986) is designed to identify where the slope of the curve in the Scree plot changes abruptly. This rate of change in the direction of the line is known as the acceleration factor, and can be estimated using the second derivative of the line. The number of factors to retain corresponds to the eigenvalue that immediately precedes the maximum value of the acceleration factor, i.e. the point in the line right before the largest change in direction. As with the other approaches, this method indicates that two factors should be retained.

Based on the conceptual concerns associated with the initial factor extraction results, as well as the various statistical indicators suggesting that either two or three factors might be more appropriate, we will fit EFA models with two and three factors using the `factanal` command to obtain ML-based solutions. We will then investigate the use of another function for fitting an EFA model in R that allows for more flexible choices regarding the methods of extraction and rotation. The three-factor EFA solution can be obtained using the `factanal` command below.

```
achievement.goal.efa.results3<-factanal(~ags1+ags
  2+ags3+ags4+ags5+ags6+ags7+ags8+ags9+ags10+ags1
  1+ags12, factors=3, rotation="promax")

achievement.goal.efa.results3

Call:
factanal(x = ~ags1 + ags2 + ags3 + ags4 + ags5 + ags6 + ags7 +ags8
+ ags9 + ags10 + ags11 + ags12, factors = 3, rotation = "promax")

Uniquenesses:
ags1 ags2 ags3 ags4 ags5 ags6 ags7 ags8 ags9 ags10 ags11 ags12
0.482 0.424 0.313 0.402 0.558 0.385 0.120 0.266 0.251 0.188 0.297 0.200

Loadings:
       Factor1    Factor2    Factor3
ags1              0.677
ags2                         0.714
ags3   0.841                -0.110
ags4   0.761
ags5              0.602
ags6              0.764
ags7              0.999     -0.101
ags8   0.832     -0.126      0.138
ags9   0.872
ags10  0.896
ags11  0.835
ags12                        0.916
```

	Factor1	Factor2	Factor3
SS loadings	4.246	2.450	1.415
Proportion Var	0.354	0.204	0.118
Cumulative Var	0.354	0.558	0.676

Factor Correlations:

	Factor1	Factor2	Factor3
Factor1	1.000	0.070	0.191
Factor2	0.070	1.000	0.633
Factor3	0.191	0.633	1.000

```
Test of the hypothesis that 3 factors are sufficient.
The chi square statistic is 157.52 on 33 degrees of freedom.
The p-value is 3.69e-18
```

The result of the chi-square test is significant, indicating that the three-factor solution may not fit the data. Again, however, given its sensitivity to sample size and stringent null hypothesis of exact model data fit, this test is probably not sufficiently reliable. For this solution, factor 1 consists of items associated with performance goal orientation (both approach and avoidance), factor 2 consists of items associated primarily with MAP, except for ags6, and factor 3 consists of items ags2 and ags12, both of which are associated with MAV. This solution appears to be somewhat more theoretically grounded than was the four-factor solution.

Results for the two-factor solution appear below.

```
achievement.goal.efa.results2<-factanal(~ags1+ags
2+ags3+ags4+ags5+ags6+ags7+ags8+ags9+ags10+ags11+
ags12, factors=2, rotation="promax")

achievement.goal.efa.results2

Call:
factanal(x = ~ags1 + ags2 + ags3 + ags4 + ags5 + ags6 +
ags7 + ags8 + ags9 + ags10 + ags11 + ags12, factors = 2,
rotation = "promax")

Uniquenesses:
ags1 ags2 ags3 ags4 ags5 ags6 ags7 ags8 ags9 ags10 ags11 ags12
0.454 0.673 0.326 0.4020.543 0.375 0.208 0.275 0.262 0.186 0.298 0.647
```

```
Loadings:
        Factor1  Factor2
ags1             0.738
ags2             0.556
ags3    0.824
ags4    0.764
ags5   -0.103    0.682
ags6             0.792
ags7             0.895
ags8    0.857
ags9    0.857
ags10   0.901
ags11   0.845
ags12   0.127    0.563


                 Factor1  Factor2
SS loadings      4.293    3.078
Proportion Var   0.358    0.256
Cumulative Var   0.358    0.614

Factor Correlations:
          Factor1  Factor2
Factor1   1.000    0.139
Factor2   0.139    1.000

Test of the hypothesis that 2 factors are sufficient.
The chi square statistic is 330.53 on 43 degrees of freedom.
The p-value is 5.15e-46
```

Once again, the chi-square test suggests that the two-factor model does not fit the data. An examination of the factor loadings reveals that factor 1 consists of mastery goal items and factor 2 consists of performance goal items. While this structure does not match the original four-factor structure proposed by the scale's authors, it does match other theoretical descriptions of the constructs that have appeared in the literature. In addition, the consensus of the statistical analyses described previously supported the two-factor solution. Therefore, taking into consideration both the theoretical and empirical evidence, it would seem that the optimal solution does indeed involve two factors, one associated with mastery goal orientation and the other with performance goal orientation.

FITTING EFA MODELS USING FA

As noted above, there are other methods for extracting factors in addition to ML. The `factanal` function can only employ ML. Therefore, if another extraction method, such as PAF, is needed, use of an alternative R function would be required. Such a function exists as a part of the `psych` library, which we have already discussed in conjunction with parallel analysis. This function, `fa`, provides the researcher with a bit more flexibility than `factanal`, particularly in terms of the methods of extraction that are available. In order to fit the four-factor model using this function, we would submit the following commands in R.

```
achievement.goal.efa.results4.paf<-fa(performance.
data, nfactors=4, residuals=TRUE, rotate="promax",
SMC=TRUE, fm="pa")
```

When calling the `fa` function, we must first provide the dataset to be factor analyzed, in this case `performance.data`. It is important to note that the only variables that can be included in this **data frame** are those involved in the EFA. All extraneous variables would need to be removed. We can indicate the number of factors to retain, the rotation to use, whether we would like residual correlations to be saved, and whether we want to use the squared multiple correlation (SMC) as the diagonal in the correlation matrix that is factor analyzed. The computer obtains this value by fitting a series of regression models in which each indicator takes the role of the dependent variable and the other indicators serve as the independent variables. As an example, in one such model ags1 would be the dependent and ags2 through ags12 would be the independent variables. The R^2 value for this model would be placed in the diagonal of the correlation matrix of all indicators, replacing the 1 that would normally appear there. Similar analyses would be conducted for each of the other 11 indicators in this case. Finally, with the `fm=` subcommand, we indicate the factor extraction algorithm to use, in this case principal axis. We can view the output from the analysis simply by typing in the name of the output object.

```
achievement.goal.efa.results4.paf
Factor Analysis using method = pa
Call: fa(r = performance.data, nfactors = 4, rotate = "promax",
  residuals = TRUE,
          SMC = TRUE, fm = "pa")
Standardized   loadings   (pattern   matrix)   based   upon
  correlation matrix
              PA1     PA2     PA3     PA4    h2     u2    com
edps744.ags1  0.05    0.73    0.03    0.04   0.56   0.44   1.0
```

```
edps744.ags2   -0.04   0.00    0.82   -0.07   0.68   0.32   1.0
edps744.ags3    0.84   0.06   -0.12   -0.08   0.71   0.29   1.1
edps744.ags4    0.71  -0.06    0.12   -0.32   0.72   0.28   1.5
edps744.ags5   -0.08   0.62    0.08   -0.05   0.46   0.54   1.1
edps744.ags6    0.04   0.73    0.06    0.03   0.59   0.41   1.0
edps744.ags7    0.00   0.97   -0.08   -0.01   0.85   0.15   1.0
edps744.ags8    0.90  -0.05    0.09    0.31   0.84   0.16   1.3
edps744.ags9    0.85   0.06   -0.06   -0.08   0.75   0.25   1.0
edps744.ags10   0.89   0.00    0.02    0.01   0.79   0.21   1.0
edps744.ags11   0.88   0.00   -0.03    0.21   0.75   0.25   1.1
edps744.ags12   0.03   0.03    0.81    0.05   0.69   0.31   1.0
```

	PA1	PA2	PA3	PA4
SS loadings	4.30	2.43	1.41	0.24
Proportion Var	0.36	0.20	0.12	0.02
Cumulative Var	0.36	0.56	0.68	0.70
Proportion Explained	0.51	0.29	0.17	0.03
Cumulative Proportion	0.51	0.80	0.97	1.00

With factor correlations of

	PA1	PA2	PA3	PA4
PA1	1.00	0.08	0.22	-0.18
PA2	0.08	1.00	0.63	-0.19
PA3	0.22	0.63	1.00	-0.06
PA4	-0.18	-0.19	-0.06	1.00

Mean item complexity = 1.1
Test of the hypothesis that 4 factors are sufficient.

The degrees of freedom for the null model are 66 and the objective function was 8.05 with Chi Square of 3430.61
The degrees of freedom for the model are 24 and the objective function was 0.21

The root mean square of the residuals (RMSR) is 0.02
The df corrected root mean square of the residuals is 0.03

The harmonic number of observations is 428 with the empirical chi square 15.78 with prob < 0.9
The total number of observations was 432 with MLE Chi Square = 90.74 with prob < 1.1e-09

```
Tucker Lewis Index of factoring reliability = 0.945
RMSEA  index  =  0.081  and  the  90%  confidence  intervals  are
   0.063 0.098
BIC = -54.91
Fit based upon off diagonal values = 1
Measures of factor score adequacy
                                           PA1 PA2  PA3 PA4
Correlation of scores with factors         0.97 0.95 0.91 0.74
Multiple R square of scores with factors   0.95 0.91 0.83 0.54
Minimum correlation of possible factor scores 0.90 0.82 0.67 0.09
```

The factor loadings appear in the Standardized loadings table, along with the communalities (h2) and the uniquenesses (u2) for each indicator variable, both of which we have discussed previously. Interpretation of the factor loadings is conducted in the same fashion as discussed above. Here, factor 1 (PA1) was associated with items ags3, ags4, ags8, ags9, ags10, and ags11, which was identical to the first factor extracted by ML with factanal for the four-factor solution. The second table includes the sum of the squared factor loadings (SS loadings), which is the numerator of the proportion of variance explained by the factor, and the proportion of variance associated with each factor from across the 12 total factors that could be obtained from this dataset (Proportion Var). This value is calculated as the sum of squared factor loadings divided by the number of variables included in the analysis. In addition, the proportion of the variance explained by each factor from the variance explained by the four factors only appears in the row Proportion Explained. The factor correlation table appears next, revealing that factors 2 and 3 were most highly correlated (0.63). Finally, various model fit statistics for the solution are presented at the end of the output. We will discuss these statistics, including equations for them, when we discuss CFA in Chapter 3. For the moment it is sufficient to state that the values of RMSR, the Tucker–Lewis index (TLI), and RMSEA all indicate that the EFA solution fits the data reasonably well. However, as noted earlier, the make-up of the factors is such that we may not find them theoretically meaningful, thus forcing us to look at other possible numbers of factors. In order to complete this example, we include the function calls and results for EFA using PAF extraction and PROMAX rotation for three and two factors with the performance data.

```
achievement.goal.efa.results3.paf<-fa(performance.
data, nfactors=3, residuals=TRUE, rotate="promax",
SMC=TRUE, fm="pa")

achievement.goal.efa.results3.paf
```

```
Factor Analysis using method = pa
Call: fa(r = performance.data, nfactors = 3, rotate = "promax",
  residuals = TRUE,
SMC = TRUE, fm = "pa")
Standardized    loadings    (pattern    matrix)    based    upon
  correlation matrix
                  PA1    PA2    PA3    h2     u2   com
edps744.ags1      0.03   0.71   0.05   0.56   0.44 1.0
edps744.ags2     -0.02   0.06   0.77   0.64   0.36 1.0
edps744.ags3      0.86   0.09  -0.13   0.71   0.29 1.1
edps744.ags4      0.75   0.05   0.04   0.59   0.41 1.0
edps744.ags5     -0.08   0.63   0.07   0.46   0.54 1.1
edps744.ags6      0.03   0.72   0.06   0.58   0.42 1.0
edps744.ags7      0.00   0.97  -0.08   0.85   0.15 1.0
edps744.ags8      0.82  -0.14   0.15   0.73   0.27 1.1
edps744.ags9      0.87   0.09  -0.08   0.75   0.25 1.0
edps744.ags10     0.89   0.00   0.02   0.80   0.20 1.0
edps744.ags11     0.84  -0.08   0.02   0.71   0.29 1.0
edps744.ags12     0.01   0.00   0.84   0.71   0.29 1.0


                        PA1    PA2  PA3
SS loadings             4.25   2.45 1.40
Proportion Var          0.35   0.20 0.12
Cumulative Var          0.35   0.56 0.67
Proportion Explained    0.52   0.30 0.17
Cumulative Proportion   0.52   0.83 1.00


With factor correlations of
     PA1  PA2  PA3
PA1 1.00 0.08 0.22
PA2 0.08 1.00 0.63
PA3 0.22 0.63 1.00



Mean item complexity = 1
Test of the hypothesis that 3 factors are sufficient.


The degrees of freedom for the null model are 66 and the object-
ive function was 8.05 with Chi Square of 3430.61
The degrees of freedom for the model are 33 and the objective
function was 0.37
```

The root mean square of the residuals (RMSR) is 0.02
The df corrected root mean square of the residuals is 0.03

The harmonic number of observations is 428 with the empirical chi square 30.65 with prob < 0.58
The total number of observations was 432 with MLE Chi Square = 158.95 with prob < 2.1e-18
Tucker Lewis Index of factoring reliability = 0.925
RMSEA index = 0.095 and the 90% confidence intervals are 0.08 0.109
BIC = -41.31
Fit based upon off diagonal values = 1
Measures of factor score adequacy

	PA1	PA2	PA3
Correlation of scores with factors	0.97	0.95	0.91
Multiple R square of scores with factors	0.94	0.91	0.83
Minimum correlation of possible factor scores	0.88	0.82	0.66

```
achievement.goal.efa.results2.paf<-fa(performance.
data, nfactors=2, residuals=TRUE, rotate="promax",
SMC=TRUE, fm="pa")
```

achievement.goal.efa.results2.paf

Factor Analysis using method = pa
Call: fa(r = performance.data, nfactors = 2, rotate = "promax",
  residuals = TRUE,
SMC = TRUE, fm = "pa")
Standardized loadings (pattern matrix) based upon
  correlation matrix

	PA1	PA2	h2	u2	com
edps744.ags1	0.00	0.74	0.54	0.46	1.0
edps744.ags2	0.07	0.63	0.41	0.59	1.0
edps744.ags3	0.83	-0.03	0.69	0.31	1.0
edps744.ags4	0.75	0.07	0.59	0.41	1.0
edps744.ags5	-0.11	0.68	0.46	0.54	1.0
edps744.ags6	0.00	0.76	0.58	0.42	1.0
edps744.ags7	-0.06	0.86	0.73	0.27	1.0
edps744.ags8	0.85	-0.03	0.71	0.29	1.0
edps744.ags9	0.86	0.01	0.74	0.26	1.0
edps744.ags10	0.90	0.00	0.81	0.19	1.0
edps744.ags11	0.85	-0.07	0.71	0.29	1.0
edps744.ags12	0.12	0.62	0.42	0.58	1.1

```
                            PA1  PA2
SS loadings                 4.27 3.11
Proportion Var              0.36 0.26
Cumulative Var              0.36 0.62
Proportion Explained        0.58 0.42
Cumulative Proportion       0.58 1.00
```

With factor correlations of
```
     PA1  PA2
PA1 1.00 0.16
PA2 0.16 1.00
```

Mean item complexity = 1
Test of the hypothesis that 2 factors are sufficient.

The degrees of freedom for the null model are 66 and the objective function was 8.05 with Chi Square of 3430.61
The degrees of freedom for the model are 43 and the objective
function was 0.8

The root mean square of the residuals (RMSR) is 0.05
The df corrected root mean square of the residuals is 0.06

The harmonic number of observations is 428 with the empirical
chi square 133.22 with prob < 3.7e-11
The total number of observations was 432 with MLE Chi
Square = 338.66 with prob < 1.4e-47

Tucker Lewis Index of factoring reliability = 0.865
RMSEA index = 0.127 and the 90% confidence intervals are
  0.114 0.139
BIC = 77.72
Fit based upon off diagonal values = 0.99
Measures of factor score adequacy
```
                                           PA1  PA2
Correlation of scores with factors         0.97 0.94
Multiple R square of scores with factors   0.94 0.88
Minimum correlation of possible factor scores 0.88 0.76
```

PRINCIPAL COMPONENTS ANALYSIS

So far, we have been discussing EFA in which the goal is to identify a (hopefully) small number of latent variables that underlie the observed indicator variables. Most often, as in the example used here, the researcher wants to investigate the latent structure underlying the indicators either because such investigation is inherently of interest (e.g. what is the nature of intelligence?) or because the latent variables represent subscales of an instrument that needs to be validated. In either case, interest is on the latent traits as entities unto themselves. However, in some instances, the researcher simply wants to reduce the dimensionality of the data by combining the indicators into a smaller number of variables, which could then be used in a subsequent analysis, such as regression. From a statistical perspective the methodology used to engage in such dimension reduction differs only somewhat from that used to fit an EFA model with PAF. As was noted earlier, with PAF the correlation matrix that is submitted to the factor analysis has on its diagonal the SMC (R^2) value for each variable. Principal components analysis (PCA) differs from PAF in that the diagonal of the correlation matrix retains the 1s rather than having them replaced by R^2. The implications of this difference from a theoretical perspective involve our beliefs about the measurement quality of the indicators. When using PCA we are implicitly assuming that the indicators are measured without error; i.e. they have perfect reliability. While this may not be a reasonable assumption to make in most (if not all) instances, it is also true that for very reliable measures the difference in the results of PCA and PAF will be fairly small because the R^2 used in the latter will be close to 1.

PCA can be conducted in R using the `princomp` function that is a part of the base set of libraries. For the achievement goal data, the command to do this would be:

```
achievement.goal.pca<-princomp(~ags1+ags2+ags3+ags4
+ags5+ags6+ags7+ags8+ags9+ags10+ags11+ags12)
```

In order to see the component loadings we would type the following:

```
achievement.goal.pca$loadings
```

```
Loadings:
Comp.1 Comp.2 Comp.3 Comp.4 Comp.5 Comp.6 Comp.7 Comp.8 Comp.9
  Comp.10 Comp.11 Comp.12
ags1 −0.342 −0.383 −0.186 −0.524 −0.264 0.553 0.135 −0.121
ags2 −0.110 −0.509 0.438 0.299 −0.658
ags3 −0.395 0.104 −0.232 0.401 0.433 0.170 −0.575 −0.205 0.156
ags4 −0.288 0.493 −0.190 0.203 −0.159 0.162 0.204 0.640
  −0.269 −0.125
ags5 −0.274 −0.257 0.128 0.145 −0.416 0.267 −0.702 −0.284
ags6 −0.357 −0.358 −0.164 −0.167 −0.138 0.653 0.112 −0.477
ags7 −0.345 −0.379 0.116 −0.115 0.118 −0.180 0.800
ags8 −0.474 0.216 −0.523 −0.305 −0.152 −0.398 −0.236 0.148 −0.299
ags9 −0.330 −0.134 0.217 −0.125 0.229 −0.689 −0.517
ags10 −0.426 −0.491 0.103 0.197 −0.149 0.698 0.106
ags11 −0.453 0.130 −0.332 0.580 −0.177 0.492 0.167 0.148
ags12 −0.139 −0.511 0.446 0.187 0.661 0.152 −0.108
Comp.1 Comp.2 Comp.3 Comp.4 Comp.5 Comp.6 Comp.7 Comp.8 Comp.9
  Comp.10 Comp.11 Comp.12
SS loadings 1.000 1.000 1.000 1.000 1.000 1.000 1.000 1.000
  1.000 1.000 1.000 1.000
Proportion Var 0.083 0.083 0.083 0.083 0.083 0.083 0.083 0.083
  0.083 0.083 0.083 0.083
Cumulative Var 0.083 0.167 0.250 0.333 0.417 0.500 0.583 0.667
0.750 0.833 0.917 1.000
```

The first table in the output includes the component loadings, which are analogous to factor loadings in EFA. Note here, however, that all 12 possible components are automatically retained by the procedure. Also, we note that the component loadings are generally lower than were the factor loadings, though the general pattern of item groupings is similar. The second table reflects the variance accounted for by each of the components. The information discussed above in relation to EFA in terms of determining the number of components of the model to retain and fit apply to PCA as well. But recall, PCA is intended to reduce the data and not necessarily identify an underlying latent structure that is directly tied to theory per se. Thus, PCA may conclude with decisions based more on statistical criteria and less on theoretical criteria in comparison to EFA.

SUMMARY

SUMMARY
2

In this chapter, we learned about the basic types of factor analysis, CFA and EFA. In particular, we saw that what differentiates them from one another is the presence of a strong guiding theory about the latent structure underlying a set of observed indicator variables, and previous empirical evidence at least partially supporting that theory (CFA), or a more general belief of what the underlying latent structure is but without strong theory and/or prior empirical evidence (EFA). We then discussed the basics of EFA, including factor extraction, the need for factor rotation, and methods for determining how many factors should be extracted, including robust but not well-used techniques. Finally, we worked through an extended example of conducting an EFA in R, and interpreting the results in terms of our latent constructs of interest. We finished the chapter with PCA, which is similar to PAF extraction in EFA, with the exception of the assumption of perfectly reliability indicators (i.e. values of 1 for the diagonal of the correlation matrix).

FURTHER READING

Fabrigar, L.R., & Wegener, D.T. (2012). *Factor Analysis*. Oxford: Oxford University Press.

Gorsuch, R.L. (1983). *Factor Analysis*. Hillsdale, NJ: Lawrence Erlbaum Associates.

Thompson, B. (2004). *Exploratory and Confirmatory Factor Analysis*. Washington, DC: American Psychological Association.

Walkey, F., & Welch, G. (2010). *Demystifying Factor Analysis: How it Works and How To Use It*. Bloomington, IN: Xlibris Corporation.

FURTHER
READING
2

REFERENCES

Bandalos, D.L., & Finney, S.J. (2010). Factor analysis: Exploratory and confirmatory. In G.R. Hancock & R.O. Mueller (eds), *The Reviewer's Guide to Quantitative Methods in the Social Sciences* (pp. 93–114). New York: Routledge.

Brown, T.A. (2015). *Confirmatory Factor Analysis for Applied Research*, 2nd edition. New York: The Guilford Press.

Fabrigar, L.R., & Wegener, D.T. (2011). *Exploratory Factor Analysis (Understanding Statistics)*. New York: Oxford University Press.

Horn, J.L. (1965). A rationale and test for the number of factors in factor analysis. *Psychometrika*, 30, 179–85.

Kaiser, H. (1960). The application of electronic computers to factor analysis. *Educational and Psychological Measurement*, 20, 141–51.

Kim, J., & Muller, C.W. (1978). *Factor Analysis: Statistical Methods and Practical Issues*. Beverly Hills, CA: Sage.

Pett, M.A., Lackey, N.R., & Sullivan, J.J. (2003). *Making Sense of Factor Analysis*. Thousand Oaks, CA: Sage.

REFERENCES
2

Raîche, G., Walls, T.A., Magis, D., Riopel, M., & Blais, J.-G. (2013). Non-graphical solutions for Cattell's scree test. *Methodology: European Journal of Research Methods for the Behavioral and Social Sciences*, 9(1), 23–6.

Thurstone, L.L. (1947). *Multiple Factor Analysis*. Chicago: University of Chicago Press.

Yakovitz, S., & Szidarovszky, F. (1986). *An Introduction to Numerical Computation*. New York, NJ: Macmillan.

Chapter 3

CONFIRMATORY FACTOR ANALYSIS

INTRODUCTION

In the previous chapter we described the general factor model, and discussed the two broad types of factor analysis, exploratory (EFA) and confirmatory (CFA). Recall that EFA is, as the name implies, exploratory in nature and is employed when either no specific theories about the latent structure underlying the observed data are clearly specified, or there is a lack of empirical work investigating this structure. In either case, sufficient information does not exist to warrant reducing the number of possible hypotheses about the factor structure to a very small number and then testing only those hypotheses. On the other hand, when strong theory does exist regarding the nature of the latent structure of the data, and there is exploratory work suggesting the nature of this structure, then CFA may be most appropriate. In this context, the researcher has both a conceptual foundation regarding the latent variables and their relationships with the observed indicators that is grounded in the literature, and results from empirical work suggesting a limited number of possible factor structures. The goal in this case is not to explore all possible latent variable patterns, as with EFA, but rather to assess which of the hypothesized or specified models is most likely given the data at hand. Figure 3.1 displays graphically the difference between the EFA and CFA models for the two-factor achievement goal orientation (i.e. Performance orientation, Mastery orientation) model examined in Chapter 2.

The left side of the figure shows the EFA model in which each observed indicator has a loading with each of the factors. This model form acknowledges our uncertainty regarding the actual nature of the latent structure. The right side of the figure shows the CFA model in which each observed indicator is linked with only one of the latent traits. In reality, the missing paths on the right exist, but have been constrained to the value of 0, reflecting our hypothesis based on the literature and prior empirical work that items ags1, ags2, ags5, ags6, ags7, and ags12

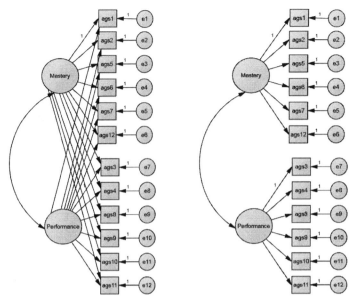

■ **Figure 3.1:**   Graphical representation of EFA and CFA models

are associated only with the Mastery factor, and that ags3, ags4, ags8, ags9, ags10, and ags11 are only associated with the Performance factor.

We presented the common factor model in equation (2.1), which explicitly shows the link between the observed indicators (y) and the latent variables (η). This model applies to both EFA and CFA, as does the relationship between the observed variable covariance matrix and the latent structure, as described in equation (2.2). For the purposes of CFA, we would make one addition to (2.1) by including an intercept term (τ), as shown in (3.1) below.

$$y = \tau + \Lambda\eta + \varepsilon \qquad\qquad\qquad \textbf{(3.1)}$$

For EFA models, τ is generally assumed to be 0, but with CFA this is not necessarily the case. Indeed, if we are interested in comparing latent variable means across groups, the model intercepts play an important role. As was true with EFA, in CFA each of these model parameters will be estimated using the variances and covariances of the observed variables. However, whereas in EFA the focus was on deciding how many factors to extract and which type of rotation to use, with CFA these issues are not a concern. We enter a CFA analysis with a predetermined factor structure in mind thereby obviating the need to worry about determining the number of factors or identifying the maximally interpretable solution using rotation. However, new considerations do emerge regarding how the model parameters should be estimated, and which of several proposed models fits the data best. It is with these issues that we will concern ourselves next, before learning how to fit CFA models using R. We begin with model parameter estimation.

MODEL PARAMETER ESTIMATION

There are a number of potential methods for estimating the parameters in model (3.1). Certainly the most common of these is **maximum likelihood** (ML), which was discussed briefly in the previous chapter. ML estimates model parameters (i.e. factor loadings, variances, covariances, intercepts, and error variances) that minimize the criterion in equation (3.2):

$$F_{\mathrm{ML}} = \frac{1}{2}\mathrm{tr}\left[\left(\left[S - \Sigma\right]\Sigma^{-1}\right)^{2}\right],$$ (3.2)

where

S = Covariance matrix among the observed indicators

Σ = Model-predicted covariance matrix among the observed indicators.

As we noted in Chapter 2, the ML algorithm relies on an assumption that the observed indicators are multivariate normal. If they are not, the estimated standard errors will be incorrect, leading to improper significance test results (Yuan, Bentler, & Zhang, 2005).

One alternative method of parameter estimation that has been shown to be effective when the indicators are not multivariate normal is **weighted least squares** (WLS), which has the following fit criterion:

$$F_{\mathrm{WLS}} = \left(S - \Sigma\right)' W^{-1}\left(S - \Sigma\right)$$ (3.3)

In (3.3) the weight matrix, W, is the asymptotic covariance matrix of the elements contained in the observed sample covariance matrix. The logic behind using this particular weight matrix is that those elements (i.e. observed variances and covariances) that have less sampling variability (i.e. smaller values in W) will receive greater weight than those elements that have greater sampling variability. A potential problem with WLS is that its computational complexity renders it less than optimal when the sample size is not large (Finney & DiStefano, 2013). A recommended approach for addressing this problem involves the use of the diagonal of

W in (3.3), rather than the entire matrix. More specifically, the fit criterion for this **diagonally weighted least squares** approach (DWLS) takes the form:

$$F_{\text{DWLS}} = \left(S - \Sigma\right)' \left(\text{diag}W\right)^{-1}\left(S - \Sigma\right.$$ (3.4)

Thus, the residuals of the observed covariance matrix are weighted not by the full covariance matrix of S, but rather only by the variances of the elements in S. To avoid the bias that would result in estimating model parameter standard errors and the model chi-square test without considering the full covariance matrix, information from W is incorporated into their estimation without the use of the full WLS approach. The reader interested in the more technical issues of this approach is referred to Wirth and Edwards (2007), Flora and Curran (2004), and Muthén, du Toit, and Spisic (1997).

The methods for estimation mentioned above only scratch the surface of the options available for estimating model parameters. These were selected because they are (a) effective, (b) widely used, and (c) available in most standard SEM software packages. At the same time, we also acknowledge that there do exist a wide array of model parameter estimation techniques. The reader will want to immerse themselves in the literature on this topic in order to gain a full understanding of the options. For this purpose, we recommend Finney and DiStefano (2013), Brown (2015), and Kline (2011). We would also add that based on our experience and available research in the area, the majority of research scenarios involving SEM can be addressed using one of these estimation methods above.

ASSESSING MODEL FIT

Once parameters have been estimated, the researcher must ascertain whether the model fits the data. Put more simply, is the model able to reproduce with accuracy the covariance matrix of the observed variables? Many ways exist to assess model fit, and we will only discuss those that have been shown to be most accurate, and that are widely available in computer software. Perhaps the most common method is the **chi-square goodness of fit test**, which we mentioned in Chapter 2. However, as we also noted there, this statistic is not particularly useful in practice because it tests the null hypothesis that $\Sigma = S$, which is very restrictive. The test will almost certainly be rejected when the sample size is sufficiently large (Bollen, 1989; 1990). In addition, the chi-square test relies on the assumption of multivariate normality of the indicators, which may not be tenable in many situations. As to this latter point, several corrections to the chi-square value have been suggested for cases where data are not multivariate normal and bias in the statistic is feared.

One of these is the Satorra–Bentler correction (Satorra & Bentler, 1994), which adjusts the standard ML-based statistic as follows:

$$\chi^2_{\text{SB}} = d^{-1} \chi^2_{\text{ML}}, \tag{3.5}$$

where

χ^2_{ML} = Standard chi-square statistic from ML

d = Scaling factor associated with the multivariate kurtosis in the observed data.

When kurtosis of the observed indicators differ, the χ^2_{SB} test has been found to be somewhat biased (e.g. Curran *et al.*, 1996). To correct for this bias, Yuan and Bentler (1997) offered a test statistic (χ^2_{YB}) that used a slightly different scaling value and that appears to outperform χ^2_{SB} in such cases. A third alternative to the standard χ^2_{ML} test statistic for use when the observed data are not multivariate normal is based on work by Bollen and Stine (1992), who proposed using a bootstrap approach to calculating estimates of the chi-square test statistic, as well as adjustments to the model standard errors when the data are not normally distributed. The bootstrap (Efron, 1982), which involves repeatedly resampling from the original sample with replacement, has a long history in statistics and is widely used in a number of applications. In the context of CFA, Bollen and Stine described a method involving the bootstrap for developing the distribution of the chi-square statistic under the null hypothesis and the corresponding development of a hypothesis test that would be robust to departures from normality. In particular, the χ^2_{ML} for the original data is calculated, and then the observed data are transformed to match the covariance matrix implied by the CFA model. This transformed dataset is then resampled using the bootstrap many times (e.g. 1000) and for each of these samples the χ^2_{ML} is calculated and saved, creating a distribution of χ^2_{ML} when the null hypothesis of good model fit is true. The original χ^2_{ML} is then compared to this distribution, and the *p*-value for the hypothesis test is the proportion of bootstrap chi-square values that exceed the χ^2_{ML} from the original dataset.

Whereas the chi-square statistics described above provide a direct test of the null hypothesis of exact model fit, researchers using CFA typically refer to a wide array of relative fit indices as well. Indeed, these may prove to be more useful in assessing the results of a CFA compared to the chi-square test, for reasons described previously. When using such fit indices, researchers are encouraged to refer to several and consider the collective results rather than taking each as an absolute up or down vote on the fit of the model. In other words, taken together what do the indices suggest about model fit? Among the most popular of such indices is the **root mean square error of approximation** (RMSEA), which is calculated as:

$$\text{RMSEA} = \sqrt{\frac{\chi_T^2 - df_T}{df_T(n-1)}}, \tag{3.6}$$

where

χ_T^2 = ML-based chi-square test for the target model; i.e. the model of interest

df_T = Degrees of freedom for the target model (number of observed covariances and variances minus number of parameters to be estimated)

n = Sample size.

By convention, values of RMSEA $\leq$ 0.05 are taken to indicate good model fit, and values between 0.05 and 0.08 are seen as indicative of adequate model fit (Kline, 2011). When RMSEA exceeds 0.08, the fit is said to be poor.

A second popular and proven fit statistic is the **comparative fit index** (CFI):

$$\text{CFI} = 1 - \frac{\max\left(\chi_T^2 - df_T, 0\right)}{\max\left(\chi_0^2 - df_0, 0\right)}, \tag{3.7}$$

where

χ_0^2 = ML-based chi-square test for the null model in which no relationships between the latent and observed variables are hypothesized to exist

df_0 = Degrees of freedom for the null model.

A closely related fit statistic to the CFI is the **Tucker–Lewis index** (TLI), sometimes also referred to as the nonnormed fit index (NNFI). It is calculated as:

$$\text{TLI} = \frac{\dfrac{\chi_0^2}{df_0} - \dfrac{\chi_T^2}{df_T}}{\dfrac{\chi_0^2}{df_0} - 1} \tag{3.8}$$

One recommendation for when a model is considered to exhibit good fit is when the values of CFI and TLI are 0.95 or higher (Hu & Bentler, 1999). Of course, as with any type of descriptive fit value, other recommendations might be found to support a different cutoff (e.g. 0.90), and no single cutoff should be taken as absolutely accurate. Rather, higher values on these indices indicate better fit of the model to the data.

A fourth index of model fit that is frequently used is the **standardized root mean square residual** (SRMR). SRMR is calculated as:

$$\text{SRMR} = \frac{\sum \left(r_{\text{observed } j,k} - r_{\text{predicted } j,k} \right)^2}{\left(p(p+1)/2 \right)}, \tag{3.9}$$

where

$r_{\text{observed } j,k}$ = Observed correlation between indicator variables j and k

$r_{\text{predicted } j,k}$ = CFA model-predicted correlation between indicator variables j and k

p = Number of observed indicator variables.

Hu and Bentler (1999) suggested that values of SRMR $\leq$ 0.08 suggest good model fit to the data.

When our interest is in comparing the fit of two or more models, we have several statistical options for making the determination. When two models are nested within one another (i.e. one model is a more constrained version of another), we can use their individual chi-square goodness of fit test statistics to create a test comparing their relative fit. This test is possible because the difference in two chi-square values is itself a chi-square, with degrees of freedom equal to the difference in the degrees of freedom for each statistic. We can calculate this statistic as:

$$\chi_C^2 - \chi_U^2 = \chi_\Delta^2, \tag{3.10}$$

with degrees of freedom equal to

$$df_C - df_U = df_\Delta, \tag{3.11}$$

where

χ_C^2 = Chi-square statistic from constrained model

χ_U^2 = Chi-square statistic from unconstrained model

df_C = Degrees of freedom for constrained model

df_U = Degrees of freedom for unconstrained model.

When χ_Δ^2 is statistically significant at the desired level of α (e.g. 0.05), we can conclude that the relative fit of the two models is statistically different; i.e. one fits better than the other.

Another statistical approach for comparing model fit involves the use of information indices, which are simply measures of variance not explained by the model, with an added penalty for model complexity. Among the most popular of these indices are the **Akaike information criterion** (AIC; Akaike, 1973), the **Bayesian information criterion** (BIC; Schwarz, 1978), and the **sample-size-adjusted BIC** (SBIC; Enders & Tofighi, 2008). Each of these statistics is based upon the model chi-square, and is interpreted such that the model with the lower value exhibits a better fit to the data. An advantage of these information indices over the chi-square difference test is that models do not need to be nested for comparisons to be conducted. The information indices are calculated as shown below.

$$\text{AIC} = \chi_M^2 + 2q \tag{3.12}$$

$$\text{BIC} = \chi_M^2 + q\ln(n)v \tag{3.13}$$

$$\text{SBIC} = \chi_M^2 + \ln\left[(n+2)/24\right]\left[\frac{v(v+1)}{2} - df\right], \tag{3.14}$$

where

χ_M^2 = Model chi-square value

q = Number of parameters estimated in the model

v = Number of observed variables

n = Sample size

df = Model degrees of freedom.

We do remind the reader that it is important not to focus only on fit statistics and indices when deciding if a model fits the data. If we maintain fit index tunnel vision we may miss other important information that could indicate a problem with the fit of the model. The analyst will want to, for example, inspect the parameter estimates to be certain the values are within the appropriate range, as well as inspect other information, such as the residuals, as was discussed with EFA. The examination of all the information will help to ensure the fit is fully evaluated.

FITTING CFA MODELS IN R USING LAVAAN

To demonstrate the application of CFA models in R, let us again consider the research problem that was the focus of Chapter 2. In particular, we were interested in investigating a hypothesized model for achievement goal orientation that involved 12 items from a scale for which it was hypothesized that there were anywhere from two to four factors. In particular, the original authors of the scale had suggested that achievement goal orientation could be best understood as consisting of four factors (MAP, MAV, PAP, PAV). Other authors have suggested that mastery goal orientation is a unified construct (i.e. combining MAP with MAV), but that PAP and PAV are separate, while still others have posited that achievement motivation really consists of two unique factors, Mastery and Performance. In addition to these well-developed theories, we also would want to identify prior work in the literature, of at least an exploratory nature, that had examined these various models and provided some preliminary evidence regarding the tenability of each. To be clear, in order for CFA to be appropriate for the problem, there should be both prior theoretical and empirical literature supporting each of the proposed models.

Prior to fitting the CFA model to the data, we need to ascertain whether the assumption of multivariate normality is tenable, given the data at hand. This can be done using **Mardia's test**, which is available with the mardia function in the psych library. The commands appear below, and the resulting output for the achievement motivation data is shown in Figure 3.2.

```
library(psych)
mardia(performance.data)
```

```
Call: mardia(x = performance.data)
Mardia tests of multivariate skew and kurtosis
Use describe(x) the to get univariate tests
n.obs = 419 num.vars = 12
b1p = 33.79 skew = 2359.47 with probability = 0
small sample skew = 2378.98 with probability = 0
b2p = 240.59 kurtosis = 40.53 with probability = 0
```

The null hypotheses of the test statistics are that the data conform to the multivariate normal distribution. In addition, the quartile plot represents the multivariate data in graphical format. As with univariate quartile plots, the solid line represents the data distribution under normality, and the scatter plot represents the actual data. If the data can be assumed to come from a multivariate normal distribution, these points would fall along the solid line. Taken together, the results of the hypothesis tests and the quartile plot suggest that it may not be tenable to assume that the data are multivariate normal. Specifically, the S-shaped curve around this line indicates a potential issue with skew. For pedagogical purposes, we will fit the data using ML under the assumption of multivariate normality, followed by the alternative methods for nonnormal data that were described above to highlight the differences. Again, for clarity's sake, we are fitting the data using both ML and an alternative approach for the purposes of demonstrating how to fit each type

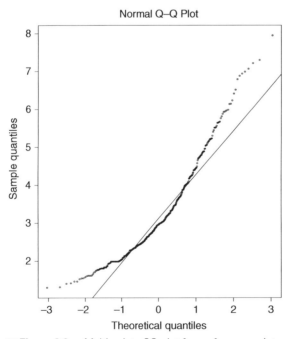

■ **Figure 3.2:**   Multivariate QQ-plot for performance data

of model using R, and to highlight differences in results for the two approaches to model parameter estimation. In actual practice, given the lack of multivariate normality that seems apparent in the previous results, we would likely not use ML and instead rely on the alternative estimation approach.

To fit the original four-factor model with ML estimation, we will use the following set of commands:

```
library(lavaan)
achievement.goal.cfa4.model<-'map=~ags1+ags5+ags7
mav=~ags2+ags6+ags12
pap=~ags3+ags9+ags11
pav=~ags4+ags8+ags10'

achievement.goal.cfa4.fit<- cfa(achievement.goal.cfa4.model,
data=performance.data)
summary(achievement.goal.cfa4.fit, fit.measures=T,
standardized=T)
```

[handwritten annotation: latent var]

The first line loads the **lavaan** library. The next four lines define or specify the model to be fit and place it in the model object achievement.goal.cfa4.model. Each line within this model defines one of the latent variables and associates them with the corresponding observed indicators. The next line creates an output file, achievement.goal.cfa4.fit, that includes the results of the CFA based on the model achievement.goal.cfa4.model and the data file performance.data. Finally, the summary command yields the output from the estimation of the model. By including fit.measures=T and standardized=T, we request the model fit statistics and standardized parameter estimates. The resulting output appears below.

```
lavaan (0.5-15) converged normally after 48 iterations

    Number of observations                            419

    Estimator                                          ML
    Minimum Function Test Statistic               328.312
    Degrees of freedom                                 48
    P-value (Chi-square)                            0.000

Model test baseline model:

    Minimum Function Test Statistic              3382.805
    Degrees of freedom                                 66
```

```
            P-value                                      0.000
User model versus baseline model:

    Comparative Fit Index (CFI)                          0.915
    Tucker-Lewis Index (TLI)                             0.884


Loglikelihood and Information Criteria:

    Loglikelihood user model (H0)                     -7014.070
    Loglikelihood unrestricted model (H1)             -6849.914


    Number of free parameters                              30
    Akaike (AIC)                                      4088.141
    Bayesian (BIC)                                    4209.277
    Sample-size adjusted Bayesian (BIC)             14114.078

Root Mean Square Error of Approximation:

    RMSEA                                                0.118
    90 Percent Confidence Interval               0.106 0.130
    P-value RMSEA <= 0.05                               0.000


Standardized Root Mean Square Residual:

    SRMR                                                0.055


Parameter estimates:

    Information                                      Expected
    Standard Errors                                  Standard


            Estimate Std.err Z-value P(>|z|) Std.lv Std.all
Latent variables:
    map =~
        ags1    1.000                               0.840   0.746
        ags5    0.774   0.057   13.564   0.000      0.650   0.682
        ags7    1.100   0.064   17.263   0.000      0.924   0.895
    mav =~
        ags2    1.000                               0.923   0.627
        ags6    0.974   0.078   12.523   0.000      0.899   0.796
        ags12   1.039   0.096   10.805   0.000      0.959   0.644
```

pap =~						
ags3	1.000				1.284	0.840
ags9	0.853	0.038	22.349	0.000	1.095	0.870
ags11	1.103	0.052	21.178	0.000	1.416	0.841
pav =~						
ags4	1.000				0.929	0.771
ags8	1.599	0.084	19.091	0.000	1.486	0.855
ags10	1.525	0.073	20.861	0.000	1.418	0.921

Covariances:

map ~~						
mav	0.709	0.079	9.000	0.000	0.914	0.914
pap	0.066	0.060	1.093	0.274	0.061	0.061
pav	0.056	0.043	1.289	0.197	0.072	0.072
mav ~~						
pap	0.163	0.072	2.265	0.023	0.138	0.138
pav	0.178	0.053	3.355	0.001	0.207	0.207
pap ~~						
pav	1.143	0.102	11.236	0.000	0.958	0.958

Variances:

ags1	0.562	0.047		0.562	0.443
ags5	0.486	0.038		0.486	0.535
ags7	0.211	0.032		0.211	0.198
ags2	1.312	0.102		1.312	0.606
ags6	0.469	0.049		0.469	0.367
ags12	1.300	0.103		1.300	0.586
ags3	0.690	0.059		0.690	0.295
ags9	0.386	0.036		0.386	0.244
ags11	0.831	0.071		0.831	0.293
ags4	0.588	0.045		0.588	0.405
ags8	0.815	0.070		0.815	0.269
ags10	0.362	0.043		0.362	0.153
map	0.706	0.083		1.000	1.000
mav	0.852	0.128		1.000	1.000
pap	1.648	0.158		1.000	1.000
pav	0.864	0.094		1.000	1.000

$\chi^2_M = 328.312$, with 48 degrees of freedom and a p-value less than 0.001, indicating that the proposed model did not fit the data, based only on the statistical test. In addition, CFI = 0.915, TLI = 0.884, SRMR = 0.055, and the model RMSEA = 0.118, with a 90% confidence interval of 0.106 to 0.130. This means that we are 90% confident that in the population the actual RMSEA would be between 0.106 and 0.130. Finally, the hypothesis test for the null hypothesis of whether RMSEA is less than or equal to 0.05 (i.e. RMSEA indicates a good fit) is less than 0.001, indicating that the null should be rejected if $\alpha = 0.05$. Taken together, these various model fit indices suggest relatively poor model–data fit. Given that the observed indicators do not follow the multivariate normal distribution, however, it is somewhat unclear to what extent the poor model fit is a function of actual model misspecification, and how much is due to the problems associated with the assumption violations.

Following the model fit statistics, we see the model parameter estimates, their standard errors, the statistic testing the null hypothesis that the estimate is equal to 0, the associated *p*-value, the standardized value when only the latent variables are standardized (`Std.lv`), and when the latent and observed variables are standardized (`std.all`). Thus, as an example, we see that the unstandardized factor loading for item ags5 is 0.774, with a standardized value of 0.682. In addition, we can see that all of the loadings are significantly different from 0. With respect to the factor covariances/correlations, the results show that MPA and MAV are strongly positively correlated with one another, as are PAP and PAV. However, the correlations of MAV and MAP with PAV and PAP are low. Finally, the largest error variances were found for ags2 and ags12, whereas the lowest error variance was associated with ags7. Among the factors, PAP had the largest variance, being essentially twice as large as the variances of any of the other factors.

As we noted above, the assumption of multivariate normality was not met for these data. Therefore, we will use alternative methods of fitting the model to determine whether better fit of the same specified model can be achieved with a more appropriate algorithm. One such approach would be to use one of the alternative approaches for calculating the chi-square statistic, such as Satorra–Bentler, Yuan–Bentler, or Bollen–Stine, in order to determine if the problem is associated primarily with the fit indices themselves, and not so much the parameter estimates. Below are the commands to request the Satorra–Bentler, Yuan–Bentler, and Bollen–Stine corrected chi-square goodness of fit test statistics, respectively. Table 3.1 shows the values for each of them.

```
achievement.goal.cfa4.satorra.fit<-cfa(achievement.goal.cfa4.model,
data=performance.data, test="Satorra.Bentler")
summary(achievement.goal.cfa4.satorra.fit, fit.measures=T,
standardized=T)
```

```
achievement.goal.cfa4.yuan.fit<-cfa(achievement.goal.cfa4.model,
data=performance.data, test="Yuan.Bentler")
summary(achievement.goal.cfa4.yuan.fit, fit.measures=T,
standardized=T)
```

```
achievement.goal.cfa4.bollen.fit<- cfa(achievement.goal.cfa4.model,
data=performance.data, test="Bollen.Stine")
summary(achievement.goal.cfa4.satorra.fit, fit.measures=
T, standardized=T)
```

Based on these results, it appears that none of the ML-based methods, nor WLS, yielded an acceptable fit for the four-factor achievement motivation model, based on set criteria. However, for the DWLS estimated model, all of the fit indices suggested that the model fit the data well. In addition, all parameter estimates were appropriate and showed no signs of misfit. Therefore, given the prior finding that the indicators were not multivariate normal, and these results suggesting that the DWLS provides acceptable model data fit, we will proceed with further analyses using the DWLS estimator to investigate other factor models for the achievement motivation data. As a final note, with the Bollen–Stine procedure the results presented are identical to those for the standard ML because the only difference in the two approaches is the method used to calculate the *p*-value for the goodness of fit test.

In order to use the DWLS estimator to investigate the fit of the three-factor model to the data, in which mastery goal orientation is a unified construct but PAP and PAV remain separate, we would define and fit the model in R as follows:

```
achievement.goal.cfa3.model<- 'mastery=~ags1+ags2+ags5+ags6+ags7+ags12
pap=~ags3+ags9+ags11
pav=~ags4+ags8+ags10'

achievement.goal.cfa3.dwls.fit<- cfa(achievement.goal.cfa3.model,
data=performance.data, estimator="WLSMV")
summary(achievement.goal.cfa3.dwls.fit, fit.measures=T,
standardized=T)
```

The fit statistics for the three-factor model appear in Table 3.1, with similar results to those for the four-factor model except for the chi-square test, which was statistically significant. Finally, we also fit the model in which Mastery and Performance were the only two factors, using the R commands that appear below.

Table 3.1: Goodness of fit statistics for the achievement motivation models

Model	Factors	χ_M^2/ p	CFI	TLI	RMSEA	SRMR
ML	4	328.3 / <0.001	0.915	0.884	0.118	0.052
Satorra	4	225.3 / <0.001	0.918	0.888	0.094	0.052
Yuan	4	258.6 / <0.001	0.905	0.869	0.102	0.052
Bollen*	4	328.3 / <0.001	0.915	0.884	0.118	0.055
WLS	4	127.3 / <0.001	0.843	0.784	0.063	0.107
DWLS	4	63.39 / 0.067	0.994	0.992	0.028	0.050
DWLS	3	90.011 / 0.001	0.986	0.982	0.043	0.059
DWLS	2	92.098 / 0.001	0.986	0.983	0.042	0.060

* The default number of bootstrap samples of 1000 was used.

```
achievement.goal.cfa2.model<-'mastery=~ags1+ags2+ags5+ags6+ags7+ags12
performance=~ags3+ags4+ags8+ags9+ags10+ags11
'

achievement.goal.cfa2.dwls.fit<- cfa(achievement.goal.cfa2.model,
data=performance.data, estimator="WLSMV")
summary(achievement.goal.cfa2.dwls.fit, fit.measures=T,
standardized=T)
```

The fit statistics appearing in Table 3.1 were virtually identical to those of the three-factor model.

The researcher faced with these results must now decide which model is most appropriate given the prevailing theories in the field and the data at hand. We have already noted that there are theoretical arguments based in the motivation literature to support each of these models. In terms of the empirical results presented here, each model fits the data well, and no one of them seems to be clearly better than the others in terms of CFI, TLI, RMSEA, or SRMR. It is true that the four-factor solution is the only one without a statistically significant chi-square test statistic. However, given the similarity in the values of the other fit measures it is not clear that this model is truly superior. In addition, because we are using the DWLS estimator, and not one of the varieties of ML, we do not have access to the information indices (AIC, BIC, SBIC) in lavaan due to the lack of the log-likelihood value needed for this purpose. How then do we decide which model is optimal? To answer this question, recall our earlier discussion in which we noted that the difference in two chi-square values is itself a chi-square, that we called χ_Δ^2 with df_Δ. Thus, we can compare the fit of the three nested models here using χ_Δ^2. We should note that because our original estimator was DWLS rather than ML, a scale correction must be applied to the chi-square values in order to yield a valid test statistic (Bryant & Satorra, 2012). In R, the anova command can be used to compare the fit of the two models, with the necessary scale correction for the DWLS estimator automatically applied. The commands and results for the tests comparing the two-, three-, and four-factor DWLS estimated models appear below.

```
anova(achievement.goal.cfa3.dwls.fit, achievement.goal.cfa2.dwls.fit)
Scaled Chi Square Difference Test (test = scaled.shifted)
```

	Df	AIC	BIC	Chisq	Chisq diff	Df diff
Pr(>Chisq)						
achievement.goal.cfa3.dwls.fit	51			90.011		
achievement.goal.cfa2.dwls.fit	53			92.097	0.13803	2
0.9333						

```
anova(achievement.goal.cfa4.dwls.fit, achievement.goal.cfa2.dwls.fit)
Scaled Chi Square Difference Test (test = scaled.shifted)
```

	Df	AIC	BIC	Chisq	Chisq diff	Df diff
Pr(>Chisq)						
achievement.goal.cfa4.dwls.fit	48			63.390		
achievement.goal.cfa2.dwls.fit	53			92.097	2.9371	5
0.7097						

```
anova(achievement.goal.cfa4.dwls.fit, achievement.goal.cfa3.dwls.fit)
Scaled Chi Square Difference Test (test = scaled.shifted)
```

	Df	AIC	BIC	Chisq	Chisq diff	Df diff
Pr(>Chisq)						
achievement.goal.cfa4.dwls.fit	48			63.390		
achievement.goal.cfa3.dwls.fit	51			90.011	2.3461	3	0.5038

None of the models fit significantly differently compared to one another. Given this result, we will want to select the most parsimonious model available, which in this case is the two-factor model. In general, when we find no significant difference in model fit, the simplest model is usually the one that we will choose.

To close out our discussion of the CFA model, let us examine the full set of results for the two-factor model of achievement motivation fit using DWLS.

```
lavaan (0.5-15) converged normally after 45 iterations
```

Number of observations		419

Estimator	DWLS	Robust
Minimum Function Test Statistic	92.098	132.825

```
Degrees of freedom                              53       53
P-value (Chi-square)                         0.001    0.000
Scaling correction factor                             0.881
Shift parameter                                      28.240
   for simple second-order correction (Mplus variant)
```

Model test baseline model:

```
Minimum Function Test Statistic           2849.173  1005.685
Degrees of freedom                              66       66
P-value                                      0.000    0.000
```

User model versus baseline model:

```
Comparative Fit Index (CFI)                  0.986    0.915
Tucker-Lewis Index (TLI)                     0.983    0.894
```

Root Mean Square Error of Approximation:

```
RMSEA                                        0.042    0.060
90 Percent Confidence Interval         0.027 0.056    0.047 0.073
P-value RMSEA <= 0.05                   0.814 0.094
```

Standardized Root Mean Square Residual:

```
SRMR                                         0.060    0.060
```

Parameter estimates:

```
Information                            Expected
Standard Errors                        Robust.sem

            Estimate Std.err Z-value P(>|z|) Std.lv Std.all
Latent variables:
  mastery =~
    ags1      1.000                              0.829  0.736
    ags2      1.103   0.102   10.760   0.000     0.914  0.621
    ags5      0.729   0.065   11.206   0.000     0.605  0.634
    ags6      1.036   0.085    2.180   0.000     0.860  0.760
    ags7      1.023   0.069   14.816   0.000     0.848  0.821
    ags12     1.164   0.103   11.255   0.000     0.965  0.647
  performance =~
    ags3      1.000                              1.267  0.828
    ags4      0.732   0.049   14.861   0.000     0.928  0.769
```

ags8	1.154	0.054	21.382	0.000	1.463	0.840
ags9	0.857	0.044	19.634	0.000	1.086	0.861
ags10	1.099	0.049	22.328	0.000	1.393	0.904
ags11	1.108	0.047	23.369	0.000	1.404	0.833

Covariances:
mastery ~~

performance	0.120	0.067	1.793	0.073	0.115	0.115

Intercepts:

ags1	5.589	0.055	101.354	0.000	5.589	4.957
ags2	5.031	0.072	69.843	0.000	5.031	3.416
ags5	6.155	0.047	131.825	0.000	6.155	6.448
ags6	5.692	0.055	102.839	0.000	5.692	5.030
ags7	5.826	0.051	115.272	0.000	5.826	5.638
ags12	5.119	0.073	70.168	0.000	5.119	3.432
ags3	5.353	0.075	71.489	0.000	5.353	3.497
ags4	6.095	0.059	103.316	0.000	6.095	5.053
ags8	5.057	0.085	59.398	0.000	5.057	2.905
ags9	5.859	0.062	94.996	0.000	5.859	4.646
ags10	5.551	0.075	73.613	0.000	5.551	3.601
ags11	4.974	0.082	60.301	0.000	4.974	2.949
mastery		0.000			0.000	0.000
performance		0.000			0.000	0.000

Variances:

ags1	0.583	0.082			0.583	0.459
ags2	1.333	0.168			1.333	0.614
ags5	0.545	0.052			0.545	0.598
ags6	0.542	0.068			0.542	0.423
ags7	0.348	0.048			0.348	0.326
ags12	1.294	0.163			1.294	0.581
ags3	0.738	0.073			0.738	0.315
ags4	0.594	0.077			0.594	0.409
ags8	0.891	0.129			0.891	0.294
ags9	0.411	0.048			0.411	0.258
ags10	0.436	0.068			0.436	0.184
ags11	0.871	0.101			0.871	0.306
mastery	0.688	0.100			1.000	1.000
performance	1.606	0.187			1.000	1.000

As we have already noted, the model fits the data well, based on all of our fit indices. In addition, all of the factor loadings were significant and positive, suggesting that the indicators were associated in the expected ways with the factors. The Mastery and Performance factors themselves were not significantly related to one another, with a correlation of 0.115. In terms of the error variances, ags2 and ags12 had the largest values, with the smallest belonging to ags7 and ags9.

SUMMARY

In Chapter 3 we were introduced to CFA, which stands as a counterpoint to EFA from Chapter 2. Specifically, when using CFA we explicitly define the relationships between the observed indicators and the latent variables, whereas with EFA we do not. As a result, with CFA we have both the benefit of more clearly defined indices of statistical fit that can be used to select from among the models the one that is optimal, and a greater burden to ensure that prior research and theory support the selection of models that we compare with one another. We also saw that with CFA a number of methods are available for estimating the model parameters, as well as several adjustments to the chi-square test and associated statistics for use with ML estimation when the data are not multivariate normal. We then presented a full example in which we applied CFA to our data and determined which model was optimal from among those that were theoretically viable.

FURTHER READING

Brown, T.A. (2015). *Confirmatory Factor Analysis for Applied Research*, 2nd edition. New York: The Guilford Press.

Fabrigar, L.R., & Wegener, D.T. (2012). *Factor Analysis*. Oxford: Oxford University Press.

Gorsuch, R.L. (1983). *Factor Analysis*. Hillsdale, NJ: Lawrence Erlbaum Associates.

Kline, R.B. (2011). *Principles and Practice of Structural Equation Modeling*, 3rd edition. New York: The Guilford Press.

Thompson, B. (2004). *Exploratory and Confirmatory Factor Analysis*. Washington, DC: American Psychological Association.

REFERENCES

Akaike, H. (1973). Information theory and an extension of the maximum likelihood principle. In B.N. Petrov & F. Caski (eds), *Proceedings of the Second International Symposium on Information Theory* (pp. 267–81). Budapest: Akademiai Kiado.

Bollen, K.A. (1990). Overall fit in covariance structure models: Two types of sample size effects. *Psychological Bulletin*, 107, 256–9.

Bollen, K.A. (1989). *Structural Equations with Latent Variables*. New York: Wiley.

Bollen, K., & Stine, R. (1992), Bootstrapping goodness of fit measures in structural equation models. *Sociological Methods and Research*, 21, 205–29.

Brown, T.A. (2015). *Confirmatory Factor Analysis for Applied Research*, 2nd edition. New York: The Guilford Press.

Bryant, F.B., & Satorra, A. (2012). Principles and practice of scaled difference chi square testing. *Structural Equation Modeling*, 19, 372–98.

Curran, P.J., West, S.G., Finch, J.F. (1996). The robustness of test statistics to nonnormality and specification error in confirmatory factor analysis. *Psychological Methods*, 1, 16–29.

Efron, B. (1982). *The Jackknife, the Bootstrap, and Other Resampling Plans*. Philadelphia, PA: Society for Industrial and Applied Mathematics.

Enders, C.K., & Tofighi, D. (2008). The impact of misspecifying class-specific residual variances in growth mixture models. *Structural Equation Modeling: A Multidisciplinary Journal*, 15, 75–95.

Finney, S.J., & DiStefano, C. (2013). Nonnormal and categorical data in structural equation models. In G.R. Hancock & R.O. Mueller (eds). *A Second Course in Structural Equation Modeling* (2nd ed., pp. 439–92). Charlotte, NC: Information Age.

Flora, D.B., & Curran, P.J. (2004). An empirical evaluation of alternative methods of estimation for confirmatory factor analysis with ordinal data. *Psychological Methods*, 9, 466–91.

Hu, L., & Bentler, P.M. (1999). Cutoff criteria for fit indexes in covariance structure analysis: Conventional criteria versus new alternatives. *Structural Equation Modeling*, 6, 1–55.

Kline, R.B. (2011). *Principles and Practice of Structural Equation Modeling*, 3rd edition. New York: The Guilford Press.

Muthén, B.O., du Toit, S.H.C., & Spisic, D. (1997). *Robust inference using weighted least squares and quadratic estimating equations in latent variable modeling with categorical and continuous outcomes*. Unpublished manuscript.

Satorra, A., & Bentler, P.M. (1994). Corrections to test statistics and standard errors in covariance structure analysis. In A. von Eye & C.C. Clogg (eds), *Latent Variables Analysis: Applications for Developmental Research* (pp. 399–419). Newbury Park, CA: Sage.

Schwarz, G.E. (1978). Estimating the dimension of a model. *Annals of Statistics* 6, 461–4.

Wirth, R.J., & Edwards, M.C. (2007). Item factor analysis: Current approaches and future directions. *Psychological Methods*, 12, 58–79.

Yuan, K.-H., & Bentler, P.M. (1997). Mean and covariance structure analysis: theoretical and practical improvements. *Journal of American Statistical Association*, 92, 767–74.

Yuan, K.-H., Bentler, P.M., & Zhang, W. (2005). The effect of skewness and kurtosis on mean and covariance structure analysis: The univariate case and its multivariate implication. *Sociological Methods & Research*, 34, 249–58.

## Chapter 4

FOUNDATIONS OF STRUCTURAL EQUATION MODELING

INTRODUCTION

Quite often in practice researchers are interested in how two or more latent constructs, such as intelligence and aptitude, are related to one another. Questions of this type can quite often be addressed using latent variable models that resemble regression or path analysis. For example, a researcher might posit a model for how the theory of planned behavior relates to college students' intentions to graduate. In this case, each construct is measured by scales consisting of ordinal items on a 1 to 5 Likert-type scale. Using the tools we learned in the previous chapter, we could express the relationships among the items and the latent constructs by fitting a CFA to each scale separately. In this chapter we will see that we can take this analysis a step further by relating the factors to one another in much the same way that we would relate observed variables to one another using regression analysis. In particular, the relationships among the factors are expressed through structural equation models (SEMs), which are very similar in spirit to regression models, but which involve latent rather than observed variables. Equation 4.1 expresses a general example in which factor η is the **endogenous** (i.e. dependent) latent variable and γ is the **exogenous** (i.e. independent) latent variable.

$$\eta = B\gamma + \zeta \tag{4.1}$$

The relationship between the two latent variables is expressed in the coefficient B, which is interpreted essentially in the same way as a regression coefficient would be. In addition, there exists random error, ζ, that is assumed to have a mean of 0 and variance of 1.

The relationships expressed in (4.1) are typically referred to as the structural part of the model, whereas the linking of observed indicators to the latent variables

(η and γ) is referred to as the measurement portion of the model. The statistical mechanisms for fitting these models and obtaining parameter estimates, as well as the tools used to assess model fit, are much the same as for fitting and assessing CFA solutions. Therefore, a great deal of what we see in this chapter will be similar to what we have already seen in Chapter 2, with the addition of interpretation of the coefficients in (4.1).

The fitting of SEMs occurs in two steps. First, the CFA models for the latent factors must be estimated and shown to fit the data well. In doing this, we are ensuring that the latent variables that we propose for inclusion in the structural model are in fact supported by the data. If the **measurement model** does not fit well, then it is not possible to go forward and estimate the structural component because the factors themselves are not dependable. Assuming that the measurement models do in fact fit the data, we can then proceed to fitting the structural components. Here, our interest is in determining whether the hypothesized model(s) expressing relationships among the factors fit the data, and in identifying the nature of the relationships themselves. As noted above, determination of model fit is done in much the same way as it is for CFA, using various indices such as RMSEA, CFI, TLI, SRMR, and the chi-square goodness of fit test. In addition, we will obtain estimates for the coefficients linking the latent variables along with standard errors and hypothesis tests.

THE IMPORTANCE OF SUBSTANTIVE THEORY IN SEM

Researchers working in SEM are typically interested in fitting models that test theories of some importance in their field of study. The example that we will focus on in this chapter involves theories about how perfectionism in college students is related to their reasons for wanting to learn material in their classes, and to their ability to control their attention and remain on task with their work. This model was not simply dreamt up by a researcher who had some data on these variables and wanted to see whether they were related to one another, but rather is the product of a careful study of the literature in the areas of perfectionism, goal orientation, and attention control. Each proposed relationship that we discuss in the following pages has multiple references supporting it. In addition, these relationships, as well as the latent constructs of perfectionism, goal orientation, and attention control, have also been examined empirically in prior research. This work involved exploratory factor analysis as well as regression modeling for observed variables. While no prior work has examined the exact models that we will fit below, there has been sufficient work done in this area that the researchers have some basis for proposing the models to be examined here. In short, prior to even proposing a model, let alone fitting it with statistical software, it is crucial that the researcher become immersed in the theory underlying their work and that the models be developed through a combination of theory and previous empirical evidence.

Why is the employment of sound theory and prior research so important? Obviously, for any research endeavor there should be ample theoretical foundations so that results can be explained in a coherent and meaningful way. This becomes especially important in the context of SEM due to the power of the statistical techniques involved, and the possibility for making logical errors as a result. The models that we fit with SEM are statistical constructs that seek to maximize prediction accuracy of covariances (or correlations) among a set of observed variables. They are obviously not cognizant of the actual theories being assessed. In addition, because we are working with covariances, directionality is not inherently present in the models. What this means is that while equation (4.1) states that η is the endogenous (dependent) variable and γ is the exogenous (independent) variable, the actual machinery doing the estimation for us does not know this. It simply tries to find the value for B (and the other model parameters) that lead to the most accurate prediction of covariances among the observed indicator variables possible. Therefore, if we are incorrect about the direction of the relationship between η and γ there is no check built into the analysis to correct us. In fact, we will obtain an estimate for B that will be interpreted as the directional relationship from γ to η. This is why the proposed models must be based on prior theory and empirical work so that we have some sound and well-supported reasons for proposing the directionality inherent in the model. This is also why it is generally wise to have multiple such models to compare with one another. It is highly unlikely that any one model is absolutely accurate in terms of the nature of the unobserved constructs and their relationships with one another. By having more than one such model (all based in theory and prior empirical evidence) we avoid a self-confirmation bias in which we obtain a good fit for a single proposed model and conclude that it must be the "right" model without comparing it to other theoretically sound models. The reader is encouraged to consider Kline's (2011) chapter "How to fool yourself with SEM" for further discussion of the importance of a well-developed and testable theory, and the pitfalls awaiting researchers who do not have one.

With this caveat regarding the importance of theory and prior empirical work firmly in place, we can now investigate fitting SEM using lavaan. We begin with a brief review of CFA in the form of fitting measurement models, and then proceed to examining three models for the same set of latent variables, and then a fourth model that adds an additional variable to the equation. We will focus on aspects

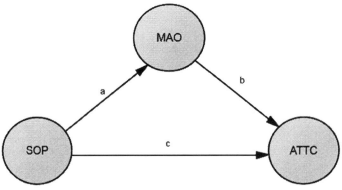

▪ **Figure 4.1:** Partially mediated model

of this analysis that are unique from what we examined in the previous chapters, and conclude with a summary of those new ideas here.

FITTING THE MEASUREMENT MODEL IN R

As noted above, the first step in fitting a SEM is to ensure that the proposed factor structure actually fits the data, prior to estimating the relationships among the factors themselves. Essentially this entails fitting CFA models as we did in Chapter 3. For the current example, we are interested in fitting and comparing the models displayed in Figure 4.1.

Specifically, Figure 4.1 represents a partially mediated model in which the relationship between the construct self-oriented perfectionism (SOP) and attention control (ATTC) is partially mediated by mastery achievement orientation (MAO). Prior to actually fitting the SEM displayed in Figure 4.1, we must first ascertain whether the measurement models for each latent variable fit the data. In other words, are the hypothesized factor structures for SOP, ATTC, and MAO supported by the data at hand? Theory suggests that the MAO factor is measured by 6 items, SOP by 13 items, and ATTC by 4 items. However, we must ascertain whether the proposed model structure is supported by our data, which we will do by fitting a CFA to each of the latent variables appearing in Figure 4.1. Below we see the R code for fitting each of the measurement models using diagonally weighted least squares estimation, followed by the resultant model fit output. Note that we have not included the full set of output in order to save space.

Mastery:
```
mastery.model<-'mastery=~ags1+ags2+ags5+ags6+ags7+ags12'
```

```
mastery.model.fit<-cfa(mastery.model, data=edps744, estimator="WLSMV")
summary(mastery.model.fit, fit.measures=T, standardized=T)
```

lavaan (0.5-15) converged normally after 34 iterations

	Used	Total
Number of observations	424	432

	DWLS	Robust
Estimator	DWLS	Robust
Minimum Function Test Statistic	30.739	78.433
Degrees of freedom	9	9
P-value (Chi-square)	0.000	0.000
Scaling correction factor		0.404
Shift parameter		2.257
for simple second-order correction (Mplus variant)		

Model test baseline model:

Minimum Function Test Statistic	1169.249	566.100
Degrees of freedom	15	15
P-value	0.000	0.000

User model versus baseline model:

Comparative Fit Index (CFI)	0.981	0.874
Tucker-Lewis Index (TLI)	0.969	0.790

Root Mean Square Error of Approximation:

RMSEA		0.076	0.135	
90 Percent Confidence Interval	0.047	0.106	0.108	0.163
P-value RMSEA <= 0.05		0.066	0.000	

Standardized Root Mean Square Residual:

SRMR	0.067	0.067

Self-oriented perfectionism:
```
self.model<-'self=~mps1+mps6+mps12+mps14+mps15+mps17+mps20+mps23+mps28+mps
32+mps34+mps40+mps42'
self.model.fit<-cfa(self.model, data=edps744, estimator= "WLSMV")
```

```
summary(self.model.fit, fit.measures=T, standardized=T)
```

lavaan (0.5-15) converged normally after 40 iterations

	Used	Total
Number of observations	413	432

	Used	Total
Estimator	DWLS	Robust
Minimum Function Test Statistic	110.570	227.625
Degrees of freedom	65	65
P-value (Chi-square)	0.000	0.000
Scaling correction factor		0.525
Shift parameter		17.196
for simple second-order correction (Mplus variant)		

Model test baseline model:

Minimum Function Test Statistic	4245.088	1543.653
Degrees of freedom	78	78
P-value	0.000	0.000

User model versus baseline model:

Comparative Fit Index (CFI)	0.989	0.889
Tucker-Lewis Index (TLI)	0.987	0.867

Root Mean Square Error of Approximation:

RMSEA		0.041	0.078	
90 Percent Confidence Interval	0.028	0.054	0.067	0.089
P-value RMSEA <= 0.05		0.860	0.000	

Standardized Root Mean Square Residual:

SRMR	0.056	0.056

ATTC:

```
attc.model<-'attc=~ats50+ats29+ats40+ats35'
attc.model.fit<-cfa(attc.model, data=edps744, estimator="WLSMV")
summary(attc.model.fit, fit.measures=T, standardized=T)
```

lavaan (0.5-15) converged normally after 33 iterations

	Used	Total
Number of observations	412	432

Estimator	DWLS	Robust
Minimum Function Test Statistic	2.934	6.542
Degrees of freedom	2	2
P-value (Chi-square)	0.231	0.038
Scaling correction factor		0.450
Shift parameter		0.023
for simple second-order correction (Mplus variant)		
Model test baseline model:		
Minimum Function Test Statistic	180.596	150.907
Degrees of freedom	6	6
P-value	0.000	0.000
User model versus baseline model:		
Comparative Fit Index (CFI)	0.995	0.969
Tucker-Lewis Index (TLI)	0.984	0.906
Root Mean Square Error of Approximation:		
RMSEA	0.034	0.074
90 Percent Confidence Interval 0.000	0.109	0.015 0.141
P-value RMSEA <= 0.05	0.527	0.197
Standardized Root Mean Square Residual:		
SRMR	0.026	0.026

The statistics for each of the measurement models indicate good fit, such that we can feel comfortable that the proposed factor structures are in fact supported by the data itself. Therefore, we can move ahead with fitting the **structural model** displayed in Figure 4.1.

FITTING THE STRUCTURAL MODEL IN R

We will first fit the partially mediated model depicted in Figure 4.1, and then consider two alternative models of the relationships among SOP, MAO, and ATTC, each of which is described later in the chapter. We will then compare the fit of these models in order to determine which of the three is optimal. The goal in this chapter is not to review all possible models for the current data, or all possible types of structural models that can be fit using lavaan. Rather, our goal is to demonstrate three common model forms in order to give you a foundation upon which to build more complex models for your own particular research problems.

In this example, Model 4.1 (Figure 4.1) proposes a model containing both direct and indirect effects linking SOP and MAO with ATTC. This model essentially says that SOP has both a direct impact on ATTC and an indirect impact through MAO. In order to express this structural model with **lavaan**, we would use the following model command:

```
model4.1 <- '
    mao=~ags1+ags2+ags5+ags6+ags7+ags12
    attc=~ats50+ats29+ats40+ats35
    sop=~mps1+mps6+mps12+mps14+mps15+mps17+mps20+mps23+mps28+mps32+
mps34+mps40+mps42

    #Direct effect
    attc~c*sop

    #Mediator effect
    mao~a*sop
    attc~b*mao

    #Indirect effect
    ab:=a*b

    #Total effect
    total:= c+(a*b)
'
```

The first section of the model specification command defines the latent variables in terms of their observed indicators. We then define the direct effect from SOP to ATTC, and label the coefficient itself c. Note that the # symbol is what is known in computer programming as a comment line indicator. R ignores everything on the line behind #. We have included the comment lines in order to remind us of what the following line of R code does. We then define the mediator effect by first linking SOP with MAO (coefficient a), and MAO with ATTC (coefficient b). The indirect effect of SOP on ATTC is the product of the mediator coefficients (a*b). Finally, we estimate the total effect for SOP on ATTC by adding the direct effect (c) to the indirect effect (a*b).

After specifying the model that we would like to fit, we then actually estimate the model parameters using the **sem** command in **lavaan**, as follows. We can obtain the parameter estimates and model fit statistics using the **summary** command, just as we did when fitting CFA models in Chapter 3. Ascertaining the fit of a SEM is identical to doing so for a CFA model. We will use the same statistical tools that we discussed in the previous chapter, including the chi-square test, RMSEA, TLI, CFI, and SRMR.

```
attcmodel1.fit<-sem(attc.model1,
     data=edps744, estimator="WLSMV")

summary(model4.1.fit, fit.measures=T, standardized=T)

lavaan (0.5-15) converged normally after 55 iterations
```

	Used	Total
Number of observations	397	432
Estimator	DWLS	Robust
Minimum Function Test Statistic	06.757	557.152
Degrees of freedom	227	227
P-value (Chi-square)	0.000	0.000
Scaling correction factor		1.131
Shift parameter		108.984
for simple second-order correction (Mplus variant)		

Model test baselinemodel:

Minimum Function Test Statistic	664.178	2435.775
Degrees of freedom	253	253
P-value	0.000	0.000

User model versus baselinemodel:

Comparative Fit Index (CFI)	0.956	0.849
Tucker-Lewis Index (TLI)	0.951	0.831

Root Mean Square Error of Approximation:

RMSEA		0.056	0.061	
90 Percent Confidence Interval	0.049	0.062	0.054	0.067
P-value RMSEA <= 0.05		0.071	0.003	

Standardized Root Mean Square Residual:

SRMR	0.070	0.070

Parameter estimates:

```
         Information                            Expected
         Standard Errors                        Robust. sem
                       Estimate Std.err Z-value P(>|z|) Std.lv Std.all
Latent variables:
  mao=~
    ags1        1.000    0.871    0.791
    ags2        1.005    0.106    9.510   0.000   0.876   0.590
    ags5        0.715    0.063   11.399   0.000   0.622   0.651
    ags6        0.933    0.088   10.627   0.000   0.812   0.734
    ags7        0.942    0.069   13.567   0.000   0.820   0.802
    ags12       1.036    0.104    9.914   0.000   0.902   0.605
  attc=~
    ats50       1.000                             1.028   0.642
    ats29       1.078    0.226    4.781   0.000   1.109   0.631
    ats40       0.799    0.172    4.640   0.000   0.822   0.437
    ats35       0.584    0.161    3.616   0.000   0.600   0.402
  sop=~
    mps1        1.000                             0.989   0.638
    mps6        1.508    0.118   12.825   0.000   1.492   0.751
    mps12       0.565    0.116    4.879   0.000   0.559   0.278
    mps14       1.253    0.091   13.729   0.000   1.239   0.788
    mps15       1.446    0.111   12.992   0.000   1.430   0.764
    mps17       0.950    0.098    9.677   0.000   0.940   0.645
    mps20       1.475    0.114   12.922   0.000   1.459   0.793
    mps23       0.775    0.075   10.316   0.000   0.766   0.525
    mps28       1.368    0.093   14.693   0.000   1.353   0.725
    mps32       0.883    0.089    9.921   0.000   0.873   0.551
    mps34       0.549    0.102    5.372   0.000   0.543   0.301
    mps40       0.715    0.073    9.795   0.000   0.707   0.587
    mps42       0.761    0.084    9.058   0.000   0.753   0.529


Regressions:
  attc~
    sop     (c) -0.004   0.074    0.058   0.954   0.004   0.004
  mao~
    sop     (a)  0.323   0.058    5.605   0.000   0.367   0.367
  attc~
    mao     (b)  0.343   0.096    3.562   0.000   0.291   0.291

Intercepts:
    ags1        5.615    0.055  101.479   0.000   5.615   5.100
    ags2        5.045    0.075   67.691   0.000   5.045   3.402
    ags5        6.156    0.048  128.074   0.000   6.156   6.436
    ags6        5.725    0.056  102.944   0.000   5.725   5.173
    ags7        5.846    0.051  113.835   0.000   5.846   5.720
```

ags12	5.118	0.075	68.270	0.000	5.118	3.431
ats50	3.768	0.080	46.846	0.000	3.768	2.354
ats29	4.136	0.088	46.841	0.000	4.136	2.354
ats40	3.562	0.095	37.645	0.000	3.562	1.892
ats35	4.610	0.075	61.447	0.000	4.610	3.088
mps1	5.212	0.078	66.880	0.000	5.212	3.361
mps6	4.073	0.100	40.825	0.000	4.073	2.052
mps12	4.494	0.101	44.387	0.000	4.494	2.231
mps14	5.360	0.079	67.823	0.000	5.360	3.408
mps15	3.864	0.094	41.061	0.000	3.864	2.063
mps17	5.589	0.073	76.366	0.000	5.589	3.838
mps20	4.088	0.092	44.227	0.000	4.088	2.222
mps23	5.378	0.073	73.247	0.000	5.378	3.681
mps28	4.615	0.094	49.191	0.000	4.615	2.472
mps32	5.312	0.080	66.749	0.000	5.312	3.354
mps34	3.753	0.091	41.448	0.000	3.753	2.083
mps40	6.073	0.061	100.303	0.000	6.073	5.040
mps42	5.627	0.072	78.646	0.000	5.627	3.952
mao	0.000				0.000	0.000
attc	0.000				0.000	0.000
sop	0.000				0.000	0.000

Variances:

ags1	0.454	0.084			0.454	0.374
ags2	1.433	0.190			1.433	0.652
ags5	0.528	0.056			0.528	0.577
ags6	0.565	0.079			0.565	0.462
ags7	0.372	0.053			0.372	0.356
ags12	1.412	0.194			1.412	0.634
ats50	1.505	0.259			1.505	0.587
ats29	1.858	0.304			1.858	0.602
ats40	2.869	0.230			2.869	0.809
ats35	1.868	0.198			1.868	0.838
mps1	1.426	0.123			1.426	0.593
mps6	1.717	0.171			1.717	0.436
mps12	3.746	0.220			3.746	0.923
mps14	0.937	0.100			0.937	0.379
mps15	1.461	0.148			1.461	0.417
mps17	1.238	0.136			1.238	0.584
mps20	1.256	0.126			1.256	0.371
mps23	1.547	0.128			1.547	0.725
mps28	1.653	0.149			1.653	0.474
mps32	1.746	0.158			1.746	0.696
mps34	2.952	0.174			2.952	0.909
mps40	0.951	0.083			0.951	0.655

mps42	1.461	0.159			1.461	0.720
mao	0.656	0.094			0.865	0.865
attc	0.969	0.260			0.916	0.916
sop	0.978	0.140			1.000	1.000

Defined parameters:

ab	0.111	0.035	3.161	0.002	0.107	0.107
total	0.107	0.073	1.463	0.143	0.103	0.103

Much of the output from an SEM is similar to that from a CFA. For example, we have estimates of the factor loading, intercept, error variance, and factor variances. For SEM we are not as interested in those parameters as we would be for a standard CFA. Given that we have already estimated the measurement models for the factors, and know that they fit the data well, we would generally not focus on the factor parameters themselves unless we note problems in the structural part of the model. Nonetheless, they are available for us to examine should we want or need to do so. Our primary focus will be on the structural parameters, including the direct and indirect effects that we specified in our model statements. Some of these effects are found under the `Regressions:` section of the output. Here we see that the coefficient linking SOP to ATTC (c) is −0.004, with a standard error of 0.074, a test statistic value of −0.058, and a p-value of 0.954. The standardized coefficients are −0.004 whether only the latent variable is standardized or the latent and observed variables are standardized. Thus, we would conclude that there is not a direct relationship between SOP and ATTC when we also include the indirect relationship through MAO. Examining the regression coefficients further, we see that there is a positive statistically significant relationship between SOP and MAO and between MAO and ATTC. These results mean that individuals with higher SOP also have a higher mastery goal orientation, and that those with a higher mastery goal orientation have higher levels of ATTC. The indirect (ab) and total effects for SOP appear at the very end of the output under the header `Defined parameters`. The indirect effect is statistically significant ($p = 0.002$) and positive with a value of 0.111. On the other hand, the total effect was not significant ($p = 0.143$).

As mentioned previously, fit of SEMs is assessed using the same tools as we employed with CFA. For Model 4.1, the chi-square goodness of fit test was statistically significant, but the CFI (0.956), TLI (0.951), RMSEA (confidence interval of 0.049 to 0.062), and SRMR all indicate that the model fits the data acceptably well for the DWLS estimation. We need to keep in mind that this good fit does not mean that this is the optimal model for the data, nor that it is the only model that fits the data well. Rather, we can conclude that the proposed model is able to accurately reproduce the covariances among the observed indicators. However, other models may fit the data equally well, or even better, and if they have theoretical support one of these alternatives might ultimately be considered superior to Model 4.1.

FITTING ALTERNATIVE SEMS

One alternative to Model 4.1 is Model 4.2, which appears in Figure 4.2.

In this case, the indirect relationship between SOP and ATTC through MAO is absent, leaving only the direct paths between MAO and ATTC, and SOP and ATTC. The commands for fitting Model 4.2 appear below, followed by the output.

```
attc.model4.2 <- '
     mao=~ags1+ags2+ags5+ags6+ags7+ags12
     attc=~ats50+ats29+ats40+ats35
     sop=~mps1+mps6+mps12+mps14+mps15+mps17+mps20+mps23+mps28+mps32+
mps34+mps40+mps42


     attc~mao+sop

     '



Attcmodel4.2.fit<-sem(attc.model4.2,
          data=edps744, estimator="WLSMV")

summary(attcmodel4.2.fit, fit.measures=T, standardized=T)

lavaan (0.5-15) converged normally after 54 iterations
```

	Used	Total
Number of observations	397	432

Estimator	DWLS	Robust
Minimum Function Test Statistic	506.757	557.152
Degrees of freedom	227	227
P-value (Chi-square)	0.000	0.000
Scaling correction factor		1.131

```
      Shift parameter                                   108.984
        for simple second-order correction (Mplus variant)
```

Model test baselinemodel:

```
   Minimum Function Test Statistic         6664.178   2435.775
   Degrees of freedom                           253        253
   P-value                                     0.000      0.000
```

User model versus baselinemodel:

```
   Comparative Fit Index (CFI)                 0.956      0.849
   Tucker-Lewis Index (TLI)                    0.951      0.831
```

Root Mean Square Error of Approximation:

```
   RMSEA                                       0.056      0.061
   90 Percent Confidence Interval     0.049    0.062      0.054   0.067
   P-value RMSEA <= 0.05                       0.071      0.003
```

Standardized Root Mean Square Residual:

```
   SRMR                                        0.070      0.070
```

Parameter estimates:
```
   Information                              Expected
   Standard Errors                         Robust.sem
```

	Estimate	Std.err	Z-value	P(>|z|)	Std.lv	Std.all
Latent variables:						
mao=~						
ags1	1.000	0.871	0.791			
ags2	1.005	0.106	9.510	0.000	0.876	0.590
ags5	0.715	0.063	11.399	0.000	0.622	0.651
ags6	0.933	0.088	10.627	0.000	0.812	0.734
ags7	0.942	0.069	13.567	0.000	0.820	0.802
ags12	1.036	0.104	9.914	0.000	0.902	0.605
attc=~						
ats50	1.000				1.028	0.642
ats29	1.078	0.226	4.781	0.000	1.109	0.631
ats40	0.799	0.172	4.640	0.000	0.822	0.437
ats35	0.584	0.161	3.616	0.000	0.600	0.402
sop=~						
mps1	1.000				0.989	0.638
mps6	1.508	0.118	12.825	0.000	1.492	0.751
mps12	0.565	0.116	4.879	0.000	0.559	0.278
mps14	1.253	0.091	13.729	0.000	1.239	0.788

mps15	0.446	0.111	12.992	0.000	1.430	0.764
mps17	0.950	0.098	9.677	0.000	0.940	0.645
mps20	1.475	0.114	12.922	0.000	1.459	0.793
mps23	0.775	0.075	10.316	0.000	0.766	0.525
mps28	1.368	0.093	14.693	0.000	1.353	0.725
mps32	0.883	0.089	9.921	0.000	0.873	0.551
mps34	0.549	0.102	5.372	0.000	0.543	0.301
mps40	0.715	0.073	9.795	0.000	0.707	0.587
mps42	0.761	0.084	9.058	0.000	0.753	0.529

Regressions:
  attc~

mao	0.343	0.096	3.562	0.000	0.291	0.291
sop	0.004	0.074	0.058	0.954	0.004	-0.004

Covariances:
  mao~~

sop	0.316	0.059	5.383	0.000	0.367	0.367

Intercepts:

ags1	5.615	0.055	101.479	0.000	5.615	5.100
ags2	5.045	0.075	67.691	0.000	5.045	3.402
ags5	6.156	0.048	128.074	0.000	6.156	6.436
ags6	5.725	0.056	102.944	0.000	5.725	5.173
ags7	5.846	0.051	113.835	0.000	5.846	5.720
ags12	5.118	0.075	68.270	0.000	5.118	3.431
ats50	3.768	0.080	46.846	0.000	3.768	2.354
ats29	4.136	0.088	46.841	0.000	4.136	2.354
ats40	3.562	0.095	37.645	0.000	3.562	1.892
ats35	4.610	0.075	61.447	0.000	4.610	3.088
mps1	5.212	0.078	66.880	0.000	5.212	3.361
mps6	4.073	0.100	40.825	0.000	4.073	2.052
mps12	4.494	0.101	44.387	0.000	4.494	2.231
mps14	5.360	0.079	67.823	0.000	5.360	3.408
mps15	3.864	0.094	41.061	0.000	3.864	2.063
mps17	5.589	0.073	76.366	0.000	5.589	3.838
mps20	4.088	0.092	44.227	0.000	4.088	2.222
mps23	5.378	0.073	73.247	0.000	5.378	3.681
mps28	4.615	0.094	49.191	0.000	4.615	2.472
mps32	5.312	0.080	66.749	0.000	5.312	3.354
mps34	3.753	0.091	41.448	0.000	3.753	2.083

mps40	6.073	0.061	100.303	0.000	6.073	5.040
mps42	5.627	0.072	78.646	0.000	5.627	3.952
mao	0.000				0.000	0.000
attc	0.000				0.000	0.000
sop	0.000				0.000	0.000

Variances:

ags1	0.454	0.084	0.454	0.374
ags2	1.433	0.190	1.433	0.652
ags5	0.528	0.056	0.528	0.577
ags6	0.565	0.079	0.565	0.462
ags7	0.372	0.053	0.372	0.356
ags12	1.412	0.194	1.412	0.634
ats50	1.505	0.259	1.505	0.587
ats29	1.858	0.304	1.858	0.602
ats40	2.869	0.230	2.869	0.809
ats35	1.868	0.198	1.868	0.838
mps1	1.426	0.123	1.426	0.593
mps6	1.717	0.171	1.717	0.436
mps12	3.746	0.220	3.746	0.923
mps14	0.937	0.100	0.937	0.379
mps15	1.461	0.148	1.461	0.417
mps17	1.238	0.136	1.238	0.584
mps20	1.256	0.126	1.256	0.371
mps23	1.547	0.128	1.547	0.725
mps28	1.653	0.149	1.653	0.474
mps32	1.746	0.158	1.746	0.696
mps34	2.952	0.174	2.952	0.909
mps40	0.951	0.083	0.951	0.655
mps42	1.461	0.159	1.461	0.720
mao	0.758	0.107	1.000	1.000
attc	0.969	0.260	0.916	0.916
sop	0.978	0.140	1.000	1.000

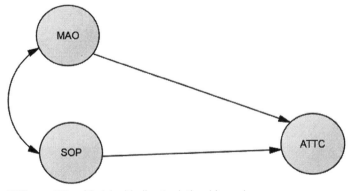

▨ **Figure 4.2:** Model with direct relationships only

In terms of fit to the data, Model 4.2 is essentially identical to Model 4.1, based on the standard statistics that we have been using. How could that be the case since we have removed one of the paths, in this case the direct relationship between SOP and MAO? The answer is that although we removed the path, we did not remove the relationship between the two variables. Notice in our output that there is a covariance between MAO and SOP. This is reflected in the double-headed line linking the two variables in Figure 4.2. Thus, the two models are actually identical in terms of their parameterization of the relationships among the latent variables. The only difference is that in Model 4.1 we made the relationship between SOP and MAO directional, whereas in Model 4.2 we did not. We have included this example in order to demonstrate one of the subtleties in latent variable modeling, namely that when relationships between variables are estimated, mathematically a covariance that is bidirectional behaves in the same fashion as a direct path that is unidirectional. In the mind of the researcher, of course, these are very different things. A covariance simply implies that the variables are related to one another but not that one impacts the other. On the other hand, a unidirectional relationship implies just that, that one latent variable can be seen as a precursor or in some sense a predictor of another. However, mathematically these two models are identical. Therefore, it is extremely important that the researcher have strong theoretical justifications for fitting one or the other of these models, as the statistics themselves will not differentiate them even though conceptually they are very different from one another.

An examination of the parameter estimates for Model 4.2 reveals essentially the same results as for Model 4.1. In particular, there is not a statistically significant direct relationship between SOP and ATTC, but there is one for MAO. In addition, MAO and SOP are significantly positively correlated with one another, such that the correlation is 0.367.

A second alternative to Model 4.1 is Model 4.3, which appears in Figure 4.3.

In this case, we have removed the direct relationship between SOP and ATTC, but maintained the indirect relationship between SOP and ATTC through MAO. The R commands to fit this model and obtain the output using lavaan appear below.

```
attc.model4.3 <- '
    mao=~ags1+ags2+ags5+ags6+ags7+ags12
    attc=~ats50+ats29+ats40+ats35
    sop=~mps1+mps6+mps12+mps14+mps15+mps17+mps20+mps2
        3+mps28+mps32+mps34+mps40+mps42
```

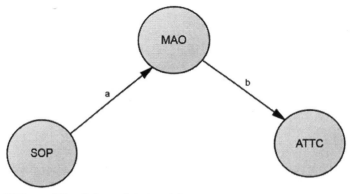

■ **Figure 4.3:** Fully mediated model

```
#Mediator effect
mao~a*sop
attc~b*mao

#Indirect effect
ab:=a*b
```

ı
```
Attcmodel4.3.fit<-sem(attc.model4.3,
        data=edps744, estimator="WLSMV")
summary(attcmodel4.3.fit, fit.measures=T, standardized=T)
```

In the interest of saving space, we will only examine output relevant to assessing model fit and to characterizing the relationships among the factors.

```
lavaan (0.5-15) converged normally after 55 iterations
```

	Used	Total
Number of observations	397	432

	DWLS	Robust
Estimator	DWLS	Robust
Minimum Function Test Statistic	506.778	527.230
Degrees of freedom	228	228
P-value (Chi-square)	0.000	0.000
Scaling correction factor		1.226

```
Shift parameter                                      113.877
   for simple second-order correction (Mplus variant)


Model test baselinemodel:
  Minimum Function Test Statistic         6664.178   2435.775
  Degrees of freedom                           253        253
  P-value                                    0.000      0.000


User model versus baselinemodel:
  Comparative Fit Index (CFI)                0.957      0.863
  Tucker-Lewis Index (TLI)                   0.952      0.848


Root Mean Square Error of Approximation:
  RMSEA                                      0.056      0.058
  90 Percent Confidence Interval    0.049    0.062      0.051    0.064
  P-value RMSEA <= 0.05                      0.078      0.027


Standardized Root Mean Square Residual:
  SRMR                                       0.070      0.070
```

The quality of fit for Model 4.3 is essentially identical to that of Model 4.1, in terms of CFI, TLI, RMSEA, and SRMR. The coefficients linking SOP, MAO, and ATTC, and the indirect effect from SOP to ATTC, appear below.

```
              Estimate Std.err Z-value P(>|z|) Std.lv Std.all
  Regressions:
    mao ~
      sop    (a)   0.323   0.058   5.553   0.000  0.367   0.367
    attc ~
      mao    (b)   0.339   0.098   3.474   0.001  0.288   0.288
  Defined parameters:
           ab      0.110   0.037   2.978   0.003  0.105   0.105
```

From these results, we can see that there is a statistically significant relationship between SOP and MAO, a significant relationship between MAO and ATTC, and a significant indirect effect from SOP to ATTC. Indeed, the parameter values along with the standard errors are very close to the values we obtained for Model 4.1.

Finally, as we discussed in the Chapter 3, it is possible to compare the fit of two nested latent variable models using the χ^2_Δ statistic, which is simply the difference in the two model chi-square values. In R this can be done using the anova command.

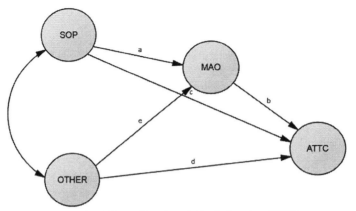

■ **Figure 4.4:** Partially mediated model including the OTHER construct

```
anova(attcmodel4.1.fit, attcmodel4.3.fit)

Scaled Chi Square Difference Test (test = scaled.shifted)

                 Df AIC BIC Chisq Chisq diff Df diff Pr(>Chisq)
Attcmodel4.1.fit 227         506.76
Attcmodel4.3.fit 228         506.78  0.0032623    1       0.9545
```

As we noted in the previous chapter, lavaan does not provide AIC and BIC values for models using DWLS estimation as we did here. However, we do obtain the χ^2_Δ test with the appropriate degrees of freedom correction (Asparouhov & Muthén, 2006). Here we see that there is not a statistically significant difference in the fit of the two models ($p = 0.9545$). Therefore, we can conclude that removing the direct path from SOP to ATTC does not degrade model fit, thereby leading us to retain the more parsimonious Model 4.3.

We would like to conclude this chapter by briefly examining a slightly more complicated model (Model 4.4), which is featured in Figure 4.4.

An additional variable has been included in the model, other-oriented perfectionism (OTHER). This is perfectionism that is driven by a desire by the student to live up to the expectations of others (e.g. parents, friends). Model 4.4 includes direct paths from SOP and OTHER to ATTC, and also indirect paths through MAO. The lavaan commands to fit this model and obtain output appear below.

```
attc.model4.4 <- '
    mao=~ags1+ags2+ags5+ags6+ags7+ags12
    attc=~ats50+ats29+ats40+ats35
    sop=~mps1+mps6+mps12+mps14+mps15+mps17+mps20+mps23+mps28+mps32+
        mps34+mps40+mps42
    other=~mps2+mps3+mps4+mps7+mps10+mps16+mps19+mps22+mps24+mps26+
        mps27+mps29+mps38+mps43+mps45

    #Direct effect
    attc~c*sop
    attc~d*other

    #Mediator effect
    mao~a*sop
    mao~e*other
    attc~b*mao

    #Indirect effect
    ab:=a*b
    eb:=e*b

    #Total effect
    total1:= c+(a*b)
    total2:= d+(e*b)

'

Attcmodel4.4.fit<-sem(attc.model4.4,
            data=edps744, estimator="WLSMV")

summary(attcmodel4.4.fit, fit.measures=T, standardized=T)
```

Portions of the output relevant to discussions of model fit and parameter estimates appear below.

```
lavaan (0.5-15) converged normally after 73 iterations
                                          Used      Total

   Number of observations                  391        432



   Estimator                              DWLS      Robust
   Minimum Function Test Statistic    2315.004   1673.553
   Degrees of freedom                      659        659
   P-value (Chi-square)                  0.000      0.000
   Scaling correction factor                        1.827
   Shift parameter                                406.755
      for simple second-order correction (Mplus variant)

Model test baselinemodel:
   Minimum Function Test Statistic   11576.370   3988.536
   Degrees of freedom                      703        703
   P-value                               0.000      0.000
User model versus baselinemodel:



   Comparative Fit Index (CFI)           0.848      0.691
   Tucker-Lewis Index (TLI)              0.838      0.671
Root Mean Square Error of Approximation:
   RMSEA                                 0.080      0.063
   90 Percent Confidence Interval  0.077  0.084   0.059   0.067
   P-value RMSEA <= 0.05                 0.000      0.000


Standardized Root Mean Square Residual:
   SRMR                                  0.093      0.093
```

From these results, we can see that the fit of Model 4.4 is substantially worse than that of the other models examined in this chapter. Indeed, independently of comparisons with fit for the other models discussed in this chapter, the fit of Model 4.4 is not very good in general. The structural parameter estimates appear below.

```
              Estimate Std.err Z-value P(>|z|) Std.lv Std.all
Regressions:
  attc~
   sop    (c)    0.052   0.104   0.498   0.618   0.049   0.049
   other  (d)   -0.196   0.200  -0.982   0.326  -0.100  -0.100
```

```
mao~
  sop      (a)    0.443    0.072    6.114    0.000    0.508    0.508
  other    (e)   -0.371    0.139   -2.667    0.008   -0.229   -0.229
attc~
  mao      (b)    0.329    0.102    3.209    0.001    0.270    0.270

Covariances:
  sop~~
  other           0.312    0.070    4.445    0.000    0.587    0.587

Defined parameters:
  ab              0.146    0.049    2.950    0.003    0.137    0.137
  eb             -0.122    0.058   -2.090    0.037   -0.062   -0.062
  total1          0.197    0.097    2.040    0.041    0.186    0.186
  total2         -0.318    0.202   -1.572    0.116   -0.162   -0.162
```

There does not exist a direct relationship between OTHER and ATTC (nor SOP and ATTC), though OTHER does have a statistically significant negative relationship with MAO. From these results we can conclude that the more a student exhibits perfectionistic attitudes as a result of other peoples' expectations, the less they want to master academic material as a result of their own desires. SOP and OTHER were significantly positively correlated (0.587), meaning that those who have higher perfectionism tendencies due to their own expectations also have higher perfectionistic tendencies due to others' expectations as well. Finally, the indirect and total effects for SOP were significant, as was the indirect effect for OTHER.

SUMMARY

In the preceding pages we have seen how CFA models can be extended and incorporated into structural models expressing relationships among latent constructs. Such models are potentially very powerful as they allow us to explore complex relationships among these constructs. At the same time, it is important to note the potential pitfalls and serious errors in our conclusions based on these models if there is not sufficient theory underlying them. Thus, it is incumbent on the researcher to have support in the literature and in theory for each of the paths included in a model. Finally, we saw that fitting these models and interpreting their results is very similar to CFA. In Chapter 5 we will extend these models further to allow for investigation of even more complex relationships among the latent variables.

FURTHER READING

Bollen, K.A. (1989). *Structural Equations with Latent Variables*. New York: John Wiley & Sons.

Hoyle, R.H. (2012). *Handbook of Structural Equation Modeling*. New York: The Guilford Press.

Kaplan, D. (2009). *Structural Equation Modeling: Foundations and Extensions*. Thousand Oaks, CA: Sage Publications.

Kline, R.B. (2011). *Principles and Practice of Structural Equation Modeling*, 3rd edition. New York: The Guilford Press.

Mueller, R.O. (1996). *Basic Principles of Structural Equation Modeling*. New York: Springer Verlag.

REFERENCES

Asparouhov, T., & Muthen, B. (2006). Robust chi-square difference testing with mean and variance adjusted test scores. *Mplus Web Notes*, 10.

Kline, R.B. (2011). *Principles and Practice of Structural Equation Modeling*, 3rd edition. New York: The Guilford Press.

## Chapter 5

SEM FOR MULTIPLE GROUPS, THE MIMIC MODEL, AND LATENT MEANS COMPARISONS

INTRODUCTION

In Chapter 4 we focused on the foundations of SEM, paying special attention to the fitting and testing of the structural components, which serve to relate latent variables to one another. In Chapter 5, we will turn our attention to the problem of comparing two or more groups with respect to SEM model parameters. We will key in on three separate approaches, including **multiple groups SEM**, the **multiple indicators multiple causes (MIMIC) model**, and comparisons of latent means. Each of these analyses extends the basic SEM framework described in Chapter 4 to accommodate differing parameter values across different groups. We will begin by examining multiple groups SEM, which serves as a precursor to investigating latent mean differences. Finally, we will conclude the chapter with the MIMIC model, and explore how it can be used to compare latent means across groups, as well as to investigate the relationship between a continuous observed covariate and a continuous latent variable.

MULTIPLE GROUPS SEM

Equations (3.1) and (4.1) expressed the CFA and SEM models, respectively. In each case, it was assumed that the basic structures of these models held across all individuals within the population. In other words, in each case, the assumption was that the model parameters estimated from the sample were correct for all members of the sample. However, such an assumption may be too strong in many situations. As an example, let's consider the mastery goal orientation factor that we worked with in the previous chapters. In particular, we may be interested in whether parameters for a CFA model are common across genders; that is, are the factor loadings, intercepts, factor variances, and error variances the same for males and females in the population? Investigation of such questions is typically referred to as invariance assessment, and model parameters that are equal across groups are said to be invariant. More formally, we refer to **factor invariance** (FI) as the case where the latent structure underlying a scale is equivalent across various groups in the population for which the instrument is intended (Millsap, 2011; Millsap & Kwok, 2004; Meredith & Millsap, 1992; McDonald, 1999). FI is necessary if we are to assume the construct comparability of a scale. Thus, in our example from Chapter 3 involving achievement motivation, only if the CFA model parameters are equivalent across genders can we interpret the meaning of mastery goal orientation to be the same for males and females. When FI does not hold in some respect, use of the latent variables measured by a scale may lead to incorrect decisions regarding individuals from the different groups (Millsap & Kwok, 2004), and inaccurate comparison of groups on the construct being measured (Steinmetz, 2013; Finch & French, 2008).

The methodology for assessing FI is based upon multiple group confirmatory factor analysis (MGCFA), a variant of multiple groups SEM. The MGCFA model is expressed as:

$$x_g = \tau_g + \Lambda_g \eta + \varepsilon_g \tag{5.1}$$

The parameters in this model are the same as in equation (3.1), with the addition of the group subscript, g, indicating that each of the parameters can differ by group. Invariance testing for the parameters in (5.1) is done sequentially using MGCFA models with increasing constraints with respect to group equality on the model parameters. The weakest type of invariance under the FI umbrella is commonly referred to as **configural invariance** (CI). Under CI, the researcher assumes only that the number of latent variables and the correspondence of observed indicators to the latent variables is the same for all groups in the population. In other words, when CI holds, the basic factor structure is equivalent across groups, but no assumptions are made about equality of the model parameters. This situation would correspond to (5.1).

If CI holds, the next level of FI to be assessed is **measurement invariance** (MI). MI refers to the case where the factor loadings are equivalent across groups. Though we refer to this type of equivalence as MI, it has also been called weak factorial invariance (Widaman & Reise, 1997), pattern invariance (Millsap, 2011), and metric invariance (Horn & McArdle, 1992). The presence of MI implies that the latent variables are being measured in the same way for members of the population subgroups under consideration (Kline, 2011; Wicherts & Dolan, 2010). The MI model is expressed as:

$$x_g = \tau_g + \Lambda\eta + \varepsilon_g \tag{5.2}$$

If MI holds, researchers typically next examine invariance of the factor model intercepts (τ), in what is often referred to as **scalar invariance** (Steenkamp & Baumgartner, 1998), or strong factorial invariance (Meredith, 1993). We will use the term scalar invariance (SI) throughout this chapter. Unlike MI, which focuses on the relationships between individual observed indicator variables and the latent trait(s) of interest, SI focuses on the means of the observed indicators in the form of the latent intercepts, τ_g. When SI holds, the researcher can conclude that any

mean differences in the observed indicators across groups are due to differences in the mean of the latent variable, η. On the other hand, when SI does not hold, such a conclusion is not warranted, such that even when the mean of the latent trait is equivalent for two groups, the means of the observed indicators that are noninvariant may differ due to group differences in τ. In addition, it is necessary to prove SI is present prior to comparing latent means across groups, which is an issue addressed later in this chapter. The SI model can be expressed as:

$$x_g = \tau + \Lambda\eta + \varepsilon_g \tag{5.3}$$

In addition to CI, MI, and SI, it is also possible to assess whether there is group invariance with respect to the unique indicator variance (ε). This type of invariance is typically referred to as **strict factor invariance** (SFI; Meredith, 1993) because it occurs only when the factor loadings, intercepts, and unique variances are invariant across groups. In addition, SFI is necessary in order to attribute group differences in the covariance structure (variances and covariances/correlations) of the observed indicators to corresponding differences at the latent variable level (Millsap, 2011). The SFI model is:

$$x_g = \tau + \Lambda\eta + \varepsilon \tag{5.4}$$

Note that the model in (5.4) is equivalent to (5.1), where all model parameters are equivalent across groups.

STEPS IN ASSESSING MODEL INVARIANCE

As noted above, the actual process of assessing model invariance involves the comparison of fit for differently constrained models, done in a sequential fashion. In step 1, the researcher will fit the CI model in which all model parameters are allowed to vary, and then a fully constrained model in which all model parameters are forced to be equal between groups. The fit of these two models is then compared using the **chi-square difference statistic** (χ^2_Δ) that was described in Chapters 3 and 4. The null hypothesis is that the fit of the two models is the same. Therefore, if this test is statistically significant we would conclude that some of the model parameters differ between the groups. If the CI and fully constrained models do not provide significantly different fit to the data, we would stop further testing and conclude that all model parameters are indeed invariant across groups, given that constraining them to be so does not diminish fit. Given a significant result in step 1, step 2 involves comparing the fully constrained model with a model in which the factor loadings are allowed to vary between groups, but all other model parameters are constrained to be equal. Again, the null hypothesis is of equivalent fit for the two models, so that a statistically significant χ^2_Δ value would mean that the models do not fit the data the same. If the fit of these two models is not equal, we would conclude that at least one of the factor loadings differs between the groups. In order to identify which loadings differ, we would select one with which to start, and constrain all others to be equal between the groups. We would then compare the fit of this model with one unconstrained factor loading against that of the fully constrained model. If the resulting χ^2_Δ is statistically significant we would keep that loading unconstrained, and move to the next factor loading. This process of comparing loading constrained and loading unconstrained models would continue until all loadings were tested and found either to be invariant or not. If any factor loadings are found not to be invariant, we would not assess invariance for the intercepts or the error terms. On the other hand, if MI was found to hold, we would move to step 3, and assess SI by constraining loadings and error variances to be equal between the groups but allowing the intercepts to vary. Again, we would compare the fit of this model with that of the fully constrained model. If the fit differs, then we would conclude that at least one of the model intercepts differs between the groups, and then proceed to search one by one to identify which are not invariant. If we find a lack of SI we would not attempt to test for SFI. However, if SI is found to hold, we would then compare a model in which loadings and intercepts are constrained to be equal between the groups and error variances are allowed to differ, in step 4 of the invariance testing procedure. The same process is used to test for SFI, with comparison of model fit between the fully constrained model and the model with error variances allowed to vary, using the χ^2_Δ test. It is also possible to test for the invariance of factor variances and covariances between the groups, in exactly the same manner as for other model parameters, comparing the fully constrained model with a model where the factor variances (or covariances) are allowed to vary. Typically, this would be done once invariance of other model parameters has been established.

MULTIPLE GROUPS CFA WITH LAVAAN

Let us now return to our example of assessing invariance for the mastery goal orientation latent variable model between genders. Recall from Chapter 3 that we found evidence to support the notion that mastery goal orientation can be thought of as a unified construct, rather than as two separate factors, which was the original proposal put forth by motivation theorists. For this model, six Likert-type items serve as the observed indicators for the latent variable MAO. The code needed to fit the CI model and to request output using lavaan appears below, followed by the output.

```
mastery.ci<-cfa(mastery.model, data=edps744, group=
"gender", estimator="WLSMV")
summary(mastery.ci, fit.measures=TRUE, standardized=
TRUE)
```

lavaan (0.5–15) converged normally after 56 iterations

	Used	Total
Number of observations per group		
2	308	312
1	116	120

Estimator	DWLS	Robust
Minimum Function Test Statistic	33.319	74.867
Degrees of freedom	18	18
P-value (Chi-square)	0.015	0.000
Scaling correction factor		0.480
Shift parameter for each group:		
2		3.953
1		1.489
for simple second-order correction (Mplus variant)		

Chi-square for each group:

2	20.773	47.238
1	12.546	27.630

```
Model test baseline model:
    Minimum Function Test Statistic      1227.416        23.036
    Degrees of freedom                         30            30
    P-value                                 0.000         0.000

User model versus baseline model:

    Comparative Fit Index (CFI)             0.987         0.904
    Tucker-Lewis Index (TLI)                0.979         0.840

Root Mean Square Error of Approximation:

    RMSEA                                   0.064         0.122
    90 Percent Confidence Interval    0.027 0.097   0.094 0.152
    P-value RMSEA <= 0.05                   0.232         0.000

Standardized Root Mean Square Residual:

    SRMR                                    0.068         0.068
    Parameter estimates:
    Information                                        Expected
    Standard Errors                                  Robust.sem

Group 1 [2]:

            Estimate Std.err Z-value P(>|z|) Std.lv Std.all
Latent variables:
    mastery =~
        ags1    1.000                              0.870  0.746
        ags2    1.018  0.110   9.273   0.000       0.886  0.584
        ags5    0.728  0.068  10.724   0.000       0.634  0.680
        ags6    1.027  0.089  11.513   0.000       0.893  0.775
        ags7    1.041  0.076  13.659   0.000       0.906  0.846
        ags12   1.054  0.104  10.153   0.000       0.918  0.620

Intercepts:
        ags1    5.601  0.067  84.049   0.000       5.601  4.800
        ags2    4.977  0.087  57.431   0.000       4.977  3.280
        ags5    6.146  0.053 115.513   0.000       6.146  6.598
        ags6    5.656  0.066  85.949   0.000       5.656  4.909
        ags7    5.844  0.061  95.488   0.000       5.844  5.454
        ags12   5.091  0.084  60.271   0.000       5.091  3.442
      mastery   0.000                              0.000  0.000
```

Variances:

	Estimate	Std.err		Std.lv	Std.all
ags1	0.604	0.108		0.604	0.444
ags2	1.517	0.208		1.517	0.659
ags5	0.466	0.048		0.466	0.537
ags6	0.529	0.077		0.529	0.399
ags7	0.327	0.052		0.327	0.285
ags12	1.345	0.195		1.345	0.615
mastery	0.757	0.127		1.000	1.000

Group 2 [1]:

	Estimate	Std.err	Z-value	P(>|z|)	Std.lv	Std.all
Latent variables:						
mastery =~						
ags1	1.000				0.720	0.710
ags2	1.270	0.188	6.762	0.000	0.914	0.663
ags5	0.903	0.148	6.084	0.000	0.650	0.632
ags6	1.029	0.153	6.708	0.000	0.741	0.697
ags7	1.082	0.122	8.893	0.000	0.779	0.852
ags12	1.272	0.210	6.063	0.000	0.916	0.596

Intercepts:

	Estimate	Std.err	Z-value	P(>|z|)	Std.lv	Std.all
ags1	5.578	0.094	59.088	0.000	5.578	5.499
ags2	5.172	0.128	40.315	0.000	5.172	3.752
ags5	6.190	0.096	64.617	0.000	6.190	6.014
ags6	5.810	0.099	58.758	0.000	5.810	5.468
ags7	5.776	0.085	67.865	0.000	5.776	6.316
ags12	5.164	0.143	36.085	0.000	5.164	3.358
mastery	0.000				0.000	0.000

Variances:

	Estimate	Std.err		Std.lv	Std.all
ags1	0.510	0.110		0.510	0.496
ags2	1.065	0.291		1.065	0.560
ags5	0.637	0.115		0.637	0.601
ags6	0.580	0.110		0.580	0.514
ags7	0.229	0.056		0.229	0.274
ags12	1.525	0.291		1.525	0.645
mastery	0.518	0.121		1.000	1.000

There were a total of 308 females (group 2) and 116 males (group 1) used in the analysis, with 4 individuals in each gender group having missing data. From these results, we also see that using DWLS estimation, the CI model appears to fit the data well, based on the CFI, TLI, RMSEA, and SRMR. The chi-square goodness of fit test is statistically significant, but given the sample size this is not completely unexpected, as we know that this test is sensitive to sample size (Brown, 2015). The software also provides us with separate parameter estimates for each of the two groups. The question of interest with invariance testing is, to what extent are sample differences in various model parameters (e.g. loadings, intercepts) indicative of true population differences, or simply the product of sampling variability? It is this question that invariance testing will answer for us.

In order to fit the fully invariant model, we will use the following lavaan commands. Notice that we indicate which of the model parameters should be constrained to equality between the groups using the group.equal= subcommand in lavaan.

```
mastery.all.equal<-cfa(mastery.model, data=edps744, group="gender",
group.equal=c("loadings", "intercepts", "residuals", "lv.variances",
"lv.covariances"), estimator="WLSMV")
summary(mastery.all.equal, fit.measures=TRUE, standardized=TRUE)

lavaan (0.5-15) converged normally after 43 iterations
```

	Used	Total
Number of observations pergroup		
2	308	312
1	116	120

Estimator	DWLS	Robust
Minimum Function Test Statistic	9.296	60.505
Degrees of freedom	35	35
P-value (Chi-square)	0.006	0.005
Scaling correction factor		1.287
Shift parameter for eachgroup:		
2		10.493
1		3.952
for simple second-order correction (Mplus variant)		

```
Chi-square for eachgroup:

2          32.020 35.366
1          27.276 25.140
```

Model test baseline model:

Minimum Function Test Statistic	227.416	623.036
Degrees of freedom	30	30
P-value	0.000	0.000

User model versus baselinemodel:

Comparative Fit Index (CFI)	0.980	0.957
Tucker-Lewis Index (TLI)	0.983	0.963

Root Mean Square Error of Approximation:

RMSEA		0.057	0.059	
90 Percent Confidence Interval	0.030	0.082	0.032	0.083
P-value RMSEA <= 0.05		0.295	0.263	

Standardized Root Mean Square Residual:

SRMR	0.094	0.094

Parameter estimates:

Information	Expected
Standard Errors	Robust.sem

Group1[2]:

	Estimate	Std.err	Z-value	P(>|z|)	Std.lv	Std.all
Latent variables:						
mastery=~						
ags1	1.000	0.797	0.726			
ags2	1.130	0.098	11.543	0.000	0.901	0.614
ags5	0.814	0.066	12.263	0.000	0.649	0.689
ags6	1.029	0.080	12.889	0.000	0.821	0.739
ags7	1.064	0.066	16.169	0.000	0.848	0.847
ags12	1.161	0.099	11.678	0.000	0.926	0.618
Intercepts:						
ags1	5.578	0.062	89.328	0.000	5.578	5.080
ags2	5.023	0.078	64.367	0.000	5.023	3.421
ags5	6.148	0.051	120.543	0.000	6.148	6.523
ags6	5.689	0.063	90.404	0.000	5.689	5.122
ags7	5.805	0.059	97.701	0.000	5.805	5.799
ags12	5.096	0.079	64.468	0.000	5.096	3.402
mastery	0.000				0.000	0.000

Variances:

ags1	0.570	0.079				0.570	0.473
ags2	1.343	0.171				1.343	0.623
ags5	0.467	0.047				0.467	0.526
ags6	0.560	0.067				0.560	0.454
ags7	0.283	0.039				0.283	0.282
ags12	1.387	0.163				1.387	0.618
mastery	0.636	0.086				1.000	1.000

Group2[1]:

	Estimate	Std.err	Z-value	P(>|z|)	Std.lv	Std.all
Latent variables:						
mastery=~						
ags1	1.000				0.797	0.726
ags2	1.130	0.098	11.543	0.000	0.901	0.614
ags5	0.814	0.066	12.263	0.000	0.649	0.689
ags6	1.029	0.080	12.889	0.000	0.821	0.739
ags7	1.064	0.066	16.169	0.000	0.848	0.847
ags12	1.161	0.099	11.678	0.000	0.926	0.618
Intercepts:						
ags1	5.578	0.062	89.328	0.000	5.578	5.080
ags2	5.023	0.078	64.367	0.000	5.023	3.421
ags5	6.148	0.051	120.543	0.000	6.148	6.523
ags6	5.689	0.063	90.404	0.000	5.689	5.122
ags7	5.805	0.059	97.701	0.000	5.805	5.799
ags12	5.096	0.079	64.468	0.000	5.096	3.402
mastery	0.044	0.092	0.480	0.631	0.055	0.055
Variances:						
ags1	0.570	0.079			0.570	0.473
ags2	1.343	0.171			1.343	0.623
ags5	0.467	0.047			0.467	0.526
ags6	0.560	0.067			0.560	0.454
ags7	0.283	0.039			0.283	0.282
ags12	1.387	0.163			1.387	0.618
mastery	0.636	0.086			1.000	1.000

Results for the fully constrained model suggest that it also fits the data well, just as did the CI model. The CFI, TLI, and RMSEA statistics are all within range to suggest good fit. This is not true of SRMR, and the chi-square goodness of fit test is also statistically significant. However, taken together, we can conclude that the fully constrained model fits the data well.

The next step in our invariance analysis is to compare the fit of the two models using the χ^2_Δ statistic. As we have seen in previous chapters, this test can be conducted in R using the anova command.

```
anova(mastery.ci, mastery.all.equal)
```

```
Scaled Chi Square Difference Test (test = scaled.shifted)
                  Df AIC BIC Chisq Chisq diff Df diff Pr(>Chisq)
mastery.ci        18         33.319
mastery.all.equal 35         59.296   20.892     17        0.2311
```

Given the non-significant result for the χ^2_Δ test, we would not reject the null hypothesis of no difference in the degree of fit between the two models, and would thereby conclude that the model parameters are invariant across the groups.

Despite the finding of full model invariance based on a comparison of the CI and fully constrained models, for pedagogical purposes, we will demonstrate how to test for each type of invariance using the MGCFA model in lavaan. We will not, however, display the full set of output for each model, leaving that for the interested reader to examine. In order to fit a model in which the factor loadings are allowed to vary between groups but all other model parameters are constrained to equality, we would use the following command, leaving "loadings" out of the group.equal= subcommand.

```
mastery.mi<-cfa(mastery.model, data=edps744, group="gender",
group.equal=c("intercepts", "residuals", "lv.variances",
"lv.covariances"), estimator="WLSMV")
summary(mastery.mi, fit.measures=TRUE, standardized= TRUE)
```

Comparison of model fit between this and the fully constrained model is again done with the anova command.

```
anova(mastery.mi, mastery.all.equal)
```

```
Scaled Chi Square Difference Test (test = scaled.shifted)
                  Df AIC BIC Chisq Chisq diff Df diff Pr(>Chisq)
mastery.mi        30         43.742
mastery.all.equal 35         59.296   6.2026      5        0.287
```

As expected, given the results comparing the fully constrained and CI models, there was not a significant difference between the fully constrained and factor loadings varying model, meaning that the loadings do not differ across groups. Similarly, we can test for SI using the following commands.

```
mastery.si<-cfa(mastery.model, data=edps_744, group="gender",
group.equal=c("loadings", "residuals", "lv.variances",
"lv.covariances"), estimator= "WLSMV")
summary(mastery.si, fit.measures=TRUE, standardized= TRUE)
anova(mastery.si, mastery.all.equal)
Scaled Chi Square Difference Test (test = scaled.shifted)
```

no
Intercept ↗

	Df	AIC	BIC	Chisq	Chisq diff	Df diff	Pr(>Chisq)
mastery.si	30		55.986				
mastery.all.equal	35		59.296		2.7578	5	0.7373

These statistically nonsignificant results indicate the presence of SI. Finally, we can test for SFI using the following commands.

```
mastery.sfi<-cfa(mastery.model, data=edps_744, group= "gender",
group.equal=c("loadings", "intercepts", "lv.variances",
"lv.covariances"), estimator="WLSMV")
summary(mastery.sfi, fit.measures=TRUE, standardized= TRUE)
anova(mastery.sfi, mastery.all.equal)

Scaled Chi Square Difference Test (test = scaled.shifted)
```

no
residuals ↗

	Df	AIC	BIC	Chisq	Chisq diff	Df diff	Pr(>Chisq)
mastery.sfi	29		48.651				
mastery.all.equal	35		59.296		10.645	6	0.1

Once again, the results for the individual parameter set match the nonsignificant results for invariance assessment of the entire model. It is important for us to note once again that in actual practice we would have stopped the invariance testing after the initial determination that the fit of the CI and fully constrained models were not significantly different. However, we went ahead and tested for MI, SI, and SFI in this example so as to demonstrate the use of lavaan for this purpose.

COMPARISON OF LATENT MEANS

Under the general aegis of MGCFA, it is possible to compare the means of one or more latent variables across groups, much as we compared the model parameters above. Traditionally, researchers who wanted to compare group means for some construct of interest, such as mastery goal orientation, would do so using analysis of variance with an observed composite score. However, such composites rest on the assumption that observed measurements (e.g. item responses) are made without error, which is quite often not tenable in practice (Brown, 2015). On the other hand, if the researcher relies on the latent variable modeling context to compare group means, such an assumption is not necessary. Using the current example, consider the case where a researcher would like to know whether males and females differ in terms of their level of mastery goal orientation. The traditional approach would be to assume items were measured without error, and add the six item scores together in order to create an observed composite score. The means for this score could then be compared between males and females using a t-test or analysis of variance. The latent variable alternative would be to use mean structure models to compare the latent means between groups. If we use this latter method in order to take advantage of its ability to correctly account for measurement error, we must first assess FI between the groups to ensure that the meaning of the latent variables is the same between them. In other words, model parameters must be shown to be equivalent prior to our comparing the latent means, using the methods demonstrated in the previous section. We do need to note here that research into the degree of invariance necessary for latent means to be comparable is still ongoing. While it is certainly true that when full FI holds, latent mean comparisons are possible, it may also be possible to compare these means even when the other model parameters are only **partially invariant** (Byrne, Shavelson, & Muthén, 1989). However, it is not known how many parameters can differ between groups, and how much such parameters can differ before means comparisons are not legitimate to make. In this chapter, we have elected to take a more conservative approach, ensuring that all model parameters are invariant prior to comparing the latent means. The reader should certainly be aware, though, that such an approach is in fact conservative and that other researchers may argue that latent means comparisons may be possible under partially invariant conditions.

In order to use the traditional analysis of variance/t-test approach for comparing group means, we would first need to create an observed composite score by summing the item responses for individual scores.

```
mastery.score<-ags1+ags2+ags5+ags6+ags7+ags12
```

We can then compare the gender means on this new variable using the t-test.

```
t.test(mastery.score~gender)

        Welch Two Sample t-test

data: mastery.score by gender
t = 0.6421, df = 221.029, p-value = 0.5215
alternative hypothesis: true difference in means is not equal to 0
95 percent confidence interval:
 -0.7753533 1.5247935
sample estimates:
mean in group 1 mean in group 2
       33.68966        33.31494
```

These results show that there is not a statistically significant difference in the groups' means on the composite score.

In order to compare the latent mastery goal orientation means between males and females, we will need to fit two models. The first constrains model loadings, intercepts, and error variances to be equal between the groups, as well as the factor means. In the second model, the loadings, intercepts, and error variances are once again constrained to be equal, but the means are allowed to vary. The commands for fitting the constrained means model, along with the model fit output, appears below. Note that in the group.equal= subcommand we include "means" to indicate that we want them constrained to equality between males and females.

```
mastery.model.equal.means<-cfa(mastery.model, data=edps744,
group="gender", group.equal=c("loadings", "intercepts", "residuals",
"lv.variances", "means"), estimator="WLSMV")
summary(mastery.model.equal.means, fit.measures=T, standardized=T)

lavaan (0.5-15) converged normally after 44 iterations
```

	Used	Total
Number of observations per group		
2	308	312
1	116	120
Estimator	DWLS	Robust
Minimum Function Test Statistic	60.101	57.743
Degrees of freedom	36	36
P-value (Chi-square)	0.007	0.012
Scaling correction factor		1.388

```
Shift parameter for eachgroup:
  2                                                    10.484
  1                                                     3.948
  for simple second-order correction (Mplus variant)
```

Chi-square for eachgroup:

```
  2                                     32.188    33.680
  1                                     27.913    24.064
```

Model test baselinemodel:

```
  Minimum Function Test Statistic      227.416   623.036
  Degrees of freedom                        30        30
  P-value                                0.000     0.000
```

User model versus baselinemodel:

```
  Comparative Fit Index (CFI)            0.980     0.963
  Tucker-Lewis Index (TLI)               0.983     0.969
```

Root Mean Square Error of Approximation:

```
  RMSEA                                  0.056     0.054
  90 Percent Confidence Interval  0.029  0.081     0.025  0.078
  P-value RMSEA <= 0.05                  0.317     0.385
```

Standardized Root Mean Square Residual:

```
  SRMR                                   0.094     0.094
```

The model fit the data well, based on the fit statistics displayed here. For the constrained model, both groups' means are set to zero. It is important to remember when dealing with latent means that they are on an arbitrary scale, and as such will typically be set to zero. When fitting the unconstrained means model, we will continue to constrain one group to have a mean of zero, while the others will be allowed to vary. In order to fit the unconstrained means model, we will use the following commands, which remove "means" from the group.equal= subcommand.

```
mastery.model.unequal.means<-cfa(mastery.model, data=edps744,
group="gender", group.equal=c("loadings", "intercepts", "residuals",
"lv.variances"), estimator="WLSMV")
summary(mastery.model.unequal.means, fit.measures=T, standardized=T)

lavaan (0.5-15) converged normally after 43 iterations
```

	Used	Total
Number of observations pergroup		
2	308	312
1	116	120

	DWLS	Robust
Estimator	DWLS	Robust
Minimum Function Test Statistic	59.296	60.505
Degrees of freedom	35	35
P-value (Chi-square)	0.006	0.005
Scaling correction factor	1.287	
Shift parameter for eachgroup:		
2		10.493
1		3.952
for simple second-order correction (Mplus variant)		

Chi-square for eachgroup:

2	32.020	35.366
1	27.276	25.140

Model test baselinemodel:

Minimum Function Test Statistic	227.416	623.036
Degrees of freedom	30	30
P-value	0.000	0.000

User model versus baselinemodel:

Comparative Fit Index (CFI)	0.980	0.957
Tucker-Lewis Index (TLI)	0.983	0.963

Root Mean Square Error of Approximation:

RMSEA		0.057	0.059	
90 Percent Confidence Interval	0.030	0.082	0.032	0.083
P-value RMSEA <= 0.05		0.295	0.263	

Standardized Root Mean Square Residual:

```
  SRMR                                    0.094      0.094
```

Parameter estimates:

```
  Information                           Expected
  Standard Errors                       Robust.sem
```

Group1[2]:

	Estimate	Std.err	Z-value	P(>|z|)	Std.lv	Std.all
Latent variables:						
mastery=~						
ags1	1.000	0.797	0.726			
ags2	1.130	0.098	11.543	0.000	0.901	0.614
ags5	0.814	0.066	12.263	0.000	0.649	0.689
ags6	1.029	0.080	12.889	0.000	0.821	0.739
ags7	1.064	0.066	16.169	0.000	0.848	0.847
ags12	1.161	0.099	11.678	0.000	0.926	0.618
Intercepts:						
ags1	5.578	0.062	89.328	0.000	5.578	5.080
ags2	5.023	0.078	64.367	0.000	5.023	3.421
ags5	6.148	0.051	120.543	0.000	6.148	6.523
ags6	5.689	0.063	90.404	0.000	5.689	5.122
ags7	5.805	0.059	97.701	0.000	5.805	5.799
ags12	5.096	0.079	64.468	0.000	5.096	3.402
mastery	**0.000**				**0.000**	**0.000**
Variances:						
ags1	0.570	0.079			0.570	0.473
ags2	1.343	0.171			1.343	0.623
ags5	0.467	0.047			0.467	0.526
ags6	0.560	0.067			0.560	0.454
ags7	0.283	0.039			0.283	0.282
ags12	1.387	0.163			1.387	0.618
mastery	0.636	0.086			1.000	1.000

Group2[1]:

```
Estimate Std.err Z-value P(>|z|) Std.lv Std.all
```
Latent variables:
  mastery=~

	Estimate	Std.err	Z-value	P(>|z|)	Std.lv	Std.all
ags1	1.000	0.797			0.726	
ags2	1.130	0.098	11.543	0.000	0.901	0.614
ags5	0.814	0.066	12.263	0.000	0.649	0.689
ags6	1.029	0.080	12.889	0.000	0.821	0.739
ags7	1.064	0.066	16.169	0.000	0.848	0.847
ags12	1.161	0.099	11.678	0.000	0.926	0.618

Intercepts:

	Estimate	Std.err	Z-value	P(>|z|)	Std.lv	Std.all
ags1	5.578	0.062	89.328	0.000	5.578	5.080
ags2	5.023	0.078	64.367	0.000	5.023	3.421
ags5	6.148	0.051	120.543	0.000	6.148	6.523
ags6	5.689	0.063	90.404	0.000	5.689	5.12
ags7	5.805	0.059	97.701	0.000	5.805	5.799
ags12	5.096	0.079	64.468	0.000	5.096	3.402
mastery	**0.044**	**0.092**	**0.480**	**0.631**	**0.055**	**0.055**

Variances:

	Estimate	Std.err	Z-value	P(>|z|)	Std.lv	Std.all
ags1	0.570	0.079			0.570	0.473
ags2	1.343	0.171			1.343	0.623
ags5	0.467	0.047			0.467	0.526
ags6	0.560	0.067			0.560	0.454
ags7	0.283	0.039			0.283	0.282
ags12	1.387	0.163			1.387	0.618
mastery	0.636	0.086			1.000	1.000

As with the constrained model, the fit was good for the model in which means were allowed to vary between groups. We have bolded the factor means in the output in order to make them easier to pick out, and from these we can see that the group 2 mean is 0.044 larger than that of group 1. In order to test whether this mean difference is statistically significant (i.e. to compare the fit of the two models), we will again use the anova command in R.

```
anova(mastery.model.unequal.means, mastery.model.equal.means)
Scaled Chi Square Difference Test (test = scaled.shifted)
```

	Df	AIC	BIC	Chisq	Chisq diff	Df diff	Pr(>Chisq)
mastery.model.unequal.means	35		59.296				
mastery.model.equal.means	36		60.101		0.23188	1	0.6301

The null hypothesis of this test is that the fit of the constrained means and unconstrained means models are the same, which is equivalent to testing whether we need to allow the groups' means to vary. Here, the p-value of 0.6341 indicates that we do not need to reject the null hypothesis and can thus conclude that the mean of the latent variable mastery goal orientation is the same for males and females.

Hancock (2001) describes the calculation of an effect size estimate comparable to Cohen's d (Cohen, 1988) that can be used to quantify the magnitude of the mean difference between pairs of latent means. This statistic is simply the difference in group latent means divided by the square root of the group latent variance. Note that the variances of the two groups are constrained to equality here, so both have the same value, 0.636. Using the results presented above, we can calculate this effect size as:

$$ES = \frac{0.044 - 0}{\sqrt{0.636}} = \frac{0.044}{0.797} = 0.055$$

Thus, the latent means differed by approximately 0.055 of a latent standard deviation, or very little.

MULTIPLE INDICATORS MULTIPLE CAUSES (MIMIC) MODEL

In Chapter 5, we have seen that it is possible to compare factor means using the MGCFA framework in which the fit of a model with group means constrained to be equal is compared with the fit of a model in which the means are allowed to vary by group. An alternative approach for comparing latent means is through the use of the MIMIC model. The MIMIC model links an observed covariate, such as gender, with a latent variable, such as mastery goal orientation, and provides an estimate of the relationships between the two. We can see a path diagram for the MIMIC model of this example in Figure 5.1. The primary point to note here is that the arrow goes from an observed variable, gender, to the factor, rather than the other way around, which is what we're used to seeing.

The MIMIC model can also be expressed as in equation (5.5).

$$\eta = Bx + \zeta \qquad\qquad (5.5)$$

Here x is the observed covariate, for example gender, and B is the coefficient linking it with the latent variable η. If B is statistically significant we would conclude that x is significantly related to the level of the factor, η. If the covariate is a dichotomous variable such as gender, then B is actually an estimate of the difference

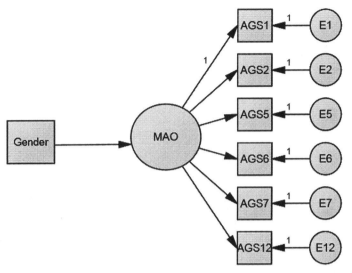

■ **Figure 5.1:** MIMIC model relating gender to mastery goal orientation (MAO)

in factor means between the groups. The R code to fit the MIMIC model using lavaan appears below, along with the resulting output.

```
mastery.mimic.model.gender<-'
mastery=~ags1+ags2+ags5+ags6+ags7+ags12
mastery~gender
'
```

mastery.mimic.gender.fit<-sem(mastery.mimic.model.gender,
data=edps744, estimator="WLSMV")
summary(mastery.mimic.gender.fit, fit.measures=T, standardized=T)
lavaan (0.5-15) converged normally after 52 iterations

	Used	Total
Number of observations	424	432
Estimator	DWLS	Robust
Minimum Function Test Statistic	34.084	74.149
Degrees of freedom	1414	
P-value (Chi-square)	0.002	0.000
Scaling correction factor	0.479	
Shift parameter	3.034	
for simple second-order correction (Mplus variant)		

Model test baselinemodel:

Minimum Function Test Statistic	173.389	607.285
Degrees of freedom	21	21
P-value	0.000	0.000

User model versus baselinemodel:

Comparative Fit Index (CFI)	0.983	0.897
Tucker-Lewis Index (TLI)	0.974	0.846

Root Mean Square Error of Approximation:

RMSEA		0.058	0.101	
90 Percent Confidence Interval	0.034	0.083	0.079	0.124
P-value RMSEA <= 0.05		0.264	0.000	

Standardized Root Mean Square Residual:

SRMR	0.061	0.061

Parameter estimates:

Information	Expected
Standard Errors	Robust.sem

	Estimate	Std.err	Z-value	P(>|z|)	Std.lv	Std.all
Latent variables:						
mastery=~						
ags1	1.000				0.831	0.738
ags2	1.078	0.098	11.015	0.000	0.895	0.604
ags5	0.767	0.064	12.066	0.000	0.637	0.665
ags6	1.031	0.078	13.158	0.000	0.856	0.758
ags7	1.040	0.066	15.793	0.000	0.864	0.839
ags12	1.102	0.096	11.428	0.000	0.916	0.613
Regressions:						
mastery~						
gender	−0.045	0.094	−0.479	0.632	−0.054	−0.024
Intercepts:						
ags1	5.672	0.166	34.248	0.000	5.672	5.038
ags2	5.114	0.186	27.460	0.000	5.114	3.452
ags5	6.217	0.132	47.246	0.000	6.217	6.488

ags6	5.778	0.171	33.765	0.000	5.778	5.117
ags7	5.906	0.170	34.676	0.000	5.906	5.732
ags12	5.196	0.191	27.217	0.000	5.196	3.479
gender	1.726	0.022	79.554	0.000	1.726	3.868
mastery	0.000	0.000	0.000			

Variances:

ags1	0.577	0.082			0.577	0.456
ags2	1.394	0.171			1.394	0.635
ags5	0.512	0.048			0.512	0.558
ags6	0.542	0.063			0.542	0.425
ags7	0.314	0.041			0.314	0.296
ags12	1.393	0.162			1.393	0.624
mastery	0.690	0.098			0.999	0.999
gender	0.199	0.010			0.199	1.000

Fitting of the MIMIC model using `lavaan` is similar to fitting other SEMs. The model fit indices for this example indicate good model fit to the data. The relationship between gender and mastery goal orientation is not statistically significant ($p = 0.632$), therefore we would conclude that the mean mastery goal orientation is not different between males and females in the population. Note that the absolute value of the estimate of B, -0.045, is essentially equal to the factor mean estimate for group 1 (labeled as 2 by lavaan) of 0.044. Recall that in the factor means modeling one group mean is set equal to zero, so that the other group's mean is really an estimate of how the two group means differ, which is precisely what the B estimate is in the MIMIC model.

The MIMIC model can also be used to relate continuous observed covariates to the latent variable. In this example, we are interested in relating the number of years of education that each participant's mother has attained, with the participant's level of mastery goal orientation. The associated MIMIC model appears in Figure 5.2.

The `lavaan` commands to fit this model and the resulting output appear below.

```
mastery.mimic.model.mom<-'
mastery=~ags1+ags2+ags5+ags6+ags7+ags12

mastery~mom_ed
'
mastery.mimic.mom.fit<-sem(mastery.mimic.model.mom,
data=edps744, estimator="WLSMV")
summary(mastery.mimic.mom.fit, fit.measures=T, standardized=T)
```

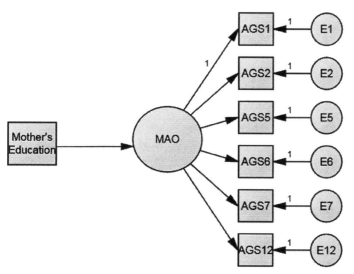

■ Figure 5.2: MIMIC model relating mother's education to mastery goal orientation (MAO)

lavaan (0.5-15) converged normally after 50 iterations

	Used	Total
Number of observations	418	432

Estimator	DWLS	Robust
Minimum Function Test Statistic	33.350	74.695
Degrees of freedom	14	14
P-value (Chi-square)	0.003	0.000
Scaling correction factor	0.464	
Shift parameter	2.781	
for simple second-order correction (Mplus variant)		

Model test baselinemodel:

Minimum Function Test Statistic	1176.142	607.009
Degrees of freedom	21	21
P-value	0.000	0.000

User model versus baselinemodel:

Comparative Fit Index (CFI)	0.983	0.896
Tucker-Lewis Index (TLI)	0.975	0.845

Root Mean Square Error of Approximation:

RMSEA			0.058	0.102
90 Percent Confidence Interval	0.033	0.083	0.080	0.125
P-value RMSEA <= 0.05			0.280	0.000

Standardized Root Mean Square Residual:

SRMR	0.061	0.061

Parameter estimates:

Information		Expected
Standard Errors		Robust.sem

	Estimate	Std.err	Z-value	P(>|z|)	Std.lv	Std.all
Latent variables:						
mastery=~						
ags1	1.000				0.836	0.741
ags2	1.055	0.096	10.984	0.000	0.882	0.598
ags5	0.784	0.063	12.374	0.000	0.655	0.681
ags6	1.025	0.079	13.043	0.000	0.857	0.758
ags7	1.035	0.066	15.751	0.000	0.865	0.840
ags12	1.072	0.095	11.336	0.000	0.896	0.604
Regressions:						
mastery~						
mom_ed	0.096	0.043	2.245	0.025	0.115	0.116
Intercepts:						
ags1	5.233	0.176	29.657	0.000	5.233	4.640
ags2	4.648	0.183	25.367	0.000	4.648	3.151
ags5	5.865	0.139	42.048	0.000	5.865	6.099
ags6	5.319	0.177	29.971	0.000	5.319	4.706
ags7	5.455	0.175	31.081	0.000	5.455	5.297
ags12	4.728	0.192	24.608	0.000	4.728	3.187
mom_ed	3.797	0.049	76.913	0.000	3.797	3.766
mastery	0.000				0.000	0.000
Variances:						
ags1	0.574	0.082			0.574	0.451
ags2	1.399	0.173			1.399	0.643

ags5	0.496	0.046		0.496	0.536
ags6	0.543	0.065		0.543	0.425
ags7	0.313	0.041		0.313	0.295
ags12	1.399	0.166		1.399	0.635
mastery	0.689	0.099		0.987	0.987
mom_ed	1.016	0.066		1.016	1.000

In this case, the estimate of B can be interpreted just like a slope in standard regression analysis. The estimate of 0.096 for mother's education (mom_ed) is statistically significant ($p = 0.025$), leading us to conclude that individuals whose mothers had more years of education had higher levels of the mastery goal orientation.

The MIMIC model is very flexible, and will easily accommodate multiple predictor variables in a single analysis. In this final example, we will include both mother's years of education and participant gender as predictors for mastery goal orientation.

```
mastery.mimic.model.mom.gender<-'
    mastery=~ags1+ags2+ags5+ags6+ags7+ags12

    mastery~mom_ed+gender

'
```

```
mastery.mimic.mom.gender.fit<-sem(mastery.mimic.model.mom.gender,
  data=edps744, estimator="WLSMV")
summary(mastery.mimic.mom.gender.fit, fit.measures=T, standardized=T)
```

```
lavaan (0.5-15) converged normally after 50 iterations
```

	Used	Total
Number of observations	418	432

	DWLS	Robust
Estimator		
Minimum Function Test Statistic	36.480	76.022
Degrees of freedom	19	19
P-value (Chi-square)	0.009	0.000
Scaling correction factor		0.504
Shift parameter		3.660
for simple second-order correction (Mplus variant)		

```
Model test baselinemodel:

    Minimum Function Test Statistic          180.109    634.626
    Degrees of freedom                            27         27
    P-value                                    0.000      0.000

User model versus baselinemodel:


    Comparative Fit Index (CFI)                0.985      0.906
    Tucker-Lewis Index (TLI)                   0.978      0.867

Root Mean Square Error of Approximation:

    RMSEA                                      0.047      0.085
    90 Percent Confidence Interval    0.023    0.070      0.065   0.105
    P-value RMSEA <= 0.05                      0.554      0.002

Standardized Root Mean Square Residual:

    SRMR                                       0.056      0.056
    Parameter estimates:
    Information                                     Expected
    Standard Errors                               Robust.sem
    Estimate Std.err Z-value P(>|z|) Std.lv Std.all
Latent variables:
    mastery=~
      ags1      1.000                                    0.835    0.740
      ags2      1.058    0.096    10.972    0.000         0.883    0.599
      ags5      0.784    0.063    12.365    0.000         0.655    0.681
      ags6      1.028    0.079    13.034    0.000         0.858    0.759
      ags7      1.034    0.066    15.722    0.000         0.863    0.838
      ags12     1.074    0.095    11.324    0.000         0.897    0.604

Regressions:
    mastery~
      mom_ed    0.097    0.043     2.263    0.024         0.116    0.117
      gender   -0.053    0.095    -0.559    0.576        -0.064   -0.028

Covariances:
    mom_ed~~
      gender    0.013    0.023     0.568    0.570         0.013    0.029
```

Intercepts:

ags1	5.376	0.302	17.815	0.000	5.376	4.767
ags2	4.799	0.320	15.005	0.000	4.799	3.253
ags5	5.977	0.243	24.600	0.000	5.977	6.216
ags6	5.466	0.308	17.758	0.000	5.466	4.836
ags7	5.603	0.309	18.134	0.000	5.603	5.441
ags12	4.881	0.328	14.890	0.000	4.881	3.290
mom_ed	3.797	0.049	76.913	0.000	3.797	3.766
gender	2.734	0.022	126.288	0.000	2.734	6.184
mastery	0.000				0.000	0.000

Variances:

ags1	0.575	0.081	0.575	0.452
ags2	1.396	0.173	1.396	0.642
ags5	0.496	0.047	0.496	0.536
ags6	0.542	0.065	0.542	0.424
ags7	0.315	0.041	0.315	0.297
ags12	1.398	0.166	1.398	0.635
mastery	0.687	0.098	0.986	0.986
mom_ed	1.016	0.066	1.016	1.000
gender	0.196	0.010	0.196	1.000

These results for mother's education and participant gender are very similar to those we obtained for each variable separately, with slight changes to the estimated values themselves, but qualitatively the same results with respect to whether and how each variable was related to mastery goal orientation.

SUMMARY

In Chapter 5 we examined extensions to SEM. In particular, we explored methods for investigating the presence of group differences in latent variable model parameters such as loadings, intercepts, error variances, and factor variances/covariances. We then extended this model to address the problem of comparing group means on a latent variable using multiple groups mean structure models. Such models may be preferable to the more commonly used observed variable methods for comparing group means such as the *t*-test or ANOVA because they correctly account for measurement error. We finished the chapter with the MIMIC model, which allows for relating observed predictor variables to the latent variables of interest. It can be used much in the same way as standard regression models, in that both categorical and continuous independent variables can be included in the model. In addition, when a categorical predictor is included, the MIMIC model

SUMMARY
5

serves as a way to compare group means with one another. If such a categorical variable has more than one category, dummy coding can be used to create variables with which group mean comparisons on the latent variable can then be made.

FURTHER READING

Hancock, G.R., & Mueller, R.O. (2013). *Structural Equation Modeling: A Second Course*. Charlotte, NC: Information Age Publishing.

Hoyle, R.H. (2012). *Handbook of Structural Equation Modeling*. New York: The Guilford Press.

Millsap, R.E. (2011). *Statistical Approaches to Measurement Invariance*. New York: Routledge, Taylor and Francis Group.

REFERENCES

Brown, T.A. (2015). *Confirmatory Factor Analysis for Applied Research*, 2nd edition. New York: The Guilford Press.

Byrne, B.M., Shavelson, R.J., & Muthén, B. (1989). Testing for the equivalence of factor covariance and mean structures: The issue of partial measurement invariance. *Psychological Bulletin*, 105(3), 456–66.

Cohen, J. (1988). *Statistical Power Analysis for the Behavioral Sciences*. Hillsdale, NJ: Lawrence Erlbaum Associates.

Finch, W.H., & French, B.F. (2008). Using exploratory factor analysis for locating invariant referents in factor invariant studies. *Journal of Modern and Applied Statistical Methods*, 7(1), 223–33.

Hancock, G.R. (2001). Effect size, power, and sample size determination for structured means modeling and MIMIC approaches to between-groups hypothesis testing of means on a single latent construct. *Psychometrika*, 66(3), 373–88.

Horn, J.L., & McArdle, J.J. (1992). A practical guide to measurement invariance in research on aging. *Experimental Aging Research*, 18, 117–44.

Kline, R.B. (2011). *Principles and Practice of Structural Equation Modeling*, 3rd edition. New York: The Guilford Press.

McDonald, R.P. (1999). *Test Theory: A Unified Treatment*. Mahwah, NJ: Lawrence Erlbaum and Associates.

Meredith, W. (1993). Measurement invariance, factor analysis, and factorial invariance. *Psychometrika*, 58, 525–43.

Meredith, W., & Millsap, R.E. (1992). On the misuse of manifest variables in the detection of measurement bias. *Psychometrika*, 57, 289–311.

Millsap, R.E. (2011). *Statistical Approaches to Measurement Invariance*. New York: Routledge, Taylor and Francis Group.

Millsap, R.E., & Kwok, O. (2004). Evaluating the impact of partial factorial invariance on selection in two populations. *Psychological Methods*, 9, 93–115.

Steenkamp, J.E.M., & Baumgartner, H. (1998). Assessing measurement invariance in cross-national consumer research. *Journal of Consumer Research*, 25, 78–90.

Steinmetz, H. (2013). Analyzing observed composite difference across groups: Is partial measurement invariance enough? *Methodology*, 9(1), 1–12.

Wicherts, J.M., & Dolan, C.V. (2010). Measurement invariance in confirmatory factor analysis: An illustration using IQ test performance of minorities. *Educational Measurement: Issues and Practice*, 29(3), 39–47.

Widaman, K.F., & Reise, S.P. (1997). Exploring the measurement invariance of psychological instruments: Applications in the substance abuse domain. In K.J. Bryan, *Alcohol and Substance Use Research* (pp. 281–324). Washington, DC: American Psychological Association.

Chapter 6

FURTHER TOPICS IN SEM

INTRODUCTION

In Chapters 4 and 5, we laid the foundation for many applications of SEM and its realization using R software. In particular, we took the CFA models that were described in Chapter 3 and put them to work in the form of structural models in Chapter 4. In Chapter 5 we saw how the models of Chapters 3 and 4 can be compared across groups, how observed covariates can be integrated into latent variable models, and how mean comparisons can be made in the latent context, avoiding some of the limitations of observed variable mean comparison techniques such as analysis of variance. In Chapter 6 we extend the SEM framework even further by examining how to model interactions among latent variables, how to fit models with feedback loops (nonrecursive models), and how to fit a recursive partitioning model known as structural equation modeling trees. Each of these techniques provides the researcher with additional tools that can be used in a wide variety of applications involving latent variables.

NONRECURSIVE SEM

In Chapter 4 we saw how to fit **recursive SEMs**, in which all of the relationships among the latent variables are unidirectional, except those involving covariances/correlations. For example, we were interested in how mastery goal orientation impacts attention control, with the arrow moving from the former to the latter. However, consider the example in Figure 6.1, in which there is an arrow from MAO to ATTC, and separately from ATTC back to MAO, creating a feedback loop. This figure describes a model in which the level of MAO predicts the level of ATTC, which in turn predicts back on the level of MAO. It is important to differentiate the two separate paths here from a single covariance/correlation between the two variables. In the latter case, we are only estimating a relationship between

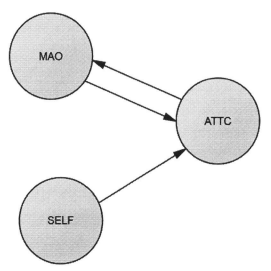

■ **Figure 6.1:** Example of nonrecursive SEM

the two factors, while in the former we estimate two unidirectional relationships simultaneously, where each variable has an impact on the other. Such models are known as **nonrecursive SEMs**, and while not as common as the recursive models that we have been focused on, they do appear in the social science research literature nonetheless.

Estimation of parameters for nonrecursive SEM is not as straightforward as in the recursive case. Results of simulation studies in this area suggest that one of the more promising methods of parameter estimation for nonrecursive models is **Two-stage least squares (2SLS)**, which tends to be more robust in modeling misspecification than other approaches for this purpose such as maximum likelihood and weighted least squares (Bollen, Kirby, Curran, Paxton, & Chen, 2007). It should also be noted that while we focus on the use of 2SLS for estimating nonrecursive model parameters, it can be used for fitting any type of SEM (Bollen, 1996). In the following section of this chapter, we will briefly describe how 2SLS works, and then demonstrate its application for fitting nonrecursive SEMs in R.

There are multiple 2SLS estimators that have been proposed for use with SEM, including an approach based on Jöreskog (1983), as well as the method used in this chapter, which was proposed by Bollen (1996), and which has proven to be perhaps the most flexible (Bollen, Kirby, Curran, Paxton, & Chen, 2007). In 2SLS estimation for SEM, latent variables are reexpressed in terms of their referent indicator variables, the loading for which is set to 1 in order to scale the factor as described in Chapter 3. In a standard CFA, the referent indicator of the latent variable η is a function of the latent variable itself, as well as a unique random error:

$$y_1 = \eta + \varepsilon_{y_1}. \tag{6.1}$$

Using simple algebra, η can be rewritten as:

$$\eta = y_1 - \varepsilon_{y_1}. \tag{6.2}$$

Similarly, the referent indicator for a second factor ξ can also be expressed as a function of its referent indicator

$$x_1 = \xi + \varepsilon_{x_1}, \tag{6.3}$$

and then rewritten as

$$\xi = x_1 - \varepsilon_{x_1}. \tag{6.4}$$

Given (6.2) and (6.4), we can express a SEM linking η and ξ in terms of only observed indicator variables and errors, thereby obviating the need to directly involve the latent variables themselves:

$$y_1 = \alpha + B\left(x_1 - \varepsilon_{x_1}\right) + \zeta. \tag{6.5}$$

We can simplify equation (6.5) to

$$y_1 = \alpha + Bx_1 - B\varepsilon_{x_1} + \zeta. \tag{6.6}$$

Model parameter values in (6.6) can be estimated using standard ordinary least squares (OLS) regression to provide estimates for the SEM in (6.7):

$$\eta = B\xi + \zeta. \tag{6.7}$$

Although the model in (6.6) is algebraically sound, the measurement error and observed predictor (x_1) on the right-hand side of the equation are correlated, leading to a violation of standard OLS assumptions. Bollen (1996) suggested the use of 2SLS in conjunction with instrumental variables (IVs) in order to avoid violating the assumption that the error term is independent of the independent variable(s). An IV is simply a variable that is correlated with x_1 but not with error. Bollen and Bauer (2004) showed that IVs can be implied by the model itself and exist internal to it in the form of observed indicator variables other than the referent. As an example, if for η variable y_2 is a second, non-referent indicator, then it could serve as an IV for the factor. Likewise, if x_2 is a non-referent indicator of ξ, then it could serve as an IV for that factor.

As the name implies, 2SLS is comprised of two analytic steps. In step 1 the variable that is correlated with error (e.g. x_1) is regressed on the set of IVs, and a predicted value, $\hat{x}_1$, is obtained. This predicted value includes only the variation associated with the IVs, and thus does not include the correlation with the error terms that created problems for the original model. This is so because the IVs themselves were selected so as to be uncorrelated with error while being correlated with x_1. In the second step, $\hat{x}_1$ replaces x_1 in equation (6.6), thus allowing for proper model identification (Bollen, 1996). Prior research has shown the 2SLS estimator to be unbiased, consistent, and asymptotically efficient, even in cases where the model has been misspecified and the data do not come from a multivariate normal distribution (Bollen, *et al.*, 2007). In short, 2SLS estimation is a very viable alternative to maximum likelihood, particularly when the assumption of multivariate normality is not met, and when the model may not be properly specified. More pertinent in the current context, 2SLS will be a very useful tool for estimating nonrecursive model parameters, such as those expressing the relationship between the two variables involved in the feedback loop in Figure 6.1.

As an example of a nonrecursive model, let's consider Figure 6.1 again. Here MAO and ATTC form a feedback loop with one another, and SELF serves as an additional predictor of ATTC. In order to fit this model using 2SLS, we will need to use the R function systemfit. We will also need to identify appropriate IVs from among the nonreferent indicators of the latent variables. Again, the reader is encouraged to refer to Bollen and Bauer (2004) for an in-depth discussion of this issue. In this case, the IVs will be one nonreferent indicator from each latent variable. In order to fit the nonrecursive model with systemfit, we will use the following command lines in R.

```
eqn1<-ats50~ags1+mps1
eqn2<-ags1~ats50
eqSystem<-list(attc=eqn1, ags=eqn2)
attc.2sls<-systemfit(eqSystem, method="2SLS", inst=
list(~ags2+mps6,
~ats29))
```

In the first two lines, we specify the equations that we would like to fit. The first (eqn1) includes the portion of the model in which MAO (ags1) and SELF (mps1) serve as predictors for ATTC (ats50). The second equation (eqn2) includes the feedback from ATTC to MAO. We then combine these equations into a single system using the list command, and call the new object eqSystem. Finally, we call the systemfit function, specify that we want to obtain model estimates using the 2SLS method, and then identify the IVs separately for each model. The first set of IVs includes ags2 and mps6, each corresponding to the two predictors in the first equation. The second IV definition includes only ats29, which corresponds to ATTC being the predictor. Remember that each of the IVs was selected because it was correlated with one of the referent indicators for each factor, but not with the model error. In order to obtain the output from the model once we have fit it, we use the summary command. Only the relevant portion of the full systemfit output is displayed below.

```
summary(attc.2sls)

2SLS estimates for 'attc' (equation 1)
Model Formula: ats50 ~ ags1 + mps1
Instruments: ~ags2 + mps6

            Estimate   Std. Error  t value  Pr(>|t|)
(Intercept) 1.4181802  0.9613273   1.47523  0.140929
ags1        0.3467024  0.2060622   1.68251  0.093242 .
mps1        0.0801444  0.1377197   0.58194  0.560933
---
Signif. codes: 0 '***' 0.001 '**' 0.01 '*' 0.05 '.' 0.1 ' ' 1


2SLS estimates for 'ags' (equation 2)
Model Formula: ags1 ~ ats50
Instruments: ~ats29

            Estimate   Std. Error  t value   Pr(>|t|)
(Intercept) 4.7286605  0.3311353   14.28015  < 2.22e-16 ***
ats50       0.2328821  0.0864773   2.69299   0.0073712 **
---
Signif. codes: 0 '***' 0.001 '**' 0.01 '*' 0.05 '.' 0.1 ' ' 1
```

Examining the output for the first equation, we see that the independent variables appear in the first column, followed by the parameter estimate (essentially a regression slope), the standard error of the estimate, the test statistic value for the null hypothesis that the coefficient = 0, and the p-value associated with the test statistic. R provides a notation system for identifying the level of significance using . and *. From these results, we would conclude that neither MAO nor SELF were significantly related to ATTC. The regression results for ATTC as a predictor of MAO appear in the next set of output. Here we see that ATTC was a statistic-ally significant predictor of MAO, with a positive slope. So, as levels of attention control increased in value so did the students' sense of mastery goal orientation. However, when controlling for self-oriented perfectionism, increases in mastery goal orientation were not associated with increased levels of attention control.

INTERACTIONS IN LATENT VARIABLE MODELS

In some instances, researchers are interested in determining whether one vari-able moderates the relationship between two other variables. For example, we might believe that mastery goal orientation is related to attention control, but that this relationship changes depending upon the level of academic frustration that an individual feels; i.e. the relationship between mastery and attention con-trol is moderated by frustration. Such moderated relationships are modeled as interactions between the two independent variables, in this case mastery orienta-tion and frustration. In the context of observed variable models such as regres-sion, interactions are quite easy to include in the model, as they are simply the products of the two independent variables. However, in SEM, interactions are not so easy to create or to include in the analysis. Given this fact, a number of approaches for estimating latent variable interactions and the associated mod-eration models have been developed over the last 30 years. Some of these are fairly complex, relying on estimation techniques rooted in quasi-maximum like-lihood and Bayesian analysis (Kelava & Nagengast, 2012; Lee, Song, & Cai, 2010; Klein & Muthén, 2007; Song & Lee, 2006). Others, such as the example demonstrated here, are based on creating latent variable interactions using prod-ucts of the individual indicator variables (Kenny & Judd, 1984). Given that this is a very fast-developing field of study in latent variable modeling, it is likely that new developments will continue to arise, and best practices will evolve. However, the method that we will demonstrate here, while certainly not optimal in all cases, has been shown to be effective in many cases, and relies only on the standard machinery underlying SEM to obtain parameter estimates for interac-tions. In addition, it can be implemented in R, making it widely accessible to all researchers who would like to use it. Despite its positive features, however, the product-based method that we describe and demonstrate below does have weak-nesses that we will address at the end of this section.

Referring back to our example, if the variables in question were observed and not latent, we could express the moderation model as:

$$\text{ATTC} = \beta_0 + \beta_1 \text{MAO} + \beta_2 \text{FRUSTRATION} + \beta_3 \left(\text{MAO} * \text{FRUSTRATION} \right) + \varepsilon.$$

(6.8)

In (6.8) the moderation effect is represented in the product of MAO and FRUSTRATION, and the assessment of its strength and significance is contained in β_3. However, given that our variables of interest are latent and not observed, it is not so easy to see how we might create an interaction between MAO and FRUSTRATION. As mentioned above, there are a number of methods available for estimating moderated latent terms in SEM. One of the oldest approaches, and one that is still widely in use, was originally proposed by Kenny and Judd (1984). Known as the product indicator method, it involves calculating products using the indicators of the two latent variables for which the moderation effect occurs, and in turn using these to establish a latent interaction term that is included in the SEM, much as $\text{MAO} * \text{FRUSTRATION}$ in equation (6.8). A number of approaches for calculating the products have been described in the literature, and Marsh, Wen, and Hau (2004) compared several of these with one another, and with maximum-likelihood-based methods as well. Based on the results of their simulation study, those authors provided two overarching guidelines for researchers wishing to use the product of indicators method:

1. Each indicator variable should be used once in the creation of product terms.
2. No indicator should be used more than once, because doing so creates correlated error terms among the product indicators.

Given these rules, it is necessary for researchers to create matched pairs of indicators in some fashion. Current recommendations suggest that if the number of indicators for the two latent variables is the same, then each set should first be ordered by the magnitude of the factor loadings obtained by fitting separate CFA models to each factor. Next, the product indicators are created by multiplying the indicator with the largest loading for one latent variable by the indicator with the largest loading for the other latent variable, and proceeding to match up the two indicators with the next largest loading, and so on. When the number of indicators differs across latent variables, then the researcher can create parcels, or groups of indicators, so that the number of parcels for each factor is the same. For example, if latent variable X has six indicators, and latent variable Y has nine indicators, then we could create three parcels of two indicators each for X and three parcels of three indicators each for Y. The mean of the indicators in each parcel is calculated to create three parcel scores for each factor. In turn, the products of these parcels' scores are then calculated in order to create the product indicators for the latent interaction term.

Use of the product indicator approach can be tedious, but is at its core fairly simple to carry out. However, there are two fairly major problems associated with this method that researchers must be aware of, and must correct for, if they are to use the method appropriately. First, the product indicators of the latent interaction term will not be normally distributed (Marsh, Wen, and Hau, 2004). Therefore, standard maximum likelihood is not appropriate for obtaining model parameter estimates. In addition, the standard chi-square difference test for comparing models will not be appropriate, nor will the standard error estimates for the model parameters. Thus, researchers using this approach will need to consider employing either a robust maximum likelihood approach such as we discussed in Chapter 3, or an alternative method for parameter estimation, including WLS or DWLS. A second potential problem associated with using the product method is that the products of the indicators will be collinear with the indicators themselves. Thus, much as is true when interactions are included in a regression model, variable centering is necessary in order to avoid the problem of collinearity (Fox, 2008). Centering simply means that the mean of the indicator variable is subtracted from each individual's value on that variable. This is done for each indicator for each predictor variable in the SEM, and then these centered indicators are used to calculate the product indicators and as indicators for the latent predictor variables used in the SEM.

In order to better understand how this process works, consider the R code below. The centered values are calculated for the indicators of MAO and FRUSTRATION, respectively.

```
MAO
ags1_c<-ags1-mean(ags1)
ags2_c<-ags2-mean(ags2)
ags5_c<-ags5-mean(ags5)
ags6_c<-ags6-mean(ags6)
ags7_c<-ags7-mean(ags7)
ags12_c<-ags12-mean(ags12)

FRUSTRATION
ats6_c<-ats6-mean(ats6)
ats17_c<-ats17-mean(ats17)
ats31_c<-ats31-mean(ats31)
ats38_c<-ats38-mean(ats38)
ats48_c<-ats48-mean(ats48)
ats58_c<-ats58-mean(ats58)
```

For each indicator of each factor involved in the interaction, a centered version is calculated for every individual in the sample. These centered variables, denoted in the R by _c, are then used to create the product indicators, below.

```
int1<-ags1_c*ats6_c
int2<-ags2_c*ats17_c
int3<-ags5_c*ats31_c
int4<-ags6_c*ats38_c
int5<-ags7_c*ats48_c
int6<-ags12_c*ats58_c
```

These product indicators must then be merged into the dataset containing the original set of variables, including the indicators for the dependent latent variable. The resulting data frame is called edps744.int.

```
edps744.int<-
data.frame(edps744.nomiss,ats6_c,ats17_c,ats31_c,ats38_c,ats48
_c,ats58_c,ags1_c,ags2_c,ags5 _c,ags6_c,ags7_c,ags12_c,int1,in
t2,int3,int4,int5
,int6)
```

We can then define and fit the model including the interaction term, int, as we demonstrate below.

```
attc.model.interaction<-'
    mastery=~ags1_c+ags2_c+ags5_c+ags6_c+ags7_c+ags12_c
    frustration=~ats6_c+ats17_c+ats31_c+ats38_c+ats48_c+ats58_c
    int=~int1+int2+int3+int4+int5+int6
    attc=~ats50+ats29+ats40+ats35

    attc~a*mastery+b*frustration+c*int
'
```

```
attc.model.interaction.fit<-sem(attc.model.interaction,
data=edps744.int, estimator="WLSMV")
summary(attc.model.interaction.fit, fit.measures=T, standardized=T)
```

Of particular importance for this discussion, notice that the predictor latent variables, mastery and frustration, both have centered indicator variables, but that the outcome variable, attc, does not. The output from this analysis appears below.

```
lavaan (0.5-15) converged normally after 86 iterations

    Number of observations                        324

    Estimator     DWLS     Robust
    Minimum Function Test Statistic        297.679    295.880
```

Degrees of freedom			203	203	
P-value (Chi-square)			0.000	0.000	
Scaling correction factor			1.514		
Shift parameter			99.202		

   for simple second-order correction (Mplus variant)

Model test baselinemodel:

Minimum Function Test Statistic		1797.459	922.060	
Degrees of freedom		231	231	
P-value		0.000	0.000	

User model versus baselinemodel:

Comparative Fit Index (CFI)		0.940	0.866
Tucker-Lewis Index (TLI)		0.931	0.847

Root Mean Square Error of Approximation:

RMSEA		0.038	0.038	
90 Percent Confidence Interval	0.028	0.047	0.028	0.047
P-value RMSEA <= 0.05		0.987	0.989	

Standardized Root Mean Square Residual:

SRMR	0.067	0.067

Parameter estimates:

Information				Expected		
Standard Errors				Robust.sem		
Estimate		Std.err	Z-value	P(>|z|)	Std.lv	Std.all
Latent variables:						
mastery=~						
ags1_c	1.000				0.805	0.727
ags2_c	1.057	0.114	9.244	0.000	0.85	10.587
ags5_c	0.836	0.071	11.734	0.000	0.673	0.717
ags6_c	1.013	0.097	10.413	0.000	0.816	0.738
ags7_c	1.049	0.082	12.809	0.000	0.844	0.831
ags12_c	1.109	0.118	9.377	0.000	0.893	0.605
frustration=~						
ats6_c	1.000				0.421	0.223
ats17_c	2.102	0.819	2.566	0.010	0.884	0.542

ats31_c		2.194	0.788	2.785	0.005	0.923	0.533
ats38_c		1.406	0.508	2.766	0.006	0.591	0.338
ats48_c		2.030	0.680	2.984	0.003	0.854	0.537
ats58_c		1.671	0.647	2.582	0.010	0.703	0.446
int=~							
int1		1.000				0.929	0.429
int2		0.549	0.330	1.664	0.096	0.510	0.225
int3		0.828	0.232	3.573	0.000	0.770	0.481
int4		0.442	0.232	1.905	0.057	0.411	0.211
int5		1.022	0.334	3.061	0.002	0.950	0.607
int6		0.439	0.275	1.597	0.110	0.408	0.169
attc=~							
ats50		1.000				0.956	0.622
ats29		1.065	0.193	5.517	0.000	1.018	0.594
ats40		0.920	0.165	5.579	0.000	0.880	0.471
ats35		0.615	0.157	3.926	0.000	0.588	0.397

Regressions:
attc~							
mastery	(a)	0.326	0.096	3.400	0.001	0.274	0.274
frustratn	(b)	-0.787	0.345	-2.282	0.023	-0.346	-0.346
int	(c)	-0.056	0.111	-0.502	0.616	-0.054	-0.054

Covariances:
mastery~~						
frustration	-0.050	0.031	-1.600	0.109	-0.147	-0.147
int	0.020	0.095	0.211	0.833	0.027	0.027
frustration~~						
int	0.033	0.049	0.675	0.500	0.085	0.085

Intercepts:
ags1_c	0.000	0.062	0.000	1.000	0.000	0.000
ags2_c	-0.000	0.081	-0.000	1.000	0.000	-0.000
ags5_c	0.000	0.052	0.000	1.000	0.000	0.000
ags6_c	0.000	0.062	0.000	1.000	0.000	0.000
ags7_c	0.000	0.057	0.000	1.000	0.000	0.000
ags12_c	0.000	0.082	0.000	1.000	0.000	0.000
ats6_c	-0.000	0.105	-0.000	1.000	-0.000	-0.000
ats17_c	0.000	0.091	0.000	1.000	0.000	0.000
ats31_c	0.000	0.096	0.000	1.000	0.000	0.000
ats38_c	0.000	0.097	0.000	1.000	0.000	0.000
ats48_c	0.000	0.089	0.000	1.000	0.000	0.000
ats58_c	0.000	0.088	0.000	1.000	0.000	0.000
int1	-0.190	0.121	-1.574	0.116	-0.190	-0.088

int2	−0.256	0.126	−2.035	0.042	−0.256	−0.113
int3	−0.233	0.089	−2.613	0.009	−0.233	−0.145
int4	−0.257	0.108	−2.375	0.018	−0.257	−0.132
int5	−0.013	0.087	−0.147	0.883	−0.013	−0.008
int6	−0.156	0.134	−1.162	0.245	−0.156	−0.065
ats50	3.852	0.086	45.044	0.000	3.852	2.506
ats29	4.179	0.095	43.849	0.000	4.179	2.440
ats40	3.583	0.104	34.511	0.000	3.583	1.920
ats35	4.627	0.082	56.090	0.000	4.627	3.121
mastery	0.000	0.000	0.000			
frustration	0.000	0.000	0.000			
int	0.000	0.000	0.000			
attc	0.000	0.000	0.000			

Variances:

ags1_c	0.578	0.088			0.578	0.471
ags2_c	1.376	0.207			1.376	0.655
ags5_c	0.427	0.045			0.427	0.485
ags6_c	0.556	0.079			0.556	0.455
ags7_c	0.319	0.041			0.319	0.309
ags12_c	1.380	0.204			1.380	0.634
ats6_c	3.371	0.197			3.371	0.950
ats17_c	1.881	0.269			1.881	0.706
ats31_c	2.143	0.263			2.143	0.716
ats38_c	2.718	0.221			2.718	0.886
ats48_c	1.803	0.190			1.803	0.712
ats58_c	1.986	0.198			1.986	0.801
int1	3.832	0.663			3.832	0.816
int2	4.861	0.681			4.861	0.949
int3	1.969	0.267			1.969	0.769
int4	3.610	0.554			3.610	0.955
int5	1.545	0.354			1.545	0.631
int6	5.631	0.858			5.631	0.971
ats50	1.448	0.199			1.448	0.613
ats29	1.898	0.247			1.898	0.647
ats40	2.708	0.243			2.708	0.778
ats35	1.852	0.190			1.852	0.843
mastery	0.649	0.106			1.000	1.000
frustration	0.177	0.119			1.000	1.000
int	0.864	0.463			1.000	1.000
attc	0.705	0.178			0.771	0.771

The model fit under DWLS appears to be good, based on the CFI, TLI, RMSEA, and SRMR. In this instance our primary interest in terms of model parameters is with regard to the regression coefficients for the latent variables. From these we can see that MAO is significantly positively related to ATTC ($\beta = 0.326$, $p = 0.001$), and that frustration is significantly negatively related to ATTC ($\beta = -0.787$, $p = 0.023$). The interaction term (`int`) is not significantly related to ATTC, meaning that there is no moderation present in the data. In other words, the relationship between mastery orientation and attention control is not influenced by an individual's level of academic frustration.

There is one final issue that must be addressed when using the product indicator approach to modeling latent interactions. The standardized coefficient for the interaction term that is produced by `lavaan` (and most other statistical software packages) is not quite correct. In order to obtain the correct standardized coefficient, we must adjust the value produced by the software using the following equation:

$$\text{INT}_{\text{correct}} = \beta_3 \left(\frac{\sqrt{\phi_{11} * \phi_{22}}}{\sqrt{\phi_{33}}} \right) = -0.054 \left(\frac{\sqrt{0.177 * 0.649}}{\sqrt{0.864}} \right) = -0.054 \left(\frac{0.339}{0.930} \right) = -0.017,$$

(6.9)

where

ϕ_{11} = Variance of latent variable 1

ϕ_{22} = Variance of latent variable 2

ϕ_{33} = Variance of interaction.

We can see that in this instance, the corrected value of the standardized coefficient is somewhat closer to zero than the uncorrected value.

STRUCTURAL EQUATION MODEL TREES

One very recent (as of the writing of this book) innovation in latent variable modeling is SEM Trees (Brandmaier, von Oertzen, McArdle, & Lindenberger, 2013). This methodology is derived from classification and regression trees (CART; Breiman, Friedman, Stone, & Olshen, 1984), as well as model-based recursive partitioning (MBRP; Zeileis, Hothorn, & Hornik, 2008). In the case of CART, a prediction model is specified including a single outcome variable and several predictors. CART begins with all members of the sample in a single grouping or node. It then searches the entire sample for the binary partition among the predictors which results in the most homogeneous split possible, in terms of the outcome variable. This split creates daughter nodes, and individuals are placed into the appropriate daughter node based upon their predictor variable value. After the initial split, CART investigates potential splits in each of the daughter nodes with the goal of creating two even more homogeneous nodes with respect to the outcome variable. This partitioning continues until further separation does not yield increased homogeneity in the outcome variable, resulting in a decision tree that differentiates the groups.

MBRP extended the CART methodology by partitioning the data based upon model parameter values (e.g. regression coefficients) rather than the simple values of the predictors. Thus, the researcher would specify a particular model, such as linear regression, and the MBRP algorithm would then follow the recursive partitioning steps described above for CART, but with the goal of making the groups as similar as possible with regard to the model parameter values, rather than the scores on the outcome variable. More specifically, the MBRP algorithm is based on the following steps:

1. Fit the model of choice (e.g. regression) to all observations in the current node (e.g. node 1).
2. Assess parameter instability (instability is simply group differences for model parameters) for each independent variable in the model, and select the one with the highest instability. If no instability is present, the algorithm stops. If instability is present, proceed to step 3.
3. Compute the split point of the model parameter value for the variable identified in step 2 that optimizes group separation.
4. Divide the node based upon this split point to create two daughter nodes in which members of the grouping variable with the most similar parameter estimates from step 3 are placed together.
5. Repeat steps 1 through 4 until stability is achieved for all model parameters.

SEM Tree is very similar to MBRP, relying on essentially the same set of steps. The difference is that rather than using parameters from an observed variable model, it defines the splits based upon SEM parameters such as factor loadings, intercepts, error variances, etc. Therefore, it can be a very useful tool for assessing model invariance for either categorical or continuous partitioning variables. In the previous chapter we examined the use of multiple groups SEM to test hypotheses about equality of model parameter values across groups such as males and females. While very useful, this approach does not lend itself easily to use with more than two groups, to cases involving more than one grouping variable of interest, or to continuous variables for which we need to assess invariance. SEM Tree, on the other hand, can easily accommodate all of these situations. It is entirely possible to have multiple partitioning variables, such as gender and ethnicity, so that we can determine whether there are interactions among them in terms of model parameter values. We can also use SEM Tree to assess invariance across values of a continuous variable, such as age or income. While still very new and in need of continued research, SEM Tree does hold the promise of being a very powerful and flexible tool for ascertaining model parameter invariance in a much wider array of situations than is currently easily done using more traditional methods. In the following, we will demonstrate the fitting of the SEM Tree model in R.

In order to fit SEM Tree to a set of data, we need to have installed both OpenMx and the semtree function. This can be done using the following two commands typed into R.

```
source('http://openmx.psyc.virginia.edu/
getOpenMx.R')
source('http://www.brandmaier.de/semtree/
getsemtree.R')
```

More information about both libraries can be found at the following websites:

OpenMx: http://openmx.psyc.virginia.edu/
SEMTrees: http://brandmaier.de/semtree/

To demonstrate the use of the trees with a continuous partitioning variable, we will examine the mastery orientation model that was described in Chapters 3 and 4. In this case, we are interested in learning whether the model structure might differ across values of the total score on the self-oriented perfectionism scale (mps_self). Recall from our earlier discussion that higher scores on this measure indicate a greater sense of self-oriented perfectionism. Of interest in the present analysis is whether individuals with differing levels of mps_self will have different latent model structures for the mastery orientation factor. In Chapter 5 we saw that such an examination could be made for a categorical variable such as gender, using multiple groups SEM. However, that approach will not work for a continuous partitioning variable such as the mps_self score. SEM Tree does, however, allow us to investigate potential differences in latent variable model structure across scores of a continuous variable.

In order to fit the SEM Tree for the mastery model, we must first create a dataset that includes only those variables that will be used as observed indicators of the factor, and the score on the partitioning variable itself. In addition, we must define which variables are latent and which are observed for OpenMx. The following set of commands does these tasks for us. First we create the dataset including the appropriate variables, and define which are manifest and which are latent.

```
tree_data<-data.frame(ags1, ags2, ags5, ags6, ags7,
ags12, mps_self)
manifests<-c("ags1", "ags2", "ags5", "ags6", "ags7",
"ags12")
latents <- c("mastery")
```

Next, we attach `tree_data` and then define the one-factor model using the OpenMx syntax framework. Again, the interested reader is referred to the OpenMx documentation for details on these commands, and the available options that can be used with it.

```
attach(tree_data)
masteryModel <- mxModel(name="Test One Factor",
        type="RAM",
        manifestVars = manifests,
        latentVars = latents,
        mxPath(from=latents, to=manifests),
        mxPath(from=manifests, arrows=2),
        mxPath(from=latents,  arrows=2,  free=FALSE,
values=1.0),
        mxPath(from="one",
            to=manifests,
            arrows=1,
            free=TRUE,
            values=1,
        ),
        mxData(observed=tree_data, type="raw")
)
```

Of particular importance in this syntax is the definition of the model terms, and the direction of the arrows from latent to manifest variables. The variable definition is carried out in `manifestVars = manifests` and `latentVars = latents`, while the path direction is carried out in `mxPath(from=manifests, arrows=2)` and `mxPath(from=latents, arrows=2, free=FALSE, values=1.0)`. We also must tell OpenMx the name of the data frame, and whether it is raw data or a covariance matrix, which we do in the subcommand `mxData(observed=tree_data, type="raw")`. After defining the model, we then call the `semtree` function and request a plot once the analysis is completed.

```
mastery.tree<-semtree(masteryModel)
plot(mastery.tree)
```

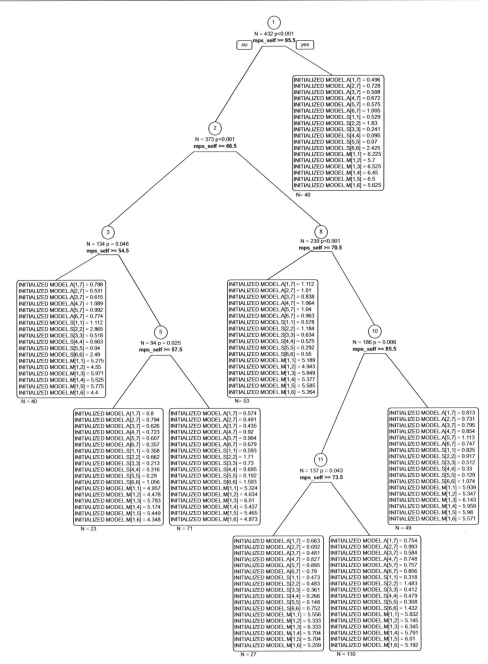

▨ **Figure 6.2:** SEM Tree plot

The resulting tree appears in Figure 6.2.

The first split occurred at an `mps_self` score of 95.5. Individuals with scores higher than this cutoff were partitioned to the right and those with lower scores were partitioned to the left. No further partitions were made in the right-hand-side group. In the leaves of the tree, the factor loadings are displayed first, and are labeled as parameter A. So, for example, the loadings for each indicator for the group with a score of 95.5 or higher, of whom there were 40 individuals, were 0.496, 0.728, 0.508, 0.672, 0.575, and 1.005. The variances and means of the indicators appear next, in the leaves of the tree.

It is also possible to obtain these estimates for the terminal nodes of the tree using the `parameters` command.

```
parameters(mastery.tree)
```

The resulting table appears below.

	4	6	7	9	12	13	14	15
INITIALIZED MODEL.A[1,7]	0.798	0.800	0.574	1.112	0.663	0.754	0.813	0.496
INITIALIZED MODEL.A[2,7]	0.531	0.794	0.491	1.010	0.692	0.993	0.731	0.728
INITIALIZED MODEL.A[3,7]	0.615	0.626	0.435	0.838	0.481	0.584	0.795	0.508
INITIALIZED MODEL.A[4,7]	1.089	0.723	0.920	1.064	0.827	0.748	0.854	0.672
INITIALIZED MODEL.A[5,7]	0.992	0.607	0.904	1.040	0.895	0.757	1.113	0.575
INITIALIZED MODEL.A[6,7]	0.774	0.357	0.679	0.963	0.790	0.856	0.747	1.005
INITIALIZED MODEL.S[1,1]	1.112	0.358	0.593	0.578	0.473	0.318	0.825	0.529
INITIALIZED MODEL.S[2,2]	2.865	0.662	1.710	1.184	0.483	1.483	0.917	1.830
INITIALIZED MODEL.S[3,3]	0.518	0.213	0.730	0.634	0.361	0.412	0.512	0.241
INITIALIZED MODEL.S[4,4]	0.663	0.316	0.695	0.575	0.266	0.479	0.330	0.095
INITIALIZED MODEL.S[5,5]	0.040	0.290	0.192	0.292	0.148	0.308	0.129	0.070
INITIALIZED MODEL.S[6,6]	2.490	1.056	1.593	0.550	0.752	1.432	1.074	2.425
INITIALIZED MODEL.M[1,1]	5.275	4.957	5.324	5.189	5.556	5.832	5.939	6.225
INITIALIZED MODEL.M[1,2]	4.550	4.478	4.634	4.943	5.333	5.145	5.347	5.700
INITIALIZED MODEL.M[1,3]	5.971	5.783	6.010	5.849	6.333	6.345	6.143	6.525
INITIALIZED MODEL.M[1,4]	5.525	5.174	5.437	5.377	5.704	5.791	5.959	6.450
INITIALIZED MODEL.M[1,5]	5.775	5.449	5.465	5.585	5.704	6.010	5.980	6.500
INITIALIZED MODEL.M[1,6]	4.400	4.348	4.873	5.264	5.259	5.192	5.571	5.625

The rows correspond to a particular model parameter (A = loadings, S = Variance, M = Mean) for the indicators, and the columns correspond to a specific terminal node of the tree. These are read from left to right, so that the column labeled "4" provides estimates for the terminal node to the far left of the tree, as this is the fourth node. As a point of reference, the first node is at the top of the tree and contains all members of the sample. This fact is made clear in Figure 6.2 as the nonterminal nodes are numbered. Thus, node 2 appears directly below and to the left of the initial node 1. Returning to the interpretation of the results, the 40 individuals in node 4 have mps_self scores below 54.5. In other words, these are individuals with the lowest level of self-oriented perfectionism. We can see from the table that the factor loadings tend to be fairly large in this node, meaning that the indicators are all strongly associated with the factor. The means of the individual indicators range from 4.4 to 5.971 on a seven-point Likert scale, and the variances from 0.04 for the fifth indicator variable (ags7) to 2.865 for the second indicator (ags2). By way of contrast, node 15 includes those 40 individuals with the highest mps_self scores, as noted previously. The pattern of loadings for this terminal node does differ in the sample from that of node 4, for example. However, SEM Tree does not provide tests comparing specific parameters with one another, but rather compares the model parameters with one another holistically. It is also possible to obtain the standard errors of the model parameters using the command se(mastery.tree).

One potential problem with all recursive-partitioning-based methods, including SEM Tree, is a tendency to overfit the sample data. In other words, the tree that is grown may be overly sensitive to relatively small perturbations in the sample, thereby creating a tree that does not generalize to the population very well. One approach for dealing with this problem is to shrink the tree somewhat, a process known as pruning, so that fewer terminal nodes are retained, and those that do remain yield a more generalizable solution. In addition, given the sample size requirements for estimating SEMs, reducing the size of the tree would result in larger samples within the individual terminal nodes, and in turn more stable parameter estimates. Within the semtree library, the prune.semtree function allows for such pruning. When using this function, the researcher can establish the maximum depth of the tree and thereby reduce the number of terminal nodes. For this example, we set the maximum depth of the pruned tree at two levels.

```
mastery.tree.pruned<-prune.semtree(mastery.tree,
  max.depth=2)
plot(mastery.tree.pruned)
```

In Figure 6.3 we can see that the initial split resulting in a terminal node with 40 individuals having mps_self scores of 95.5 or higher remains. On the other side of the tree, there are two terminal nodes with the left side including individuals with mps_self scores less than 66.5 and the right side including those with scores between 66.5 and 95.5. As before, we can examine the model parameters in order to gain an understanding of the nature of these groups. One other point to note

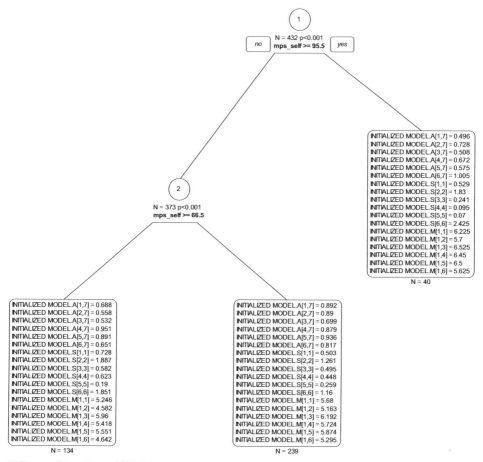

■ **Figure 6.3:** Pruned SEM Tree

is that the two nodes on the left side include 134 and 239 individuals, respectively, which should provide us with more confidence in the stability of the model parameter estimates.

SUMMARY

In Chapter 6, we have focused on some more advanced issues in SEM. In particular, we learned how to address two more complex issues in the latent variable paradigm, the nonrecursive (or feedback loop) model, and the moderation model. In addition, we also learned about a very new (as of the writing of this book) development in the world of SEM, namely SEM Tree models, which may prove useful for invariance testing research. In each case, we saw how R can be brought to bear on these situations and how the resulting output can be interpreted. Each of these models represents an important extension of SEM for use in dealing with specific research problems.

FURTHER READING

Hancock, G.R., & Mueller, R.O. (2013). *Structural Equation Modeling: A Second Course*. Charlotte, NC: Information Age Publishing.
Hoyle, R.H. (2012). *Handbook of Structural Equation Modeling*. New York: The Guilford Press.

REFERENCES

Bollen, K.A. (1996). An alternative two stage least squares (2SLS) estimator for latent variable equations. *Psychometrika*, 61, 109–21.
Bollen, K.A., & Bauer, D.J. (2004). Automating the selection of model-implied instrumental variables. *Sociological Methods and Research*, 32, 425–52.
Bollen, K.A., Kirby, J.B., Curran, P.J., Paxton, P.M., & Chen, F. (2007). Latent variable models under misspecification: Two-stage least squares (2SLS) and maximum likelihood (ML) estimators. *Sociological Methods and Research*, 36, 48–86.
Brandmaier, A.M., von Oertzen, T., McArdle, J.J., & Lindenberger, U. (2013). Structural equation model trees. *Psychological Methods*, 18(1), 71–86.
Breiman, L., Friedman, J., Stone, C.J., & Olshen, R.A. (1984). *Classification and Regression Trees*. New York: Wadsworth.
Fox, J. (2008). *Applied Regression Analysis and Generalized Linear Models*. Los Angeles: Sage Publications.
Jöreskog, K.G. (1983). Factor analysis as an error in variable model. In H. Wainer & S. Messick (eds), *Principles of Modern Psychological Measurement* (pp. 185–96). Hillsdale, NJ: Lawrence Erlbaum.
Kelava, A., & Nagengast, B. (2012). A Bayesian model for the estimation of latent interaction and quadratic effects when latent variables are nonnormally distributed. *Multivariate Behavioral Research*, 47, 717–42.
Kenny, D.A., & Judd, C.M. (1984). Estimating the non-linear and interactive effects of latent variables. *Psychological Bulletin*, 96, 201–10.
Klein, A.G., & Muthén, B.O. (2007). Quasi-maximum likelihood estimation of structural equation models with multiple interaction and quadratic effects. *Multivariate Behavioral Research*, 42(4), 647–73.
Lee, S.Y., Song, X.Y., & Cai, J.H. (2010). A Bayesian approach for nonlinear structural equation models with dichotomous variables using logit and probit links. *Structural Equation Modeling*, 17, 280–302.

Marsh, H.W., Wen, Z., & Hau, K.T. (2004). Structural equation models of latent interactions: Evaluation of alternative estimation strategies and indicator construction. *Psychological Methods*, 9(3), 275–300.

Song, X.Y., & Lee, S.Y. (2006). Bayesian analysis of structural equation models with nonlinear covariates and latent variables. *Multivariate Behavioral Research*, 41, 337–65.

Zeileis, A., Hothorn, T., & Hornik, K. (2008). Model-based recursive partitioning. *Journal of Computational and Graphical Statistics*, 17(2), 492–514.

Chapter 7

GROWTH CURVE MODELING

INTRODUCTION

In several previous chapters, we have described latent variable modeling in the context of factor analysis, structural equations, and multiple groups analyses. In this chapter, we turn our attention to yet another application of latent variable analyses, in this case for the modeling of change in observed variables over time using **growth curve models (GCMs)**. The most common scenario in which such an analysis would prove useful involves a case where the researcher has gathered data on a sample at multiple points in time, and the research question of primary interest is: do scores on these measures change over time in a linear (or nonlinear) fashion? In addition, the researcher might also be interested in whether there is a relationship between an individual's starting point on the measurement of interest and their change trajectory, as well as whether the change trajectories of two (or more) processes are related to one another. These questions, as well as others, can be directly addressed using GCMs. In this chapter, we will first provide sufficient background into the theory of GCMs so that the reader will feel comfortable using them in practice. We will then turn our attention to the fitting of these models using R, starting with fairly simple ones and moving to fitting more complex relationships in the data.

There exist a number of tools for evaluating change in one or more measurements over time. For example, repeated measures analysis of variance (ANOVA) allows a researcher to compare means of a single measurement taken at multiple points in time. This model can easily be extended to incorporate multiple such measurements in a repeated measures multivariate analysis of variance (MANOVA). In addition, multilevel models can be used to assess change over time, where the individual measurements are treated as level-1 observations, and the members of the sample are treated as level-2 data (Snijders & Bosker, 1999). Another option for researchers interested in modeling longitudinal data is GCM, sometimes also referred to as latent growth curve modeling. In this paradigm, we bring to bear the flexibility and power associated with latent variable models to the problem of understanding change over time in a set of measurements. As an example, a researcher might have collected test scores from a sample of students each year over four years. A primary question of interest in such a case would be whether the scores change in a systematic fashion over time. In particular, it might be hypothesized that the scores improve over time in a linear fashion. In order to assess this hypothesis, we could use any of the methods described above. ANOVA, multilevel models, and GCM would all allow us to assess whether there is a linear increase in scores across the four years. However, GCM offers some distinct advantages that the other two methods do not. Specifically, because GCM is a latent variable technique we have access to all of the approaches that have been described in previous chapters under the umbrella of SEM, such as the MIMIC model, multiple group modeling, and structural models with multiple latent variables. As we will see below, this added flexibility makes GCM very appealing when dealing with investigating change over time.

GROWTH CURVE MODELS

The key to understanding GCM is to realize that the latent variables in this case are the initial status of the construct being measured, and the change in that construct over time. The GCM appears in Figure 7.1.

We see that there are two latent variables, the Intercept (initial status) and the Slope (rate of growth). Rather than being freely estimated as is generally the case in latent variables models, the loadings linking the observed measurements with each latent trait are constrained to be specific values, reflecting the hypothesis regarding the type of growth to be measured. For example, in order to model linear growth, we would set the loadings for the Slope term to be 0, 1, 2, and 3, such that the equal distance between values reflects the linear growth trajectory. With regard to the intercept, the coefficients are all set to 1, and this will be the case regardless of the hypothesis regarding change over time. Because the coefficient for the initial time point in Figure 7.1 is set to 0, its mean is the estimate for the mean of the Intercept latent variable. More generally, the mean of the latent intercept is the mean of the measurement with a coefficient of 0 for the latent growth variable. Thus, if we were more interested in estimating the mean of the final status, rather than initial, we could use the coefficients $-3, -2, -1, 0$ for the slope term. Finally, note that the GCM will provide an estimate of the covariance (correlation) between the slope and the intercept, or between the change in scores and the initial status.

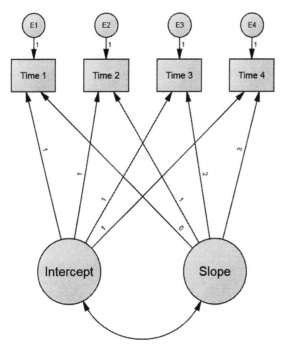

◼ **Figure 7.1:** Example growth curve model with four time points

In the following sections of this chapter, we describe how to fit a variety of GCMs, from the basic linear model of Figure 7.1 to more complex models including non-linear terms and observed and latent covariates. The growth command in the lavaan library allows us to easily fit a variety of such models. In addition, it is important to note that in the following pages we cover a variety of such models, but there are others available to the reader as well. Therefore, we encourage the interested reader to use this chapter as a starting point upon which they can build more complex models as the need arises.

FITTING LINEAR GROWTH CURVE MODELS IN R

In this example, we have data on a language assessment that was given to a group of 410 elementary school students beginning in the fall of 2003, and continuing twice a year through spring, 2006. Our primary interest is in determining whether there is linear growth in the scores over this time, which would indicate improvements in language usage by the students. Prior to fitting this model, however, it will be helpful for us to examine our data graphically as a way of better understanding the nature of the relationship between time and test score. In order to do this, we will use the `ggplot` function that is a part of the `ggplot2` library in

R. We will first need to construct a data frame that is in long rather than wide format. Wide format is how the data needs to be organized for fitting the GCM in lavaan, where wide simply means that each individual in the dataset appears in one line and each measurement taken over time appears in a column. However, what we would like to do is plot the mean scores across time, which will necessitate creating a new dataset in which one column contains the variable time and a second column contains the mean language test score for each year. The following commands do this in R.

```
lf3_mean<-mean(lf3)
ls4_mean<-mean(ls4)
lf4_mean<-mean(lf4)
ls5_mean<-mean(ls5)
lf5_mean<-mean(lf5)
ls6_mean<-mean(ls6)

gcm_mean<-rbind(lf3_mean, ls4_mean, lf4_mean, ls5_mean,
lf5_mean, ls6_mean)
gcm_time<-rbind(1,2,3,4,5,6)
gcm_mean.dataframe<-data.frame(gcm_mean, gcm_time)
```

The first block of code simply calculates the means for each test score across all examinees, saving them in new variables. Then, we stack these means on top of one another in the correct temporal order, using the rbind command. We create a time index variable with values 1–6 to denote the six measurement times. Finally, we combine the vectors created by the two rbind commands into a data frame using the data.frame command. The resulting dataset looks as follows:

```
gcm_mean.dataframe
```

	gcm_mean	gcm_time
lf3_mean	188.8293	1
ls4_mean	199.0293	2
lf4_mean	200.4902	3
ls5_mean	207.9268	4
lf5_mean	208.4220	5
ls6_mean	213.3049	6

We can now use this data frame in conjunction with ggplot to create a line graph of the test scores.

```
ggplot(gcm_mean.dataframe, aes(gcm_time, gcm_mean,
group=1))+geom_line()+geom_point()
```

Given the large number of excellent references on using `ggplot`, we will not explore all possible uses of the command. However, we will briefly describe the preceding code, and then display the resulting graph. When using `ggplot`, we must first identify the dataframe containing the data, in this case `gcm_mean.dataframe`. The plot itself is created using the `aes` subcommand, which has three arguments. The first argument is the variable that will denote the values on the *x*-axis. In this example, the *x*-axis will be the time index variable that we created, `gcm_time`. The second argument is the variable containing the actual scores (`gcm_mean`), and the third argument is the grouping variable. In this example, we do not have any groups and indicate this with the `group=1` statement. Finally, we request that individual data points (`geom_point`) be plotted, and then connected with a line (`geom_line`). For each of these subcommands, we can manipulate characteristics of the line and the points within the `()`. Again, the interested reader is encouraged to investigate how to do this through one of the several excellent online tutorials available for `ggplot`. The resulting graph appears in Figure 7.2.

It appears that there was an increase in scores over the measurement periods, with steeper increases from fall to spring (1 to 2, 3 to 4, and 5 to 6) then from spring to fall (2 to 3, 4 to 5), perhaps reflecting the impact of the summer vacation.

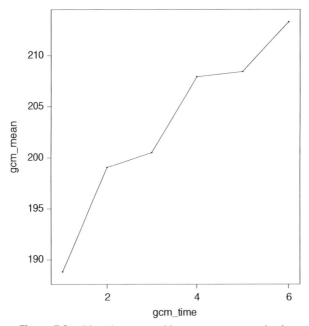

■ **Figure 7.2:**   Mean language achievement test scores by time

In order to fit the linear GCM with `lavaan`, we will use the following commands:

```
lang.growth.model1<-'
i=~1*lf3+1*ls4+1*lf4+1*ls5+1*lf5+1*ls6
s=~0*lf3+1*ls4+2*lf4+3*ls5+4*lf5+5*ls6
'

lang.growth.model1.fit<-growth(lang.growth.model1, data=gcm_data)
```

First we must specify the model with two latent variables, the intercept (i) and the slope (s). As discussed above, the intercept is an estimate of the initial value of the construct being measured, in this case language usage skills. The slope provides information about the average amount of linear change in the scores between each consecutive measurement. Note that for the intercept, all of the measurements are assigned a coefficient value of 1, whereas we model linear growth with the slope by assigning each successive measurement a coefficient value one unit larger than that assigned to the previous measurement. By assigning the first measurement (lf3) a coefficient value of 0, we set the value of the intercept to be the estimate of the mean starting point for the sample; i.e. the mean language score in fall, 2003. We then fit the model using the `lavaan` function `growth`. In order to obtain the model parameter estimates, we use the `summary` command, which is similar to what we have done with other models described in previous chapters.

```
summary(lang.growth.model1.fit)
```

```
lavaan (0.5-15) converged normally after 171 iterations

    Number of observations                          410

    Estimator                                        ML
    Minimum Function Test Statistic             236.222
    Degrees of freedom                               16
    P-value (Chi-square)                          0.000

Parameter estimates:

    Information                                Expected
    Standard Errors                            Standard
```

```
Estimate Std.err Z-value P(>|z|) Std.lv Std.all
```
Latent variables:

i=~

	Estimate	Std.err	Z-value	P(>|z|)	Std.lv	Std.all
lf3	1.000				16.657	0.854
ls4	1.000				16.657	0.983
lf4	1.000				16.657	1.031
ls5	1.000				16.657	1.157
lf5	1.000				16.657	1.227
ls6	1.000				16.657	1.279

s=~

	Estimate	Std.err	Z-value	P(>|z|)	Std.lv	Std.all
lf3	0.000				0.000	0.000
ls4	1.000				2.006	0.118
lf4	2.000				4.012	0.248
ls5	3.000				6.018	0.418
lf5	4.000				8.023	0.591
ls6	5.000				10.029	0.770

Covariances:

i~~

	Estimate	Std.err	Z-value	P(>|z|)	Std.lv	Std.all
s	80	2.993	−8.347	0.000	−0.748	−0.748

Intercepts:

	Estimate	Std.err	Z-value	P(>|z|)	Std.lv	Std.all
lf3	0.000				0.000	0.000
ls4	0.000				0.000	0.000
lf4	0.000				0.000	0.000
ls5	0.000				0.000	0.000
lf5	0.000				0.000	0.000
ls6	0.000				0.000	0.000
i	192.837	0.877	219.862	0.000	11.577	11.577
s	4.205	0.135	31.256	0.000	2.096	2.096

Variances:

	Estimate	Std.err	Z-value	P(>|z|)	Std.lv	Std.all
lf3	102.934	9.597			102.934	0.271
ls4	55.366	5.488			55.366	0.193
lf4	67.279	5.571			67.279	0.258
ls5	43.347	3.761			43.347	0.209
lf5	42.158	3.830			42.158	0.229
ls6	41.408	4.655			41.408	0.244
i	277.453	22.111			1.000	1.000
s	4.024	0.549			1.000	1.000

When interpreting the results of the GCM, our primary interest is in the slope estimate, which tells us whether there is linear change over time. For this example, the unstandardized estimate is 4.205, which is statistically significant from 0

($p < 0.001$). Thus, we can conclude that there is positive linear change in test scores over time, and that from one measurement to the next the average amount of such growth is just over four points. The mean starting score on the assessment was 192.837, and based on the statistically significant negative covariance (-24.98; $p < 0.001$), we can conclude that individuals with higher starting scores experienced less linear growth than did those with lower starting scores. Because we requested the standardized estimates, R also provides the correlation between i and s, which was -0.748, indicating that the negative relationship between the starting value and change over time was fairly strong.

FITTING NONLINEAR GROWTH CURVE MODELS IN R

We are not limited to fitting only linear change trajectories with GCMs. For example, if we have a hypothesis and/or empirical evidence to suggest that the change in language test scores follows a quadratic trend over time, we can fit such a model and test whether the quadratic change term is statistically significant. In order to do so, we would simply use the following commands in R. Note that the quadratic term (q) is specified by taking the squares of the coefficients used in the linear specification.

```
lang.growth.model2<-'
i=~1*lf3+1*ls4+1*lf4+1*ls5+1*lf5+1*ls6
s=~0*lf3+1*ls4+2*lf4+3*ls5+4*lf5+5*ls6
q=~0*lf3+1*ls4+4*lf4+9*ls5+16*lf5+25*ls6
'
lang.growth.model2.fit<-growth(lang.growth.model2,
data=gcm_data)
summary(lang.growth.model2.fit, standardized=TRUE)
lavaan (0.5-15) converged normally after 241 iterations
```

Number of observations	410
Estimator	ML
Minimum Function Test Statistic	161.860
Degrees of freedom	12
P-value (Chi-square)	0.000

Parameter estimates:

Information	Expected
Standard Errors	Standard

Estimate Std.err Z-value P(>|z|) Std.lv Std.all

Latent variables:
  i=~
    lf3   1.000   17.108   0.900
    ls4   1.000   17.108   0.998
    lf4   1.000   17.108   1.051
    ls5   1.000   17.108   1.221
    lf5   1.000   17.108   1.255
    ls6   1.000   17.108   1.316
  s=~
    lf3   0.000   0.000   0.000
    ls4   1.000   3.339   0.195
    lf4   2.000   6.679   0.410
    ls5   3.000   10.018   0.715
    lf5   4.000   13.358   0.980
    ls6   5.000   16.697   1.285
  q=~
    lf3   0.000   0.000   0.000
    ls4   1.000   0.444   0.026
    lf4   4.000   1.777   0.109
    ls5   9.000   3.997   0.285
    lf5   16.000   7.106   0.521
    ls6   25.000   11.103   0.854

Covariances:
  i~~
    s   -35.299   8.565   -4.121   0.000   -0.618   -0.618
    q   1.554   1.349   1.152   0.249   0.205   0.205
  s~~
    q   -1.158   0.814   -1.423   0.155   -0.781   -0.781

Intercepts:
    lf3   0.000   0.000   0.000
    ls4   0.000   0.000   0.000
    lf4   0.000   0.000   0.000
    ls5   0.000   0.000   0.000
    lf5   0.000   0.000   0.000
    ls6   0.000   0.000   0.000
    i   190.029   0.919 206.822   0.000   11.108   11.108
    s   7.320   0.348   21.006   0.00   2.192   2.192
    q   -0.562   0.061   -9.260   0.000   -1.266   -1.266

```
Variances:
    lf3        68.574      10.472                    68.574       0.190
    ls4        59.632       5.630                    59.632       0.203
    lf4        71.886       5.934                    71.886       0.271
    ls5        33.659       3.462                    33.659       0.171
    lf5        45.023       4.057                    45.023       0.242
    ls6        38.933       7.010                    38.933       0.230
    i         292.686      24.977                     1.000       1.000
    s          11.152       4.853                     1.000       1.000
    q                                                 1.000       1.000
```

The quadratic term is statistically significant ($p < 0.001$) and negative (-0.562), indicating that there is a quadratic change, such that the rate of increase in scores over time is slowing. The quadratic term is not significantly correlated with either the starting value or the linear change over time. Fitting a cubic model would simply involve cubing the linear coefficients and adding another line to the model specification. Of course, fitting such higher-order models can yield results that are sometimes difficult to interpret, and require more observed variables so that we have sufficient information in order to obtain the model parameter estimates. In addition, it is recommended that the researcher fitting such complex structure to the data have a priori hypotheses that would suggest the possible existence of such relationships in the data.

INCLUDING COVARIATES IN GROWTH CURVE MODELS

Just as with other SEMs, it is possible to add observed variable covariates to the GCM specification. For example, we might want to know whether the linear growth over time is the same for females (coded as 1) and males (2), and whether the mean starting point is the same for the genders. In order to do so, we would simply include sex in what amounts to a MIMIC model specification. The R code to do this appears below. Here we simply include equations relating the observed variable sex with both i and s.

```
lang.growth.model1.mimic<-'
i=~1*lf3+1*ls4+1*lf4+1*ls5+1*lf5+1*ls6
s=~0*lf3+1*ls4+2*lf4+3*ls5+4*lf5+5*ls6

i~sex
s~sex
'
lang.growth.model1.mimic.fit<-growth(lang.growth.model1.mimic,
data=gcm_data)
```

```
summary(lang.growth.model1.mimic.fit, standardized=TRUE)

lavaan (0.5-15) converged normally after 175 iterations
```

Number of observations				410
Estimator				ML
Minimum Function Test Statistic				241.931
Degrees of freedom				20
P-value (Chi-square)				0.000

```
Parameter estimates:
```

Information				Expected	
Standard Errors				Standard	

	Estimate	Std.err	Z-value	P(>|z|)	Std.lv	Std.all
Latent variables:						
i=~						
lf3	1.000				16.656	0.854
ls4	1.000				16.656	0.983
lf4	1.000				16.656	1.032
ls5	1.000				16.656	1.157
lf5	1.000				16.656	1.227
ls6	1.000				16.656	1.279
s=~						
lf3	0.000				0.000	0.000
ls4	1.000				2.005	0.118
lf4	2.000				4.011	0.248
ls5	3.000				6.016	0.418
lf5	4.000				8.021	0.591
ls6	5.000				10.026	0.770
Regressions:						
i~						
sex	-4.247	1.745	-2.434	0.015	-0.255	-0.127
s~						
sex	0.476	0.269	1.770	0.077	0.237	0.118
Covariances:						
i~~						
s	-24.466	2.958	-8.271	0.000	-0.744	-0.744

Intercepts:

lf3	0.000				0.000	0.000
ls4	0.000				0.000	0.000
lf4	0.000				0.000	0.000
ls5	0.000				0.000	0.000
lf5	0.000				0.000	0.000
ls6	0.000				0.000	0.000
i	199.075	2.706	73.557	0.000	11.952	11.952
s	3.506	0.417	8.417	0.000	1.749	1.749

Variances:

lf3	103.284	9.614		103.284	0.271
ls4	55.530	5.494		55.530	0.193
lf4	67.066	5.556		67.066	0.257
ls5	43.290	3.757		43.290	0.209
lf5	42.145	3.829		42.145	0.229
ls6	41.380	4.652		41.380	0.244
i	272.915	21.800		0.984	0.984
s	3.965	0.546		0.986	0.986

These results show that there is a statistically significant relationship between the sex of the examinee and the initial score ($p = 0.015$), but not between sex and the change over time ($p = 0.077$). The difference in mean starting scores was 4.247, with males, who were coded as the higher number, having the lower mean given the negative value of the coefficient. It is also interesting to note that the estimates of the mean values for both i and s change somewhat when we include the observed covariate, sex.

ASSESSING CHANGE OVER TIME IN MULTIPLE VARIABLES SIMULTANEOUSLY

In addition to including one or more observed covariates, we can also examine the relationship between two latent change variables using the GCM. For example, perhaps we would like to know (a) whether language and reading test scores change linearly over time, and (b) whether change in one is correlated with change in the other. Examining such a relationship is possible using the following model specification:

```
lang.growth.model3<-'
lang_i=~1*lf3+1*ls4+1*lf4+1*ls5+1*lf5+1*ls6
lang_s=~0*lf3+1*ls4+2*lf4+3*ls5+4*lf5+5*ls6
```

```
read_i=~1*rf3+1*rs4+1*rf4+1*rs5+1*rf5+1*rs6
read_s=~0*rf3+1*rs4+2*rf4+3*rs5+4*rf5+5*rs6
'

lang.growth.model3.fit<-growth(lang.growth.model3, data=gcm_data)
summary(lang.growth.model3.fit, standardized=TRUE)
lavaan (0.5-15) converged normally after 322 iterations
```

Number of observations		410

Estimator		ML
Minimum Function Test Statistic		791.330
Degrees of freedom		64
P-value (Chi-square)		0.000

Parameter estimates:

Information	Expected
Standard Errors	Standard

	Estimate	Std.err	Z-value	P(>|z|)	Std.lv	Std.all
Latent variables:						
lang_i=~						
lf3	1.000				16.691	0.858
ls4	1.000				16.691	0.984
lf4	1.000				16.691	1.036
ls5	1.000				16.691	1.158
lf5	1.000				16.691	1.224
ls6	1.000				16.691	1.292
lang_s=~						
lf3	0.000				0.000	0.000
ls4	1.000				2.029	0.120
lf4	2.000				4.058	0.252
ls5	3.000				6.087	0.422
lf5	4.000				8.116	0.595
ls6	5.000				10.145	0.785
read_i=~						
rf3	1.000				17.070	0.795
rs4	1.000				17.070	0.938
rf4	1.000				17.070	0.965
rs5	1.000				17.070	1.060
rf5	1.000				17.070	1.112
rs6	1.000				17.070	1.159

```
read_s=~
  rf3        0.000                              0.000      0.000
  rs4        1.000                              1.581      0.087
  rf4        2.000                              3.163      0.179
  rs5        3.000                              4.744      0.295
  rf5        4.000                              6.325      0.412
  rs6        5.000                              7.907      0.537

Covariances:
  lang_i~~
    lang_s    -25.364    2.995    -8.467    0.000    -0.749    -0.749
    read_i    296.697   21.906    13.544    0.000     1.041     1.041
    read_s    -24.645    2.608    -9.449    0.000    -0.934    -0.934
  lang_s~~
    read_i    -28.169    2.860    -9.851    0.000    -0.813    -0.813
    read_s      4.512    0.418    10.790    0.000     1.406     1.406
  read_i~~
    read_s    -18.213    2.946    -6.182    0.000    -0.675    -0.675

Intercepts:
  lf3        0.000                              0.000      0.000
  ls4        0.000                              0.000      0.000
  lf4        0.000                              0.000      0.000
  ls5        0.000                              0.000      0.000
  lf5        0.000                              0.000      0.000
  ls6        0.000                              0.000      0.000
  rf3        0.000                              0.000      0.000
  rs4        0.000                              0.000      0.000
  rf4        0.000                              0.000      0.000
  rs5        0.000                              0.000      0.000
  rf5        0.000                              0.000      0.000
  rs6        0.000                              0.000      0.000
  lang_i   192.782    0.878   219.598    0.000    11.550    11.550
  lang_s     4.217    0.135    31.313    0.000     2.079     2.079
  read_i   188.212    0.916   205.449    0.000    11.026    11.026
  read_s     4.511    0.130    34.761    0.000     2.853     2.853

Variances:
  lf3      100.155    8.276              100.155    0.264
  ls4       55.671    4.729               55.671    0.194
  lf4       66.025    5.093               66.025    0.254
```

ls5	44.434	3.554		44.434	0.214
lf5	44.518	3.681		44.518	0.239
ls6	39.101	3.993		39.101	0.234
rf3	170.177	12.642		170.177	0.369
rs4	.369	5.835		73.369	0.222
rf4	84.213	6.329		84.213	0.269
rs5	54.836	4.386		54.836	0.211
rf5	49.946	4.179		49.946	0.212
rs6	45.263	4.490		45.263	0.209
lang_i	278.581	22.143		1.000	1.000
lang_s	4.117	0.546		1.000	1.000
read_i	91.379	24.155		1.000	1.000
read_s	2.501	0.530		1.000	1.000

Note that the specification of the linear change models for language and reading is identical except for the variable names themselves. The growth command in lavaan will automatically estimate the covariances among the reading and language intercepts and slopes. Prior to examining these, however, we might first look at the estimates of change for each. In both cases there was a positive linear change in test scores, each of somewhat more than four points between testing periods, on average. In addition, the mean starting value for reading was approximately 188 whereas it was just under 193 for language. As we noted previously, there was a negative relationship between the initial score and the growth rate for language, and a similar result was apparent for reading as well. Finally, the relationship between the rates of growth in language and reading test scores was positive, given the covariance (4.512). This result means that students with stronger linear growth in their language performance also experienced stronger linear growth in their reading performance. The estimated correlation here is 1.406, which is clearly out of the −1 to 1 bounds for correlations. This result indicates that the standardized relationship between linear growth for the two tests is difficult to estimate given that it is so very close to 1. It is possible to conclude, however, that the relationship in growth trajectories for language and reading scores in the population is likely to be relatively strong and positive.

As was the case for language scores alone, it is possible to examine graphically the growth trajectories for the language and reading tests together, using the following ggplot command. A new dataset is once again created in long format, including means for both language and reading, as well as an indicator for time that is numbered 1 through 6; the resulting plot is shown in Figure 7.3.

```
rf3_mean<-mean(rf3)
rs4_mean<-mean(rs4)
rf4_mean<-mean(rf4)
```

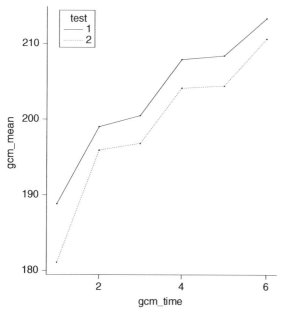

■ **Figure 7.3:** Mean language and reading achievement test scores by time

```
rs5_mean<-mean(rs5)
rf5_mean<-mean(rf5)
rs6_mean<-mean(rs6)

gcm_mean<-rbind(rf3_mean, rs4_mean, rf4_mean, rs5_
mean, rf5_mean, rs6_mean)
gcm_time<-rbind(1,2,3,4,5,6)
test<-as.factor(c(1,1,1,1,1,1,2,2,2,2,2,2))

gcm_mean_read.dataframe<-data.frame(gcm_mean,
gcm_time)

gcm_mean_both.dataframe<-rbind(gcm_mean.dataframe,
gcm_mean_read.dataframe)
gcm_mean_both.dataframe<-cbind(gcm_mean_both.
dataframe,test)

ggplot(gcm_mean_both.dataframe, aes(gcm_time, gcm_
mean, linetype=test))+geom_line()+geom_point()
```

SUMMARY

In this chapter, we focused on the use of latent variable models for the investigation of change over time. The GCM described here provides the researcher with a flexible and easy to use tool for assessing the nature of change over time, through the modeling of linear and quadratic (or other higher-order) models. Such models can also include observed covariates in the form of the MIMIC model, and multiple latent variables that can also be time dependent, as was demonstrated here. In addition to yielding estimates of change over time, the GCM also provides the researcher with measures of the relationship between growth and initial status, and between growth in two different variables. Other analyses that are available in the context of GCMs are multiple groups models allowing for the testing of invariance of growth and initial status, as well as models in which the latent growth variable can be used as a predictor of another latent variable. In short, the flexibility of SEMs that we have seen repeatedly can be extended quite easily to the measurement of change over time through GCMs.

FURTHER READING

Duncan, T.E., Duncan, S.C., & Strycker, L.A. (2006). *An Introduction to Latent Variable Growth Curve Modeling*. Mahwah, NJ: Lawrence Erlbaum Associates, Publishers.

Kline, R.B. (2011). *Principles and Practice of Structural Equation Modeling*, 3rd edition. New York: The Guilford Press.

Little, T.D. (2013). *Longitudinal Structural Equation Modeling*. New York: The Guilford Press.

Mirman, D. (2014). *Growth Curve Analysis and Visualization using R*. Boca Raton, FL: CRC Press.

REFERENCES

Snijders, T., & Bosker, R. (1999). *Multilevel Analysis: An Introduction to Basic and Advanced Multilevel Modeling*. Thousand Oaks, CA: Sage Publications.

## Chapter 8

MIXTURE MODELS

INTRODUCTION

To this point, the focus of our book has been on latent variables that are continuous in nature, such as the factors that we discussed in Chapters 2 through 7. In this chapter, we will turn our attention to the situation where the latent variable is categorical, consisting of a small number of discrete classifications in the population. As with other latent variable models, such **mixture models** include observed indicators that are directly impacted by the unobserved latent variable. The observed indicators can be categorical variables themselves, or they can be continuous. In addition, the latent mixtures can be characterized by different parameters (e.g. regression coefficients) for statistical models involving observed variables. In all cases, the presumption underlying mixture models is the same as what we assumed for the factor models that were the focus of previous chapters, namely that the latent (categorical) variable is the direct antecedent of the observed indicators, whatever form they may take. In this chapter, we will learn how to fit and interpret the results for a latent class and mixture regression models using the R software package. It needs to be noted that this is not intended to be an exhaustive examination of the topic, but rather a solid introduction from which the interested reader can launch into more specific areas of practice, which we will touch on briefly throughout the chapter. We start with a brief introduction to latent class analysis and mixture regression models, followed by a more extensive review of how to work with these models using R.

LATENT CLASS MODELS

We will begin our discussion of mixture models by considering perhaps the most basic of these, the latent class model. Figure 8.1 shows a simple latent class model with three indicator variables, V1, V2, and V3, which can be either categorical

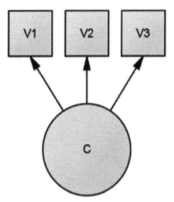

■ **Figure 8.1:**   Example latent class model

or continuous, and a single latent variable, C, consisting of a small number of categories.

Latent class analysis (LCA) was first introduced in the late 1960s by Lazarsfeld and Henry (1968). LCA is typically conducted in an exploratory manner in which, much like with EFA (Chapter 2), firmly grounded a priori hypotheses regarding the number or nature of the latent classes underlying the data may not be available (Collins & Lanza, 2010). It might be the case that the researcher has some general ideas about how many and what types of classes exist in the population, but these ideas are not so well established as to be dealt with in a confirmatory way. It should be noted here that it is possible, though beyond the scope of this book, to fit confirmatory LCA models using specific model constraints. In typical exploratory LCA the researcher would fit several models to the data, each being differentiated from the others by the number of latent classes. The relative fit of these models is then compared in order to identify the optimal number of classes. Comparative fit is assessed via indices designed to determine which model can best reproduce the observed data. Among these statistics for assessing model fit are the AIC and BIC that we discussed in regards to CFA in Chapter 3. In addition, there are the chi-square and likelihood ratio goodness of fit tests, the Lo–Mendell–Rubin (Lo, Mendell, & Rubin, 2001; Nylund, Asparouhov, & Muthén, 2007) test, and the bootstrap likelihood ratio test (McLachlan & Peel, 2000). In addition to relying on such statistical assessments of model fit, the researcher must also consider the substantive coherence of the latent classes when selecting a model (Bauer & Curran, 2004). This issue is important in the same way that interpretability is a key criterion in determining the optimal number of factors in EFA. That is, the final LCA solution must be defensible based on the types of individuals that have been grouped together, with regard to their responses on the indicators used in the analysis, as well as other potentially pertinent variables, such as demographic characteristics.

The standard LCA model linking a matrix of observed indicators X with the latent class variable Y describes the relationship between latent class membership and the response pattern to the observed variables as:

$$\pi_{1,2,3\ldots,jt}^{X_1 X_2 X_3 \ldots X_j, Y} = \sum_{t}^{T} \pi_t^Y \Pi \pi_{jt}^{X_j | Y},$$

(8.1)

where

π_t^Y = Probability that a randomly selected individual will be in class t of latent variable Y

$\pi_{jt}^{X_j | Y}$ = Probability that a member of latent class t will provide a particular response to observed indicator j.

The model in equation (8.1) asserts that responses to the observed variables are conditionally independent of one another given a particular latent class in Y (Goodman, 2002). This basic LCA model is characterized by two types of parameters: (a) the probability of a particular response for an observed variable conditional on latent class membership, and (b) the probability of being in a specific latent class, t, both of which will be important in interpreting the results of the model.

It is possible to incorporate one or more covariates into model (8.1), where the independent variable(s) predicts latent class membership. This relationship between the latent class and the covariate(s) is expressed in terms of a logistic regression model. The inclusion of one or more covariates can aid the researcher in both better understanding the nature of the latent class solution (i.e. what the classes mean), and improving the ability of the latent class solution itself to correctly recover the actual classes in the population. Such covariates should be selected with care, focusing on variables that have a theoretical relationship to the classes that are expected to exist in the population. The LCA model with covariate z_k is expressed as:

$$\pi_{1,2,3\ldots,jt}^{X_1 X_2 X_3 \ldots X_j, Y} = \sum_{t}^{T} \left(\pi_t^Y \mid z_k \right) \Pi \pi_{jt}^{X_j | Y}.$$

(8.2)

An extension of the LCA model in (8.1) is the latent class regression model, sometimes known as the mixture regression model. This technique identifies latent classes in the population based upon coefficients in a model (e.g. linear regression), rather than by means of the responses to the observed variables. As an example, a researcher might be interested in the relationship between a dependent variable and one or more independent variables. Furthermore, she might believe that there are differences in the nature of this relationship among subgroups in the population. For example, the model of interest might examine the relationship between scores on a measure of academic achievement (dependent variable) and family income (independent variable) using simple linear regression. The latent class regression model would seek to identify subgroups within the population across which the coefficient of family income in a regression model differed. As with LCA, the researcher might have some predetermined ideas, based in theory, regarding the number and composition of these latent classes, but not sufficient prior evidence with which to develop formal hypotheses about them. Latent class regression models could then be used in an exploratory manner to identify such subgroups in the population, and to obtain estimates of these model parameters. The simple linear mixture regression model is expressed as:

$$\pi^{X_1 X_2 X_3 \ldots X_j, Y}_{1,2,3 \ldots, jt} = \sum_t^T \pi_t^Y \left(m_i = \beta_0 + \beta_1 f_{1i} + \epsilon_i \right), \tag{8.3}$$

where

m_i = Dependent variable value for individual i

f_{1i} = Independent variable value for individual i

β_1 = Coefficient relating m_i to f_{1i}

β_0 = Model intercept

ϵ_i = Random error for individual i.

The latent classes in mixture regression models are defined by differences in the model parameters β_0 and β_1.

FITTING A BASIC LCA IN R

In order to demonstrate the fitting of LCA models in R, we will consider the following example. A researcher administered a survey to a group of 374 adolescents, asking them whether they viewed each of 17 ideals as potentially important to them in their future lives. The items were answered as either yes (1) or no (2). In addition, the researcher also collected scores on a meaning in life scale, where higher scores indicated that the respondent viewed their lives as having more meaning. The 17 ideals appear below:

1. Help others
2. Serve God
3. Make the world better
4. Change the way people think
5. Create something new
6. Make things beautiful
7. Fulfill duties
8. Do right thing
9. Live life to the fullest
10. Make money
11. Discover new things
12. Earn the respect of others
13. Support family/friends
14. Serve country
15. Have fun
16. Be successful
17. Have a good career

The researcher was particularly interested in whether there exist a small number of latent classes of individuals that can be clearly differentiated by their prospective purpose in life. She has some general hypotheses about the existence of such groups, believing that there may be between three and five in the population. Further, she believes that one group is likely to have an overall sense of purpose across all items, while another may have virtually no sense of purpose. A third hypothesized group is expected to have an other-oriented sense of purpose, and a fourth group may be better characterized as having an inner-focused sense of purpose. However, these hypothesized groups have not been empirically validated in previous work, making the current study exploratory in nature.

We will begin by fitting models for 3, 4, and 5 latent classes using the poLCA function in the poLCA library. In order to fit the model, we must first specify the latent class model in terms of the observed variables. This is done with the following lines of R code:

```
attach(purpose.lca)
f<-cbind(v1,v2,v3,v4,v5,v6,v7,v8,v9,v10,v11,v12,v13
,v14,v15,v16,v17)~1
```

First, we must attach the data file of interest, `purpose.lca`. Next, we create an object in which the 17 observed variables (items) are combined and set equal to 1. Finally, we fit the model for three latent classes using the following command:

```
purpose.class3.nocovariate<-poLCA(f,purpose.
lca,nclass=3)
```

The output is saved in the object `purpose.class3.nocovariate`. Within the poLCA function, we indicate the object that includes the actual model (`f`), the dataset including the variables in `f`, and then the number of latent classes. To see the results of the analysis, we simply type the name of the output file, and the resulting output appears.

```
Conditional item response (column) probabilities,
by outcome variable, for each class (row)

$v1
          Pr(1)   Pr(2)
class 1: 1.0000  0.0000
class 2: 0.9277  0.0723
class 3: 0.7395  0.2605


$v2
          Pr(1)   Pr(2)
class 1: 0.7644  0.2356
class 2: 0.6385  0.3615
class 3: 0.5202  0.4798


$v3
          Pr(1)   Pr(2)
class 1: 0.9949  0.0051
class 2: 0.8368  0.1632
class 3: 0.7524  0.2476


$v4
          Pr(1)   Pr(2)
class 1: 0.8124  0.1876
class 2: 0.4594  0.5406
class 3: 0.4077  0.5923


$v5
          Pr(1)   Pr(2)
class 1: 0.9223  0.0777
class 2: 0.2972  0.7028
class 3: 0.5079  0.4921
```

```
$v6
          Pr(1)   Pr(2)
class 1: 0.9623  0.0377
class 2: 0.3878  0.6122
class 3: 0.5432  0.4568

$v7
          Pr(1)   Pr(2)
class 1: 0.9699  0.0301
class 2: 0.7959  0.2041
class 3: 0.5057  0.4943

$v8
          Pr(1)   Pr(2)
class 1: 0.9908  0.0092
class 2: 0.9235  0.0765
class 3: 0.7416  0.2584

$v9
          Pr(1)   Pr(2)
class 1: 0.9785  0.0215
class 2: 0.9349  0.0651
class 3: 0.7058  0.2942

$v10
          Pr(1)   Pr(2)
class 1: 0.7174  0.2826
class 2: 0.6439  0.3561
class 3: 0.1238  0.8762

$v11
          Pr(1)   Pr(2)
class 1: 0.9688  0.0312
class 2: 0.6537  0.3463
class 3: 0.4407  0.5593

$v12
          Pr(1)   Pr(2)
class 1: 0.9943  0.0057
class 2: 0.8763  0.1237
class 3: 0.3403  0.6597

$v13
          Pr(1)   Pr(2)
class 1: 0.9965  0.0035
```

```
class 2: 0.9847  0.0153
class 3: 0.7617  0.2383


$v14
          Pr(1)   Pr(2)
class 1: 0.7059  0.2941
class 2: 0.4457  0.5543
class 3: 0.2392  0.7608


$v15
          Pr(1)   Pr(2)
class 1: 0.9874  0.0126
class 2: 0.9786  0.0214
class 3: 0.4935  0.5065


$v16
          Pr(1)   Pr(2)
class 1: 0.9825  0.0175
class 2: 0.9921  0.0079
class 3: 0.3011  0.6989


$v17
          Pr(1)   Pr(2)
class 1: 0.9480  0.0520
class 2: 0.9398  0.0602
class 3: 0.3186  0.6814
Estimated class population shares
  0.4166  0.4381  0.1453


Predicted class memberships (by modal posterior prob.)
    0.4305  0.4305  0.139


============================================================
Fit for 3 latent classes:
============================================================
number of observations: 374
number of estimated parameters: 53
residual degrees of freedom: 321
maximum log-likelihood: -2586.876

AIC(3): 5279.753
BIC(3): 5487.738
G^2(3): 1562.913 (Likelihood ratio/deviance statistic)
X^2(3): 912036.4 (Chi-square goodness of fit)
```

The first section of the output includes the response probabilities for each latent class on each item. Recall that a response of 1 means Yes and a response of 2 means No. Thus, for item 1 (Help others), the proportion of individuals responding Yes in the first latent class was 1.00, with 0.9277 of the second class, and 0.7395 of the third class also responding Yes. For item 5 (Create something new), 0.9223 of class 1 indicated Yes, as did 0.2972 of class 2 and 0.5079 of class 3. We could interpret the rest of the item response patterns by latent classes in a similar fashion. The proportion of individuals classified into each latent class appears after the item response probabilities. We can see that the first class consisted of 0.4166 of the 374 individuals in the sample, while class 2 consisted of 0.4305 of the sample, and class 3 0.1453. The modal posterior probabilities of class membership appear next. These values are very similar to the estimated class population shares in the previous table, but represent the mean of the modal class probabilities for each individual in the sample.

Finally, we are presented with the model fit information for the three-latent-class solution. This table includes the total sample size used to fit the model, followed by the number of estimated parameters, the model degrees of freedom (sample size − estimated parameters), and the maximum log-likelihood value for the solution. Relative model fit can be assessed using the AIC and BIC, which have been described in previous chapters. As a reminder, these values are calculated using the likelihood value adjusted by a penalty for model complexity. When comparing models, the one with the smaller AIC or BIC is considered to be better fitting. Two absolute goodness of fit statistics are also included in the fit table. Both G^2 and χ^2 test the null hypothesis of good model to data fit; i.e. the model is able to accurately reproduce the observed item response patterns for individuals in the sample. Thus, a statistically significant result would indicate that the model does not fit the data well. While in theory such a straightforward method of assessing absolute fit of a model to data would be desirable, research has shown that neither of these statistics is particularly accurate for identifying the correct number of latent classes (Nylund, *et al.*, 2007), which is reflected in R by the lack of p-values for these statistics. As mentioned above, the most appropriate tools for this purpose are the Lo–Mendell–Rubin test and the bootstrap likelihood ratio test, neither of which are available with the poLCA library. Thus, in order to identify the optimal model we will rely on the BIC and AIC, which can be compared across models.

We will now fit the four and five latent class models using the R commands below. The model fit information for each solution appears immediately after the commands.

```
purpose.class4.nocovariate<-poLCA(f,purpose.
lca,nclass=4)
purpose.class5.nocovariate<-poLCA(f,purpose.
lca,nclass=5)
=========================================================
Fit for 4 latent classes:
=========================================================
number of observations: 374
number of estimated parameters: 71
residual degrees of freedom: 303
maximum log-likelihood: -2557.669

AIC(4): 5257.339
BIC(4): 5535.961
G^2(4): 1504.499 (Likelihood ratio/deviance statistic)
X^2(4): 882880.8 (Chi-square goodness of fit)
=========================================================
Fit for 5 latent classes:
=========================================================
number of observations: 374
number of estimated parameters: 89
residual degrees of freedom: 285
maximum log-likelihood: -2515.95

AIC(5): 5209.899
BIC(5): 5559.158
G^2(5): 1421.059 (Likelihood ratio/deviance statistic)
X^2(5): 451022 (Chi-square goodness of fit)
```

Based upon the AIC the five-latent-class solution appears to provide better fit to the data than either the three- or four-class solution; i.e. it had the lowest AIC value. However, the BIC would suggest that the four-class solution is optimal in terms of model fit. Below are the class proportions for the four- and five-class solutions.

```
Estimated class population shares
0.145 0.4078 0.0818 0.3654
Estimated class population shares
0.1521 0.2349 0.4484 0.0326 0.1319
```

In the five-class solution class 4 has only 12 individuals (0.0326*374), whereas the smallest class (3) in the four-class solution includes 31 people (0.0818*374). Considering the BIC and AIC results in conjunction with the class sizes, we would argue that the four-class is preferable to the five-class solution, as it may provide a better fit, is more parsimonious, and does not include any very small classes. Below are the item response patterns by latent class membership for the four-class solution.

```
$v1
          Pr(1)   Pr(2)
class 1: 0.7364  0.2636
class 2: 1.0000  0.0000
class 3: 0.9400  0.0600
class 4: 0.9278  0.0722


$v2
          Pr(1)   Pr(2)
class 1: 0.5277  0.4723
class 2: 0.8322  0.1678
class 3: 0.0000  1.0000
class 4: 0.7059  0.2941


$v3
          Pr(1)   Pr(2)
class 1: 0.7476  0.2524
class 2: 0.9917  0.0083
class 3: 1.0000  0.0000
class 4: 0.8094  0.1906


$v4
          Pr(1)   Pr(2)
class 1: 0.3977  0.6023
class 2: 0.8063  0.1937
class 3: 0.7387  0.2613
class 4: 0.4160  0.5840


$v5
          Pr(1)   Pr(2)
class 1: 0.5033  0.4967
class 2: 0.9051  0.0949
class 3: 0.7491  0.2509
class 4: 0.2322  0.7678


$v6
          Pr(1)   Pr(2)
class 1: 0.5394  0.4606
class 2: 0.9503  0.0497
```

```
class 3: 0.9375  0.0625
class 4: 0.2936  0.7064

$v7
           Pr(1)   Pr(2)
class 1: 0.5058  0.4942
class 2: 0.9895  0.0105
class 3: 0.6448  0.3552
class 4: 0.8117  0.1883

$v8
           Pr(1)   Pr(2)
class 1: 0.7360  0.2640
class 2: 0.9876  0.0124
class 3: 0.8383  0.1617
class 4: 0.9499  0.0501

$v9
           Pr(1)   Pr(2)
class 1: 0.7003  0.2997
class 2: 0.9761  0.0239
class 3: 1.0000  0.0000
class 4: 0.9261  0.0739

$v10
           Pr(1)   Pr(2)
class 1: 0.1284  0.8716
class 2: 0.7296  0.2704
class 3: 0.4624  0.5376
class 4: 0.6704  0.3296

$v11
           Pr(1)   Pr(2)
class 1: 0.4451  0.5549
class 2: 0.9516  0.0484
class 3: 0.8108  0.1892
class 4: 0.6433  0.3567

$v12
           Pr(1)   Pr(2)
class 1: 0.3403  0.6597
class 2: 0.9912  0.0088
class 3: 0.8778  0.1222
class 4: 0.8819 0.1181
```

$v13
```
           Pr(1)    Pr(2)
class 1:  0.7571   0.2429
class 2:  0.9938   0.0062
class 3:  1.0000   0.0000
class 4:  0.9862   0.0138
```

$v14
```
           Pr(1)    Pr(2)
class 1:  0.2431   0.7569
class 2:  0.7620   0.2380
class 3:  0.0000   1.0000
class 4:  0.4874   0.5126
```

$v15
```
           Pr(1)    Pr(2)
class 1:  0.4927   0.5073
class 2:  0.9865   0.0135
class 3:  1.0000   0.0000
class 4:  0.9749   0.0251
```

$v16
```
           Pr(1)    Pr(2)
class 1:  0.2997   0.7003
class 2:  0.9815   0.0185
class 3:  1.0000   0.0000
class 4:  0.9912   0.0088
```

$v17
```
           Pr(1)    Pr(2)
class 1:  0.3174   0.6826
class 2:  0.9413   0.0587
class 3:  1.0000   0.0000
class 4:  0.9339   0.0661
```

We will not review these results item by item in great detail, but will look at a few for illustrative purposes. The goal of examining the item response patterns is to develop a coherent and substantively meaningful description of the classes, much in the way that we examined how items group together in EFA (Chapter 2) in order to develop a meaningful description of the factors. Item 1 (Help others) was endorsed by most members of each class. However, endorsement patterns for item 2 (Serve God) differed by class for this sample, with those in class 2 providing the highest such rates, followed by class 4, class 1, and class 3, for which no members endorsed it. Another item with a great deal of item endorsement variation across groups was number 4 (Change the way people think). Latent class 2 provided the largest proportion of endorsements, followed by latent class 3, and then classes 1 and 4, both of which were well below 50%. Based on the results for all 17 items, a rough description of the classes might be as follows:

Latent class 1: Make the world a better place

Latent class 2: Endorses all aspects of purpose in life

Latent class 3: Endorses all aspects of purpose, except for serving God and country

Latent class 4: Endorses all aspects of purpose, except for those in the area of creativity.

Of course, a more detailed consideration of these results in light of hypotheses about the nature of purpose in adolescents would be necessary in order to provide a complete and accurate description of the results. However, we hope that this example has provided the reader with the general flavor of how such interpretation is typically carried out.

FITTING AN LCA MODEL WITH COVARIATES IN R

As discussed in the beginning of the chapter, it is possible to fit a latent class model in which not only are classes investigated based upon responses to a set of variables as in the previous example, but also a covariate predicting latent class membership is included in the analysis as well. Such a covariate would be selected based upon theoretical relationships with the expected latent classes, with this part of the model itself taking the form of logistic regression, in which the dependent variable is the latent class membership and the independent variable(s) are the covariate(s) of interest. In the current example the covariate of interest is a separate scale score measuring meaning in life, such that higher scores on the scale reflect a greater belief that life has meaning. Of interest is whether meaning in life scores are related to latent class membership. It is important to recall that inclusion of the covariate will impact the latent class solution itself, meaning that the actual class membership results, and the attendant item response probabilities, with and without the covariate, will not be identical. In order to fit the LCA with a covariate, we would use the following command structure in R.

```
f2<-cbind(v1,v2,v3,v4,v5,v6,v7,v8,v9,v10,v11,v12,v1
3,v14,v15,v16,v17)~meaning.score
purpose.class4.covariate<-poLCA(f2,purpose.
lca,nclass=4)
```

The only difference in model setup is that we replace the ~1 from the standard LCA with ~meaning.score, the name of the covariate of interest. If we wanted to include more than one covariate, such as gender, we would simply type that as ~meaning.score+gender. The results for the four-class solution with a covariate appear below.

```
Conditional item response (column) probabilities,
by outcome variable, for each class (row)

$v1
          Pr(1)   Pr(2)
class 1: 1.0000  0.0000
class 2: 1.0000  0.0000
class 3: 0.7735  0.2265
class 4: 1.0000  0.0000

$v2
          Pr(1)   Pr(2)
class 1: 1.0000  0.0000
class 2: 0.8039  0.1961
class 3: 0.1568  0.8432
class 4: 1.0000  0.0000

$v3
          Pr(1)   Pr(2)
class 1: 1.0000  0.0000
class 2: 1.0000  0.0000
class 3: 0.6429  0.3571
class 4: 1.0000  0.0000

$v4
          Pr(1)   Pr(2)
class 1: 0.5283  0.4717
class 2: 0.8472  0.1528
class 3: 0.3871  0.6129
class 4: 0.5820  0.4180

$v5
          Pr(1)   Pr(2)
class 1: 0.1926  0.8074
class 2: 1.0000  0.0000
class 3: 0.4599  0.5401
class 4: 0.6305  0.3695
```

```
$v6
         Pr(1)   Pr(2)
class 1: 0.4157  0.5843
class 2: 0.9634  0.0366
class 3: 0.5225  0.4775
class 4: 0.5741  0.4259

$v7
         Pr(1)   Pr(2)
class 1: 0.8765  0.1235
class 2: 0.9873  0.0127
class 3: 0.6021  0.3979
class 4: 0.8267  0.1733

$v8
         Pr(1)   Pr(2)
class 1: 1.0000  0.0000
class 2: 0.9797  0.0203
class 3: 0.7997  0.2003
class 4: 0.9224  0.0776

$v9
         Pr(1)   Pr(2)
class 1: 0.9577  0.0423
class 2: 0.9736  0.0264
class 3: 0.8955  0.1045
class 4: 0.6644  0.3356

$v10
         Pr(1)   Pr(2)
class 1: 0.6194  0.3806
class 2: 0.7697  0.2303
class 3: 0.5356  0.4644
class 4: 0.0590  0.9410

$v11
         Pr(1)   Pr(2)
class 1: 0.7057  0.2943
class 2: 0.9764  0.0236
class 3: 0.6523  0.3477
class 4: 0.3640  0.6360
```

```
$v12
          Pr(1)   Pr(2)
class 1: 0.8811  0.1189
class 2: 0.9950  0.0050
class 3: 0.7564  0.2436
class 4: 0.4662  0.5338

$v13
          Pr(1)   Pr(2)
class 1: 1.0000  0.0000
class 2: 0.9913  0.0087
class 3: 0.9042  0.0958
class 4: 0.8744  0.1256

$v14
          Pr(1)   Pr(2)
class 1: 0.5968  0.4032
class 2: 0.7298  0.2702
class 3: 0.2507  0.7493
class 4: 0.4493  0.5507

$v15
          Pr(1)   Pr(2)
class 1: 0.9682  0.0318
class 2: 0.9860  0.0140
class 3: 0.9042  0.0958
class 4: 0.4498  0.5502

$v16
          Pr(1)   Pr(2)
class 1: 1.0000  0.0000
class 2: 0.9911  0.0089
class 3: 0.7997  0.2003
class 4: 0.4229  0.5771

$v17
          Pr(1)   Pr(2)
class 1: 0.9263  0.0737
class 2: 0.9677  0.0323
class 3: 0.8120  0.1880
class 4: 0.2919  0.7081
Estimated class population shares
0.2668  0.3435  0.307  0.0827
```

```
Predicted class memberships (by modal posterior prob.)
0.2594 0.3583 0.2995 0.0829


==========================================================
Fit for 4 latent classes:
==========================================================
2 / 1
                   Coefficient Std. error t value Pr(>|t|)
(Intercept)      36.78583        0.02787 1319.827         0
meaning.score   -12.25046        0.07398 -165.588         0
==========================================================
3 / 1
                   Coefficient Std. error t value Pr(>|t|)
(Intercept)      69.14663   0.10804        640.011         0
meaning.score   -27.84820   0.21608       -128.879         0
==========================================================
4 / 1
                 Coefficient Std. error t value Pr(>|t|)
(Intercept)     -35.21883    0.02533      -1390.231        0
meaning.score    11.34939    0.07600        149.336        0
==========================================================
number of observations: 374
number of estimated parameters: 74
residual degrees of freedom: 300
maximum log-likelihood: -2432.216


AIC(4): 5012.431
BIC(4): 5302.826
X^2(4): 29509207 (Chi-square goodness of fit)
```

Perhaps the first aspect of the results to notice is that model fit, as measured by AIC and BIC, appears to be better for the four-class solution with the covariate than without. We also notice that the estimated class proportion shares change with the inclusion of the covariate, signaling some changes in the composition of the groups. Furthermore, it is also entirely possible that the group number assigned by poLCA to individuals in the sample has changed, even while the basic nature of the group remains the same. This phenomenon, known as label switching, occurs because the designation of the class membership number is arbitrary. In other words, if we were to use LCA with a new sample from the same population we may well obtain very similar results to those displayed here in terms of the size and item response probabilities of the latent classes. However, the actual numeric designations assigned to the classes might not correspond to those assigned in this case, so that latent class 1 for this sample might be assigned a class number of 3 for another sample, even while the nature of the classes would be the same, so that class 1 in sample 1 is essentially the same in character as class 3 in sample 2. In the same way, inclusion of a covariate may result in such label switching even though the nature of the latent class is the same. We can determine the extent to which such code switching has occurred through an examination of the item response patterns and the characterization of the latent classes, as we described above.

Of particular interest in this section of the chapter is the examination of the results for the covariate's relationship with latent class membership. This is reflected in the section of the output labeled `Fit for 4 latent classes:`. The analysis reported here is for a multinomial logistic regression model (Agresti, 2013) in which the dependent variable is the latent class membership, with class 1 serving as the reference category. The relationship between the meaning in life scale score and each of the other latent classes versus the first class is reflected in the table. As an example of interpreting these results, the coefficient for meaning in life with respect to latent class 2 versus 1 is −12.25046, and is statistically significant. This means that higher scores on the meaning in life scale are associated with class 1 as opposed to class 2; i.e. class 1 has higher meaning in life scores than does class 2. Similarly, latent class 1 also has higher meaning in life scores than does class 3, but not than class 4, which has the significantly higher meaning scores.

FITTING MIXTURE REGRESSION MODELS IN R

In addition to LCA, we can also fit **mixture regression models** using R. At the beginning of this chapter we mentioned the basic idea surrounding this extension of LCA, in which class membership is based upon differences in the parameters for a regression analysis, rather than the observed indicator variable response patterns as is the case for LCA. In the following section we will describe the use of the `flexmix` library of functions for fitting mixture regression models to data. The example to be examined here involves scores from a set of instruments focused on Civics education that was given to 453 American 15-year-old high school students. Of particular interest in the current analyses are scores on measures of citizenship and patriotism. Higher scores on the citizenship scale reflect a greater sense of responsibility as a citizen of the nation. Higher patriotism scores indicate that an individual feels a stronger sense of patriotism toward the nation in which they live, in this case the USA. In the current analysis, we will focus on a simple linear regression model in which patriotism serves as the independent variable, and citizenship as the dependent, in order to determine whether one's sense of patriotism is associated with one's sense of responsibility as a citizen, and whether this relationship differs across various subgroups in the data. We believe that within the population there are different classes of individuals with regard to the strength and nature of this relationship, such that it might be stronger for some types of adolescents than others. However, we do not have sufficient information with which to build formal hypotheses regarding the number or nature of these groups, making this an exploratory analysis.

When fitting the mixture regression model, we will first want to attach the dataset of interest, and load the flexmix library.

```
attach(civics)
library(flexmix)
```

The flexmix function that we will use to fit the data does not accommodate missing observations. Therefore, we will need to create a separate dataset that excludes all missing values, using the command below.

```
civics.nomiss<-na.omit(civics)
```

This dataset now contains no missing data. Once the data are ready, we will first fit a mixture regression model for two latent classes. As with LCA, we will want to fit several models that differ based on the number of latent classes present, and then compare the fit of these to determine which is statistically optimal.

```
mixture.regression.model2<-flexmix(citizenship~
patriotism, data=civics.nomiss, k=2)
```

By typing the name of the flexmix object, we obtain the following output, which reveals the size of each latent class, and the fact that the algorithm converged.

```
mixture.regression.model2

Call:
flexmix(formula = citizenship ~ patriotism, data = civics.
nomiss, k = 2)

Cluster sizes:
1 2
58 395
convergence after 40 iterations
```

Using the summary command, we can obtain the prior probabilities of membership in each class, the class sizes, the number of individuals in the sample with a posterior probability greater than 0 for each class, and the ratio of the number of individuals assigned to each class and the number of individuals with posterior probabilities greater than 0. Finally, the AIC and BIC values are provided allowing us to compare fit across models with different numbers of latent classes.

```
summary(mixture.regression.model2)
Call:
flexmix(formula = citizenship ~ patriotism, data = civics.
nomiss, k = 2)
          prior size post>0 ratio
Comp.1 0.257 58    453   0.128
Comp.2 0.743 395   439   0.900
'log Lik.' -933.2052 (df=7)
AIC: 1880.41 BIC: 1909.222
```

In order to obtain parameter estimates with the associated hypothesis test results we will use the refit function from the flexmix library. This function fits the regression model for each class separately using the R glm function, and the posterior probability of latent class membership as the weight. Thus, individuals with low posterior probability values for a given class (i.e. those who are unlikely to belong to that class) will play a small role in the parameter estimation for that class, when compared to those with larger posterior probabilities. Once we have used refit, we can ask for the summary of the resulting object to obtain the following results.

```
mixture.regression.model2.refit<-refit(mixture.
regression.model2)
summary(mixture.regression.model2.refit)
$Comp.1
                Estimate Std. Error z value Pr(>|z|)
(Intercept) 5.11212     1.72115 2.9702 0.002976 **
patriotism  0.58128     0.17043 3.4107 0.000648 ***
---
Signif. codes: 0 '***' 0.001 '**' 0.01 '*' 0.05 '.' 0.1 ' ' 1


$Comp.2
                Estimate Std. Error z value Pr(>|z|)
(Intercept) 9.383468    0.464769  20.1895 < 2e-16 ***
patriotism  0.084760    0.047634   1.7794 0.07518 .
---
Signif. codes: 0 '***' 0.001 '**' 0.01 '*' 0.05 '.' 0.1 ' ' 1
```

From these results we can see that for the first latent class (`Comp.1`) the relationship between the patriotism and citizenship scores was positive and statistically significant at the $\alpha = 0.05$ level. Thus, for this class individuals who felt more patriotic also had a greater sense of their duties as citizens. On the other hand, for the second latent class, this relationship was not statistically significant at the $\alpha = 0.05$ level. Given that the second latent class is the larger of the two, we can conclude that for most individuals there is not a relationship between one's feeling of patriotism and self-perceived duties as a citizen, but for a small group of individuals a positive relationship between these variables does exist.

One primary tool for determining the degree of separation between the latent classes is the **rootogram**, which is a histogram featuring the posterior probability of latent class membership on the x-axis, and the square root of the latent class size on the y-axis. Well-separated solutions are marked by a rootogram with peaks near 1 and 0 on the x-axis, and low bars in the middle posterior probability range. Rootograms can be obtained in flexmix using the following command, with the output shown in Figure 8.2.

```
plot(mixture.regression.model2)
```

These results demonstrate that the two classes are reasonably well separated, with relatively few individuals having posterior probabilities in the middle range.

As with LCA, we will want to fit mixture regression models with differing numbers of classes and then compare model fit to determine which might prove to be optimal. Below is the R code for the three-class solution, followed by the resulting refitted output.

```
mixture.regression.model3<-flexmix(citizenship~patriotism,
data=civics.nomiss, k=3)
summary(mixture.regression.model3)
mixture.regression.model3.refit<-refit(mixture.regression.model3)
summary(mixture.regression.model3.refit)
plot(mixture.regression.model3)
Call:

flexmix(formula   =   citizenship   ~   patriotism,   data   =   civics.
nomiss, k = 3)
```

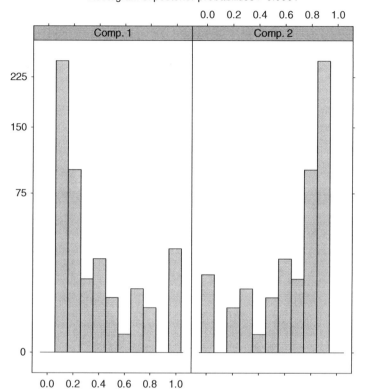

■ Figure 8.2: Rootogram for the two-latent-class solution for the mixture regression model

```
              prior  size  post>0  ratio
Comp.1        0.357   125     443  0.282
Comp.2        0.217    53     453  0.117
Comp.3        0.426   275     430  0.640

'log Lik.' -927.8764 (df=11)
AIC: 1877.753 BIC: 1923.028

$Comp.1
              Estimate Std. Error z value    Pr(>|z|)
(Intercept)   6.55416     1.47925  4.4307  0.000009392 ***
patriotism    0.39530     0.15463  2.5563      0.01058 *
---
Signif. codes: 0 '***' 0.001 '**' 0.01 '*' 0.05 '.' 0.1 ' ' 1
$Comp.2
              Estimate  Std. Error  z value   Pr(>|z|)
(Intercept)   4.54727      1.99779   2.2762   0.022837 *
patriotism    0.64828      0.20109   3.2238   0.001265 **
```

```
---
Signif. codes: 0 '***' 0.001 '**' 0.01 '*' 0.05 '.' 0.1 ' ' 1

$Comp.3
             Estimate  Std. Error   z value  Pr(>|z|)
(Intercept)  11.79390     1.16343   10.1372  <2e-16 ***
patriotism   -0.17996     0.12464   -1.4439  0.1488
---
Signif. codes: 0 '***' 0.001 '**' 0.01 '*' 0.05 '.' 0.1 ' ' 1
```

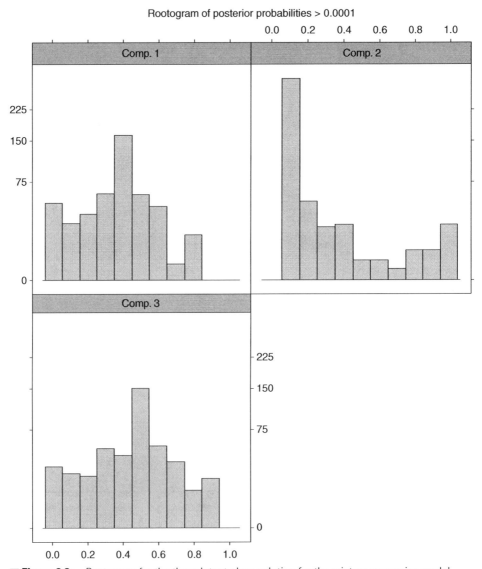

▦ **Figure 8.3:** Rootogram for the three-latent-class solution for the mixture regression model

When reading these results, we would first consider the relative fit of the two- and three-class models in terms of AIC and BIC. We can see that fit for the two-class solution is better if we consider the BIC but not the AIC. An inspection of the rootogram plot for the three-group solution in Figure 8.3 shows that, given the relatively large number of cases with posterior probabilities hovering in the middle of the distribution, classes 1 and 3 both exhibit quite a bit of overlap with the other classes. Therefore, it appears that the two-class solution provides a better-differentiated set of latent classes, though neither model demonstrated clearly better fit based upon the relative fit indices. Finally, the regression results for the three-latent-class model show that for classes 1 and 2, there is a statistically significant positive relationship between patriotism and citizenship, whereas for class 3 the relationship is not statistically significant. While for the sample the relationship between the two variables is stronger for latent class 2 than for class 1, we cannot conclude from these results that this difference is present in the population; i.e. the two sample coefficients (0.39530 and 0.64828) have not been statistically compared with one another. As a final note, we could certainly continue fitting models to the data in order to find the optimal solution from a wider range of options than just two and three classes. The method for carrying this out in R would be just as demonstrated above, and the interpretation of the results would be done in precisely the same manner as we have used for comparing the two- and three-class solutions, including referral to AIC and BIC, as well as an examination of the rootogram and a consideration of the substantive results of the analysis.

SUMMARY

In this chapter we have focused on analyses for the case when the latent variable of interest is categorical rather than continuous. We described both latent class analysis and mixture regression models, which allow for identification of a finite (and hopefully small) number of groups of individuals based upon a set of observed variables, or relationships among such variables. These tools can be quite useful in identifying subgroups within the population which might otherwise not be clearly defined. Two additional issues should be noted at this point. First, as presented above, both LCA and mixture regression are exploratory in nature. This fact places a burden on the researcher, who must carefully interpret the results with an eye toward whether they match previously existing theories about the population, as well as prior empirical work in the area. Much as is the case with EFA (Chapter 2), one can very easily be misled by such exploratory results as they may be very specific to the given sample. Therefore, when possible, checking model fit with a cross-validation sample is recommended when possible. Second, as with factor analysis, it is possible to conduct a confirmatory latent class analysis in which specific patterns in variable means or regression relationships that are suggested by theory are explicitly tested using parameter constraints. Such modeling is beyond the purview of this chapter, but the researcher should be aware of it, and of the opportunities that such confirmatory models present for theory testing.

FURTHER READING

Collins, L.M., & Lanza, S.T. (2010). *Latent Class and Latent Transition Analysis*. Hoboken, NJ: John Wiley & Sons, Inc.

Hagenaars, J.A., & McCutcheon, A.L. (2002). *Applied Latent Class Analysis*. Cambridge: Cambridge University Press.

Hancock, G.R., & Samuelsen, K.M. (2008). *Advances in Latent Variable Mixture Models*. Charlotte, NC: Information Age Publishing.

McCutcheon, A.L. (1987). *Latent Class Analysis*. Thousand Oaks, CA: Sage Publications.

McLachlan, G., & Peel, D. (2000). *Finite Mixture Models*. New York: John Wiley & Sons, Inc.

REFERENCES

Agresti, A. (2013). *Categorical Data Analysis*. Hoboken, NJ: John Wiley & Sons.

Bauer, D.J., & Curran, P.J. (2004). The integration of continuous and discrete latent variable models: Potential problems and promising opportunities. *Psychological Methods*, 9(1), 3–29.

Collins, L.M., & Lanza, S.T. (2010). *Latent Class and Latent Transition Analysis*. Hoboken, NJ: John Wiley & Sons, Inc.

Goodman, L.A. (2002). Latent class analysis: The empirical study of latent types, latent variables, and latent structures. In: J.A. Hagenaars & A.L. McCutcheon (eds), *Applied Latent Class Analysis*. Cambridge: Cambridge University Press.

Lazarsfeld, P.F., & Henry, N.W. (1968). *Latent Structure Analysis*. Boston: Houghton Mifflin.

Lo, Y., Mendell, N., & Rubin, D. (2001). Testing the number of components in a normal mixture. *Biometrika*, 88, 767–78.

McLachlan, G., & Peel, D. (2000). *Finite Mixture Models*. New York: John Wiley & Sons, Inc.

Nylund, K.L., Asparouhov, T., & Muthén, B.O. (2007). Deciding on the number of classes in latent class analysis and growth mixture modeling: A Monte Carlo simulation study. *Structural Equation Modeling*, 14(4), 535–69.

Chapter 9

ITEM RESPONSE THEORY FOR DICHOTOMOUS AND POLYTOMOUS ITEMS

INTRODUCTION

Item response theory (IRT) refers to a set of statistical models designed for use with responses to items on tests, questionnaires, and other such instruments in order to obtain estimates of individuals' levels on the construct measured by the scale as a whole. For example, a commonly used model is the **three-parameter logistic (3PL) model** which contains one parameter specific to the respondents (person parameter) and three parameters specific to the items. The person parameter is the estimate of the latent trait being measured by the scale (e.g. reading ability, depression), and is referred to as theta (θ). The item parameters include the location on the latent trait scale (b parameter), their ability to differentiate among individuals with different levels of the construct (a parameter), and in some instances the likelihood that an individual will endorse the item due solely to chance or guessing (c parameter). The construct itself is a latent variable that is measured by the set of items, which serve the role of indicators much as the observed variables in the factor analysis models described in Chapters 2 and 3. See Lord and Novick (1968), Muthén and Lehman (1985), and Thissen, Steinberg, and Wainer (1993) for a discussion on the relationship between the IRT and factor analysis parameters.

IRT models can be divided into two broad families based on whether they utilize dichotomous items (two categories only) or polytomous items with three or more categories. In the following pages we will provide a brief introduction to classical test theory, followed by descriptions of several IRT models, for both dichotomous and polytomous items, followed by a description of fitting each model using R. Finally, we discuss the assessment and comparison of model fit using various statistical tools in order to decide which model might be most appropriate for a given set of data. The goal of this chapter is to demonstrate the correct use and interpretation of IRT models using the R software package. Therefore, the technical discussion of the various models will not be emphasized. However, we do provide sufficient detail for the reader to acquire the foundational knowledge to begin to use each model. Those readers who are interested in a more comprehensive treatment of specific topics discussed in this chapter will be provided with appropriate references for further reading.

CLASSICAL TEST THEORY IN R

Prior to actually studying the IRT models, it is useful for us to first investigate the data that will serve as the example throughout this chapter. We will use ten items taken from a sixth-grade mathematics achievement test from a large national testing program. The items are scored as correct (1) or incorrect (0) for the 7130 examinees in the sample. We must first import the data into R from its current home in SPSS, using the methods described in Chapter 1. We will name the data mathg6 in R.

Once the data are imported, a next step is to obtain some basic descriptive information about the responses, such as the proportion of individuals correctly answering each item, an index of classical test theory **item discrimination**, and an estimate of the correlation between the item response and the total test score. All of this information is provided by the psychometric package in R, using the following commands.

```
library(psychometric)
item.exam(mathg6, discrim=TRUE)
```

First, we use the library command to gain access to the functions in psychometric. Then we can use the item.exam function, with the first argument being the dataset name (note that the data contains only the item responses), and the second requesting an estimate of classical test theory item discrimination. The resulting output appears below.

The Item.total column includes point-biserial correlation coefficient values between the individual items and the total score, while the Item.Tot.woi is the point-biserial between each item and the total score with that item omitted. **Item difficulty** in classical test theory (CTT) is simply the proportion of individuals answering the item correctly. CTT item discrimination is calculated by first identifying the group of examinees with the highest test scores (top third in the case

Item	Item.total	Item.Tot.woi	Difficulty	Discrimination
V1	0.439	0.299	0.836	0.314
V2	0.528	0.370	0.732	0.497
V3	0.534	0.370	0.693	0.550
V4	0.589	0.441	0.718	0.579
V5	0.554	0.381	0.576	0.636
V6	0.605	0.459	0.704	0.606
V7	0.494	0.309	0.575	0.578
V8	0.601	0.453	0.699	0.619
V9	0.620	0.478	0.706	0.628
V10	0.372	0.286	0.946	0.137

of the `psychometric` package) and those with the lowest scores (bottom third), and then calculating the difference in the proportion answering the item correctly in each group.

As an example of interpreting these CTT item statistics, consider item 1 (V1). It had a correlation of 0.44 with the total score when it was included in the calculation, and 0.30 when omitted from the total score. Thus, individuals with higher sum scores on the instrument as a whole were more likely to answer the item correctly. Approximately 84% of all examinees (Difficulty = 0.836) answered the item correctly, and the difference in the proportion correct between the highest and lowest scoring groups was 0.32. We could employ Ebel's criteria (1969) for categorizing item discrimination values where values greater than 0.40 indicate an item is satisfactory, values between 0.30 and 0.39 suggest items need minimal to no revision, values between 0.20 and 0.29 suggest item revision, and values less than or equal to 0.19 suggest potential item deletion.

For a norm-referenced assessment, it is ideal for average item difficulty values to be approximately 0.50 for a given subtest or at the composite score level. We could employ the following criteria to categorize item difficulty: values below 0.30 indicated a difficult item, values greater than 0.30 but less than 0.70 indicated a satisfactory item, and values greater than 0.70 indicated an easy item. It is expected that there is a range of items in terms of difficulty on each subtest which are ordered from least difficult to most difficult (Nunnally & Bernstein, 1994).

We can also obtain an estimate of internal consistency reliability for the exam using the `alpha` function in the `psychometric` package. Reliability is most often defined as the consistency of an instrument for a sample (Nunnally & Bernstein, 1994). It can be estimated in a number of ways, including Cronbach's α, which for dichotomous items is known as the KR20 statistic. It is calculated as

$$KR20 = \frac{j}{j-1}\left(1 - \frac{\sum_{j=1}^{J} p_j q_j}{s^2}\right).$$ **(9.1)**

Here, j is the number of items, p_j is the proportion of individuals correctly answering item j, and q_j is the proportion of individuals answering item j incorrectly. Finally, s^2 is the variance of the sum score on the test. KR20 ranges between 0 and 1, with higher values indicating greater internal consistency; i.e. higher reliability for the sample. The command and resulting output for this procedure, along with the command to obtain a two-tailed confidence interval, appear below.

```
alpha(mathg6)
$alpha
[1] 0.724

$lambda2
[1] 0.730

alpha.CI(0.7245, 10, 7130, level=0.95, onesided=FALSE)
LCL      ALPHA            UCL
1 0.7149 0.7245 0.7340
```

The KR20 of the test for this sample is estimated using the `alpha` command from the `psychometric` library. The estimate for these data is 0.725, suggesting that for this sample the performance on the items is fairly consistent. We obtain a confidence interval for the estimate of reliability with the `alpha.CI` command. In this case, we supply the reliability value obtained in the previous step (0.725), followed by the number of items, the sample size, the desired level of confidence, and whether we want the interval to be one-sided or not. In this case we requested a 95% two-sided confidence interval (e.g., `onesided=FALSE`), which indicated that in the population the actual internal consistency reliability of the scale lies between 0.715 and 0.735.

DICHOTOMOUS IRT

Fitting the Rasch model in R

Of course, while classical test theory provides some useful information about the test and items, it is not as informative for that purpose as is IRT (Hambleton,

Swaminathan, & Rogers, 1991). Thus, we will turn our attention to the fitting of IRT models to the math data, starting with the model for dichotomous data with the least number of parameters, the **Rasch model**. All IRT models, including Rasch, express the relationship between an examinee's level of the latent trait (e.g. math ability) and the probability of endorsing a given item (e.g. answering the item correctly) in the form of a logistic model. These IRT models rest on three foundational assumptions: (1) **monotonicity** – the relationship between the latent trait and the probability of item endorsement is monotonically increasing, (2) **unidimensionality** – only a single latent trait is being measured by the set of items, and (3) **local independence** – when the latent trait is controlled for, there is no correlation between item responses. We devote a later chapter to assessing these assumptions using the R software package.

The Rasch model is expressed as

$$P\left(x_j = 1 \mid \theta, b_j\right) = \frac{e^{\left(\theta, -b_j\right)}}{1 + e^{\left(\theta, -b_j\right)}}. \tag{9.2}$$

In equation (9.2), x_i is the response to item j with 1 being correct in the context of an achievement test. An individual's level of the latent trait being measured is represented by θ, and the item location is b_j. For this example θ corresponds to an examinee's math ability while b_j is the difficulty of item j. An important strength of IRT models is that item difficulty and examinee ability are placed on the same scale. Therefore, it is possible to directly compare where an individual lies on the latent trait with the location of any item on the instrument. In addition, b and θ are both centered on 0, which represents average or typical location for both. The Rasch model is a special case of what is known as the **one-parameter logistic (1PL) model**. What distinguishes the Rasch model from the general 1PL is that the item discrimination value (a) is set equal to 1. Discrimination refers to the ability of an item to differentiate among examinees with different levels of the latent trait of interest. Items with larger discrimination values are better able to do this than items with smaller values. All 1PL models hold discrimination equal across items, with the Rasch model setting this value to 1 while other 1PL models estimate a from the data. The 1PL model can be expressed as:

$$P\left(x_j = 1 \mid \theta, b_j\right) = \frac{e^{a\left(\theta, -b_j\right)}}{1 + e^{a\left(\theta, -b_j\right)}}. \tag{9.3}$$

Fitting of the Rasch model in R is accomplished through the ltm library of functions. As described in Chapter 1, prior to conducting the analysis the user will need to first install the library into their version of R. Once this is complete, the following commands can be used to estimate the Rasch model for the mathematics exam data.

```
library(ltm)
mathg6.rasch<-rasch(mathg6, constraint=cbind(ncol
(mathg6)+1, 1))
```

The rasch function is specifically designed for fitting both the Rasch and 1PL models. We differentiate between the two models using the constraint command. For the Rasch model, we set the item discrimination parameter values to 1 for all items with the following: constraint=cbind(ncol(mathg6)+1, 1). The first argument is simply the set of item response data. Note that for all of these commands, the data set only contains the item responses, and nothing else. We then set the item discrimination value to 1 with the +1, 1 part of the function call. The results of the analysis are contained in the output object mathg6. rasch. In order to view the item parameter estimates, standard errors, and model fit statistics, we use the summary command.

```
summary(mathg6.rasch)
Call:
rasch(data = mathg6, constraint = cbind(ncol(mathg6) + 1, 1))

Model Summary:
log.Lik            AIC          BIC
-36771.04 73562.08 73630.8

Coefficients:
            value  std.err z.vals
Dffclt.V1  -1.97   0.03    -53.76
Dffclt.V2  -1.23   0.03    -38.71
Dffclt.V3  -1.00   0.03    -32.55
Dffclt.V4  -1.14   0.03    -36.48
Dffclt.V5  -0.37   0.02    -12.87
Dffclt.V6  -1.06   0.03    -34.22
Dffclt.V7  -0.37   0.02    -12.68
Dffclt.V8  -1.04   0.03    -33.53
Dffclt.V9  -1.08   0.03    -34.65
Dffclt.V10 -3.37   0.05    -59.79
Dscrmn      1.00           NA     NA
```

```
Integration:
method: Gauss-Hermite
quadrature points: 21

Optimization:
Convergence: 0
max(|grad|): 0.031
quasi-Newton: BFGS
```

The output includes the actual model call, essentially a restatement of our commands, followed by information on the fit of the model to the data, including the log-likelihood value (`logLik`), the Akaike information criterion (`AIC`), and the Bayesian information criterion (`BIC`). As we discussed in Chapter 3, these latter two values can be used to compare the relative fit of models for the same set of data, as a part of a model selection strategy, which will be demonstrated in detail later in the chapter. As was true for CFA models, each of these statistics is a penalized version of the -2 log-likelihood ($-2\ln L$), with more complex models containing more parameters being penalized more heavily. The $-2\ln L$ itself is a measure of how close the predicted item responses based on the estimated model are to the actual item responses in the data. Lower values of this statistic indicate a closer alignment of the two (i.e., the model predicts the actual item responses well). The $-2\ln L$ tends to decrease in value as more parameters are added to the model, regardless of whether the additional parameters actually contribute markedly to the accuracy of the predictions. The AIC and BIC for the IRT models are calculated as

$$\text{AIC} = -2\ln L + 2p \tag{9.4}$$

$$\text{BIC} = -2\ln L + \ln(N)p. \tag{9.5}$$

Here, N is the total sample size and p is the number of item parameters being estimated. We will come back to these indices later in the chapter, when we compare the relative fit of the IRT models in order to determine which may be optimal. However, suffice it to say for the moment that smaller values of these indices indicate better model fit.

In addition to model fit information, the `summary` command also provides individual item parameter estimates, along with their standard error and the z statistic testing the null hypothesis that the parameters are 0 in the population. The output is organized so that the item difficulty estimates (`Dffclt`) for the items appear first, followed by item discrimination (`Dscrmn`). For the Rasch model, the single discrimination value common to all items was set equal to 1, and because it was constrained rather than estimated from the data, there is no standard error. Remember from our previous discussion that the item difficulty estimates (Dffclt.V1, etc.) are centered at 0, so that negative values represent relatively easy items and positive values indicate relatively more difficult items. An examination of these results suggests that all of the items were somewhat easy, with item 10 being the easiest, and items 5 and 7 being the most difficult. The standard errors of the estimates measure sampling variation, with relatively larger values indicating more such variability. In other words, item difficulty values with larger standard errors exhibit more difference in value from sample to sample than do those with smaller standard errors. The z value is the ratio of the item parameter estimate and standard error. Large absolute values (greater than 2) would indicate that the item parameter is unlikely to be 0 in the population.

In addition to the actual item parameter values, an IRT model can also be described graphically in the form of the **item characteristic curve (ICC)**, which places examinee location on the latent trait being measured (e.g. math ability) on the x-axis and the probability of endorsing an item (e.g. providing a correct response) on the y-axis. In R, the user can obtain the ICCs for all of the items in a single graph (see Figure 9.1) using the plot(mathg6.rasch,type=c("ICC")) command.

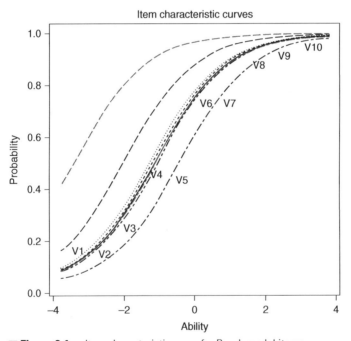

■ **Figure 9.1:** Item characteristic curve for Rasch model items

The relationship between ability and the probability of a correct response is monotonically increasing for all items. That is, the more math ability an individual possesses, the greater the probability of their correctly answering the item. In addition, we can see the relative difficulty of the items based upon their locations in the graph. For example, item 10 is the easiest, given its position furthest to the left on the *x*-axis, while items 5 and 7 are the furthest to the right, indicating that they are the most difficult. In R, it is also possible to plot the ICC for one item or a subset of items, rather than the entire item set. This is particularly useful when the test consists of a large number of items, making it difficult to interpret individual item plots when all are placed on the same graph together. As an example, let us plot the ICC for items 7 and 9 using the command `plot(mathg6.rasch,type=c("ICC"), items=c(7,9))`. Notice that the addition to this command from our previous example is the `items=c(7,9)` subcommand, which specifies that we only want the plot for items 7 and 9 (see Figure 9.2).

In addition to the ICC, we can also use R to plot the item information curves (IIC) for the items. **Item information** refers to the degree to which an item reduces the uncertainty in estimation of the latent trait value for an individual (de Ayala, 2009). It is calculated as

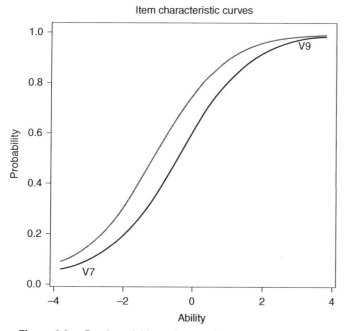

■ **Figure 9.2:** Rasch model item characteristic curves for items 7 and 9

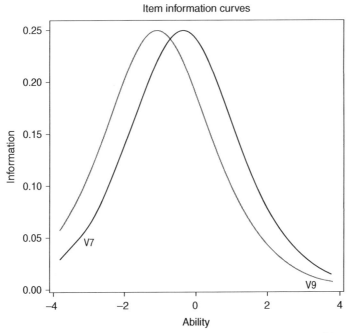

Figure 9.3: Rasch model item information curves for items 7 and 9

$$I_j = a^2 \left(p_j \left(1 - p_j \right)\right),$$ (9.6)

where a^2 is the item discrimination value squared, and p_j is the proportion of individuals correctly responding to item j. For the Rasch model, a is set equal to 1 for all items, so that I_j is $\left(p_j \left(1 - p_j\right)\right)$. Larger values of I_j for a specific range of the ability distribution indicate that the item provides relatively more information regarding the latent trait in that region than in other parts of the distribution. The IIC provides a graphical mechanism for evaluating at which levels of ability a given item provides the most (and least) information. We can use the `plot` command to obtain the IIC for items 7 and 9, as shown in Figure 9.3. Note that the only difference between this and the previous use of the command is the subcommand `type=c("IIC")` rather than `type=c("ICC")`.

```
plot(mathg6.rasch,type=c("IIC"), items=c(7,9))
```

Based on these IICs, we can conclude that item 9 provides maximum information for estimating θ around values of -1.5, while item 7 provides maximum information just below $\theta = 0$. The IICs for all of the items can be produced in a single

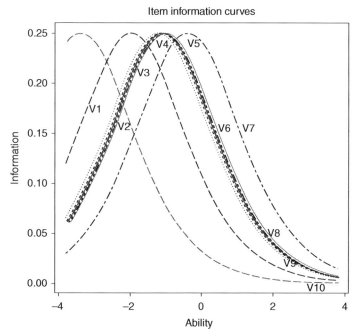

■ Figure 9.4: Rasch model item information curves for all items

plot, so that the researcher can learn which items provide the most information for specific levels of the latent trait: `plot(mathg6.rasch,type=c("IIC"))`; the output is shown in Figure 9.4. Based on these plots, it would appear that most of the items provide maximum information around a θ of -1.

In addition to item information, we may also be interested in assessing the total information (I) about θ provided by the test as a whole. Total test information is the sum of the individual item information values, under the assumption of local independence. We can visualize I with respect to the latent trait using a total information curve (TIC). Interpretation of the TIC is similar to that of the IICs, with the focus on information provided by the total instrument across the range of θ. Using a value of 0 in the `items=c()` subcommand will produce the TIC, as seen in Figure 9.5.

```
plot(mathg6.rasch,type=c("IIC"), items=c(0))
```

The test appears to provide maximum information for examinees with a latent trait value around -1, or those with somewhat below average math ability. We can also obtain a numeric estimate for I across the entire distribution of θ, or a portion thereof, which may prove useful in comparing the relative utility of models for a

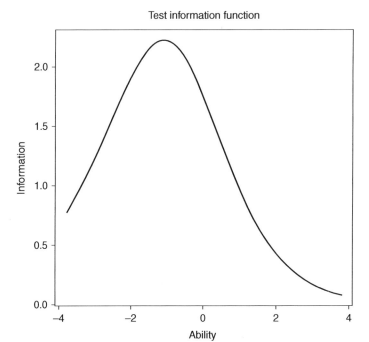

Test information function

▪ **Figure 9.5:** Rasch model test information function

given set of data. As an example, we can get the total information for the instrument across all values of the latent trait by using:

```
information(mathg6.rasch, c(-10,10))

Call:
rasch(data = mathg6, constraint = cbind(ncol(mathg6) + 1, 1))

Total Information = 10
Information in (-10, 10) = 10 (100%)
Based on all the items
```

The subcommand c(-10,10) identifies the range of θ for which information is requested. In this case, we request essentially all possible values of the latent trait. The total information provided by the test in this range is 10, which is equal to 100% of all information possible for this instrument under the Rasch model. If we were only interested in the amount of information the instrument will provide for those with above average math ability we would use the subcommand c(0,10):

```
Call:
rasch(data = mathg6, constraint = cbind(ncol(mathg6) + 1, 1))
```

```
Total Information = 10
Information in (0, 10) = 2.47 (24.75%)
Based on all the items
```

In this range of the latent trait the total information yielded by the test is 2.47, or 24.75% of the total information provided by the Rasch model of this math test. Conversely, approximately 75% of the information in this test is provided for ability levels below 0.

An issue of some importance for researchers is the degree to which the proposed model fits the item response data. We can address this issue at both the item and total instrument levels, in terms of either absolute or relative fit. Absolute fit indices are based upon the degree to which predicted item responses made by the model correspond to the actual item responses observed in the data. If these predictions are sufficiently close to the observed values, we conclude that the model fits the data well. Relative fit refers to the comparative performance of one model with another in regards to these predictions. So, in the first case we are asking the question "Does the model do a good job of predicting the item response patterns?", while in the second instance the question is "Does the model do a better job of predicting the item response patterns than other competing models?" We will address the assessment of absolute fit next, and save discussion of the relative fit question for later in the chapter.

Assessing absolute model fit for the Rasch model

The assessment of absolute model fit can be conducted using a chi-square test of the null hypothesis that the model fits the data. The chi-square statistic is defined as

$$\chi^2 = \sum \frac{\{O_r - E_r\}}{E_r},$$

(9.7)

where O_r equals the observed number of examinees with item response pattern r, and E_r is the model expected (predicted) number of examinees with item response pattern r. In other words, once the model parameters are estimated, they are used to predict item responses for every examinee. Then, the actual (observed) number of individuals with a particular set of responses on the ten items (e.g. 1101001101) is counted, and compared with the predicted number of individuals with this same pattern. If the frequency of observed and model-predicted individuals for each response pattern are close to one another, we can conclude that the model fits the data well. Theoretically, the resulting statistic is distributed as a chi-square. However, under many conditions it does not in fact conform to the chi-square distribution, making it improper for testing model fit (Tam & Li, 1997). Therefore, an alternative approach based on the bootstrap procedure may be preferable in most circumstances. The bootstrap model goodness of fit test can be implemented in R, and works as follows:

Step 1:   Estimate the IRT model parameters (e.g. Rasch) from the data.
Step 2:   Calculate the χ^2 goodness of fit statistic for this model.
Step 3:   Randomly generate item and person parameters using the parameter estimates obtained in step 1 as the population-generating values.
Step 4:   Simulate item response data using the parameter values generated in step 3.
Step 5:   Calculate the χ^2 goodness of fit statistic for the simulated data using the IRT model utilized in step 1 (e.g. Rasch).
Step 6:   Repeat steps 2 through 5 B (e.g. 1000) times in order to create a distribution of the χ^2 under the null hypothesis that the model fits the data.
Step 7:   Compare the χ^2 value from step 2 with the distribution created in step 6, and calculate the p-value, which corresponds to 1-percentile of the observed χ^2.

In order to obtain the bootstrap chi-square test of overall model fit for a 1PL or Rasch model, we would use the command GoF.rasch(mathg6.rasch, B=1000). The B=1000 subcommand requests that 1000 bootstrap samples under the null hypothesis be generated. The reader is cautioned that the bootstrap procedure can take a long time to conduct, particularly for larger samples and more items. The resultant output for our example appears below.

```
Bootstrap Goodness-of-Fit using Pearson chi-squared
Call:

rasch(data = mathg6, constraint = cbind(ncol(mathg6) + 1, 1))
Tobs: 2212.44
# data-sets: 1001
p-value: 0.001
```

The significant result here indicates that the Rasch model does not adequately fit the data.

Similarly to model fit, a test can also be used to determine whether the model fits for the individual items as well. In this case, the statistic is calculated by comparing the frequency of individuals correctly responding to the item for a given (very small) range of values of θ, with the model-predicted frequency. The R command is item.fit(mathg6.rasch, simulate.p.value=TRUE). If we select FALSE for the simulate.p.value command, the standard chi-square distribution will be used, whereas TRUE would utilize the bootstrap methodology described previously.

```
Item-Fit Statistics and P-values

Call:

rasch(data = mathg6, constraint = cbind(ncol(mathg6) + 1, 1))
Alternative: Items do not fit the model
Ability Categories: 10
Monte Carlo samples: 100


        X^2          Pr(>X^2)
V1    201.01    0.17
V2    245.48    0.12
V3    253.54    0.11
V4    451.83    0.01
V5    253.16    0.29
V6    496.27    0.01
V7    108.85       1
V8    535.23    0.01
V9    609.34    0.01
V10   306.15    0.01
```

As with the model fit assessment, significant results for item fit indicate that the model does not accurately fit responses for the individual items. Therefore, we would conclude that for this example the model did not fit items 4, 6, 8, 9, or 10 well.

Obtaining latent trait estimates for the Rasch model

Our focus so far has been on learning about the attributes of the items that make up the scale of interest, and assessing whether the model fits the data. IRT models also provide estimates of the measured latent trait (θ) for individuals in the sample. These latent trait values can be obtained with R, and used in subsequent analyses quite easily. In order to save the θ estimates from the Rasch model, we would use the factor.scores command that is part of the ltm library.

```
theta.rasch<-factor.scores(mathg6.rasch)
```

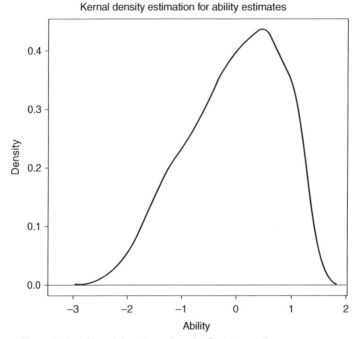

Kernal density estimation for ability estimates

■ **Figure 9.6:** Plot of theta based on the Rasch model

The object **theta.rasch** contains the θ estimate and standard error for each individual in the sample, and the item response patterns corresponding to each θ. In order to obtain basic descriptive statistics for θ we would use the command **summary(theta.rasch$score.dat$z1)**. Within **theta.rasch**, the latent trait estimate itself is contained within the set **score.dat** in the variable labeled **z1**. The output from **summary** appears below.

Min.	1st Qu.	Median	Mean	3rd Qu.	Max.
-2.49	-1.14 -	0.83 -	0.78	-0.52	1.06

We can see that the mean math ability for the sample is -0.7854, with the lowest being -2.4910 and the highest being 1.0630. The standard deviation of the latent trait is obtained with the command **sqrt(var(theta.rasch$score.dat$z1))**, yielding the value 0.5712838. We can also plot the latent trait using **plot(theta.rasch)**. From this plot, shown in Figure 9.6, we can see that the distribution of math ability is somewhat negatively skewed.

The actual **theta.rasch** object includes the following information, which we can obtain by simply typing **theta.rasch**.

```
Call:
rasch(data = mathg6, constraint = cbind(ncol(mathg6) + 1, 1))

Scoring Method: Empirical Bayes

Factor-Scores for observed response patterns:
V1 V2 V3  V4  V5  V6  V7  V8  V9  V10  Obs  Exp  z1     se.    z1
 1  0  0   0   0   0   0   0   0    0   17  7.690 -2.491 0.622
```

This is the first of 673 lines in the output (one line for every observed item response pattern). The first column, containing 1, indicates that this is the first line in the output. The next ten columns represent the responses on the items. Thus, this first pattern represents those who answered all ten items incorrectly. The Obs column contains the number of examinees who fit this pattern, 17, while Exp represents the expected number predicted by the model. Finally, the z1 column is the actual θ estimate for this response pattern, while se.z1 is the standard error of the latent trait. Again, there will be a similar line of output for every observed response pattern in the data.

Fitting the 1PL model in R

Fitting of the 1PL model in R is very similar to fitting the Rasch, and the types of output available for the 1PL are very similar. To fit the 1PL without restricting item discrimination values to 1, we use the command mathg6.1pl<-rasch(mathg6), followed by summary(mathg6.1pl) to obtain the item parameter estimates and AIC/BIC values. As with the Rasch model results, output for the 1PL model is captured in the object mathg6.1pl.

```
Call:
rasch(data = mathg6)

Model Summary:
    log.Lik          AIC        BIC
 -36610.62 73243.24 73318.83

Coefficients:
               Value std.err z.vals
Dffclt.V1 -1.61  0.03  -46.61
Dffclt.V2 -1.01  0.02  -35.81
Dffclt.V3 -0.83  0.02  -30.77
Dffclt.V4 -0.94  0.02  -34.02
Dffclt.V5 -0.31  0.02  -12.83
```

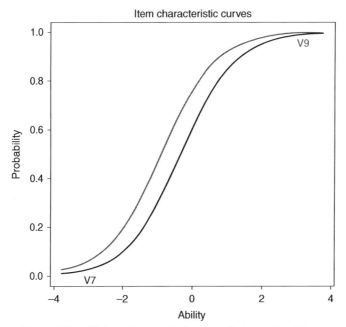

■ **Figure 9.7:** 1PL item characteristic curves for items 7 and 9

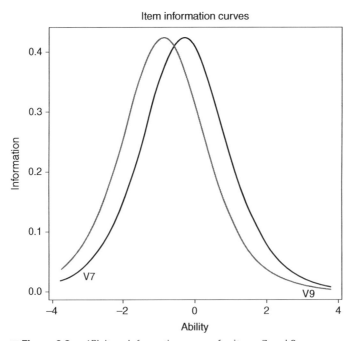

■ **Figure 9.8:** 1PL item information curves for items 7 and 9

```
Dffclt.V6   -0.87  0.02  -32.17
Dffclt.V7   -0.31  0.02  -12.64
Dffclt.V8   -0.85  0.02  -31.60
Dffclt.V9   -0.89  0.02  -32.52
Dffclt.V10  -2.74  0.05  -50.17
Dscrmn       1.30  0.01   69.33


Integration:
method: Gauss-Hermite
quadrature points: 21


Optimization:
Convergence: 0
max(|grad|): 0.047
quasi-Newton: BFGS
```

The labels are identical to those we saw with the Rasch model. First, we note that the discrimination value (Dscrmn) estimated in common for all of the items is 1.302. Second, the item difficulties (Dffclt) were somewhat different in the 1PL from the Rasch, though in general these differences were not particularly large. We can use the AIC and BIC statistics to compare the relative fit of the two models, with the better-fitting model being the one with the smaller values, as discussed above. Given that the 1PL (AIC = 73243.24, BIC = 73318.83) model had lower values for both statistics than did the Rasch (AIC = 73562.08, BIC = 73630.8), we would conclude that it provides a better fit to the data, based on these statistics. As a reminder, later in the chapter we will devote time to comparing the fit of the IRT models and deciding on the optimal one for these data.

As with the Rasch model, we will want to examine the ICCs and IICs for individual items. Once again, let us use items 7 and 9 for the example of each graph for the 1PL model.

```
plot(mathg6.1pl,type=c("ICC"), items=c(7,9))
plot(mathg6.1pl,type=c("IIC"), items=c(7,9))
```

The ICCs (Figure 9.7) and IICs (Figure 9.8) for these items are very similar for the 1PL as for the Rasch model, with the IICs being slightly narrower than the Rasch-based IICs.

The total information provided by the 1PL model is 13.02, which is slightly larger than the 10 associated with the Rasch model.

```
information(mathg6.1pl, c(-10,10))

Call:
rasch(data = mathg6)

Total Information = 13.02
Information in (-10, 10) = 13.02 (100%)
Based on all the items
```

If we are interested only in those students who have above average ability, the amount of information provided by the 1PL would be 3.06, which is approximately 23.5% of the total test information. This value represents a somewhat lower proportion of information attributable to the upper half of the θ distribution than we saw with the Rasch.

```
information(mathg6.1pl, c(0,10))

Call:
rasch(data = mathg6)

Total Information = 13.02
Information in (0, 10) = 3.06 (23.51%)
Based on all the items
```

The total test information curve and information for each of the items in the same graph appear in Figures 9.9 and 9.10, with the appropriate R commands being shown below. As we saw with items 7 and 9, the general shape of these plots was similar for the 1PL as for the Rasch model.

```
plot(mathg6.1pl,type=c("IIC"), items=c(0))
plot(mathg6.1pl,type=c("IIC"))
```

Finally, we can obtain model and item fit information as we did for the Rasch model. We will use the GoF.rasch command to obtain the fit test for the 1PL model, and once again request 1000 bootstrap samples. We can also test fit for the individual items with the item.fit command, appearing below.

```
GoF.rasch(mathg6.1pl, B=1000).

Bootstrap Goodness-of-Fit using Pearson chi-squared

Call:
rasch(data = mathg6)

Tobs: 1831.99
# data-sets: 1001
```

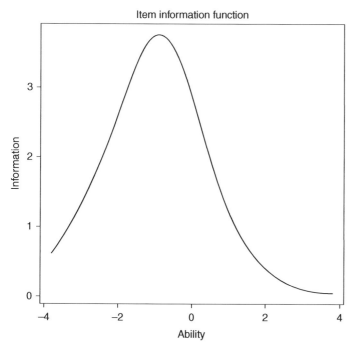

■ **Figure 9.9:** 1PL test information curve

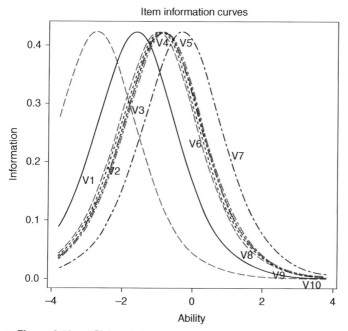

■ **Figure 9.10:** 1PL item information curves for all items

```
p-value: 0.001

item.fit(mathg6.1pl, simulate.p.value=TRUE)

Item-Fit Statistics and P-values

Call:

rasch(data = mathg6)
Alternative: Items do not fit the model
Ability Categories: 10
Monte Carlo samples: 100

         X^2      Pr(>X^2)
V1     137.48 0.42
V2     134.73 0.63
V3     132.86 0.74
V4     290.40 0.01
V5     130.62 0.99
V6     324.62 0.01
V7     32.80 1
V8     355.50 0.01
V9     418.69 0.01
V10   245.58 0.01
```

The significant result of the model fit test suggests that, as was true for the Rasch model, the 1PL does not fit the data well. In addition, it appears that the fit for items 4, 6, 8, 9, and 10 was not good.

We may also be interested in the distribution of the latent trait, and can use the following commands to first save the estimates in an object called **theta.1pl** and then plot them (see Figure 9.11).

```
theta.1pl<-factor.scores(mathg6.1pl)
plot(theta.1pl)
```

The distribution of θ for the 1PL model is similar to that for the Rasch, with evidence of negative skewness. We will also examine descriptive statistics for the latent trait, including its standard deviation, which we will calculate.

```
summary(theta.1pl$score.dat$z1)
    Min.   1st Qu. Median   Mean    3rd Qu.    Max.
 -2.3600 -1.0610 -0.7864 -0.7409 -0.5069 1.0260
```

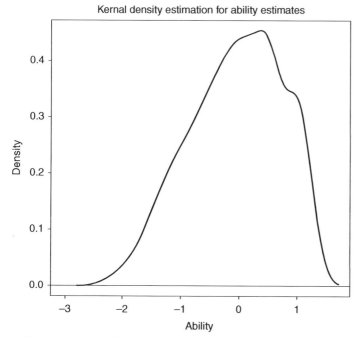

Kernal density estimation for ability estimates

■ **Figure 9.11:** 1PL distribution of theta

```
sqrt(var(theta.1pl$score.dat$z1))
[1] 0.5136693
```

We see similar values for both the mean and standard deviation for the 1PL as for the Rasch model.

Fitting the 2PL model in R

Recall that for both the Rasch and 1PL models, a single item discrimination value exists for all of the items, either set at 1 in the case of Rasch or a single estimated value for the 1PL. However, this tacit assumption of equal discrimination across items may not be reasonable in many cases, leading researchers to investigate the fit of the **two-parameter logistic model (2PL)**, which allows for unique discrimination values for each item. The 2PL model takes the form:

$$P\left(x_j = 1 \mid \theta, b_j\right) = \frac{e^{a_j\left(\theta, -b_j\right)}}{1 + e^{a_j\left(\theta, -b_j\right)}}. \qquad \textbf{(9.8)}$$

To fit this model to our math achievement data, we will use a new function, ltm, from the ltm library. The syntax for doing so is:

```
mathg6.2pl<-ltm(mathg6~z1)
```

Once again, we create an output object containing the results of the 2PL model (mathg6.2pl), that can be used for subsequent analyses and graphical displays. Following the ltm function, we include the name of the data file containing the items and ~z1, which indicates that we are fitting a 2PL model by allowing each item to have its own item discrimination value. In order to view the item parameter estimates, we use the summary command, just as we did for the Rasch and 1PL models.

The format of the 2PL output is virtually identical to that of the previous models, including the relative fit indices, followed by the item parameter estimates, with the addition that each item has a unique item discrimination value (Dscrmn). Indeed, we can see that the discrimination values of the items do indeed differ from one another, suggesting that using a single value as in the 1PL is probably not optimal. The discrimination values were all greater than 1 except for item 7. In addition, items 9 and 10 had the highest values, indicating that they are best at differentiating among individuals with different levels of the latent trait. In terms of relative fit, the AIC and BIC values for the 2PL model are somewhat smaller than those of the 1PL and Rasch, suggesting that allowing different discrimination values for the items improves model fit.

```
summary(mathg6.2pl)

Call:
ltm(formula = mathg6 ~ z1)

Model Summary:
    log.Lik          AIC          BIC
-36427.71 72895.41 73032.86

Coefficients:
                  value std.err z.vals
Dffclt.V1 -1.91    0.07 -25.03
Dffclt.V2 -1.10    0.04 -26.57
Dffclt.V3 -0.90    0.03 -24.55
Dffclt.V4 -0.85    0.02 -29.59
Dffclt.V5 -0.34    0.02 -12.36
Dffclt.V6 -0.78    0.02 -28.78
Dffclt.V7 -0.41    0.03 -11.74
Dffclt.V8 -0.76    0.02 -28.45
```

```
Dffclt.V9  -0.74     0.02 -30.03
Dffclt.V10 -2.30     0.07 -29.30
Dscrmn.V1   1.00       0.04 20.57
Dscrmn.V2   1.13       0.04 24.41
Dscrmn.V3   1.12       0.04 24.95
Dscrmn.V4   1.56       0.05 26.62
Dscrmn.V5   1.15       0.04 25.93
Dscrmn.V6   1.61       0.06 26.86
Dscrmn.V7   0.85       0.03 22.73
Dscrmn.V8   1.63       0.06 26.90
Dscrmn.V9   1.85       0.06 26.63
Dscrmn.V10  1.74     0.10 17.44


Integration:
method: Gauss-Hermite
quadrature points: 21


Optimization:
Convergence: 0
max(|grad|): 0.0030
quasi-Newton: BFGS
```

With respect to the item parameters, we see that item difficulty values for the 2PL changed somewhat when compared to the other models, though these differences were generally not very large. Furthermore, the relative ordering of items in terms of least to most difficult remained much the same, regardless of the model used.

Below are the commands for obtaining the ICCs and IICs for items 7 and 9 for the 2PL model.

```
plot(mathg6.2pl,type=c("ICC"), items=c(7,9))
```

We see from Figure 9.12 that the item with the largest discrimination value (V9) has a more quickly increasing function across levels of θ than does item 7, which had the lowest discrimination value. Therefore, relatively small changes in ability are associated with fairly large changes in the probability of a correct item response for item 9, when compared with item 7. This difference in the relationship between ability and the probability of a correct item response demonstrates the impact of different item discrimination values. The IICs for these items (see Figure 9.13) can be obtained using the command `plot(mathg6.2pl,type=c("IIC"), items=c(7,9))`.

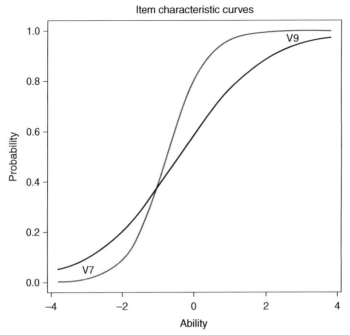

■ **Figure 9.12:** 2PL item characteristic curves for items 7 and 9

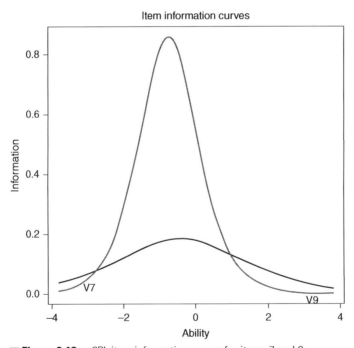

■ **Figure 9.13:** 2PL item information curves for items 7 and 9

The impact of allowing different discrimination values is readily apparent in the amount of information provided by each item. While the maximum information about θ provided by each item peaks between -0.5 and -1, the absolute amount is much greater for V9 than V7. In other words, the item with the larger a provided more information about the latent trait across most of its distribution, with the exception of what lies in the tails, below -3 and above 1.5. Therefore, a test developer interested in assessing examinees with average or slightly below average math ability would obtain much more precise estimates of their θ values from item 9 than item 7. We can also quantify the amount of information that a researcher might expect to obtain from the 2PL model across the entire math ability distribution, or only its upper half.

```
information(mathg6.2pl, c(-10,10))

Call:
ltm(formula = mathg6 ~ z1)


Total Information = 13.72
Information in (-10, 10) = 13.72 (100%)
Based on all the items
```
```
information(mathg6.2pl, c(0,10))

Call:
ltm(formula = mathg6 ~ z1)


Total Information = 13.72
Information in (0, 10) = 2.94 (21.46%)
Based on all the items
```

These results show that the 2PL model provides slightly more information than the 1PL across the entire ability distribution (13.72 versus 13.02), but not for the upper half (2.94 versus 3.06). In other words, estimates of the latent trait for individuals who have above average math ability would actually be a bit more precise using the 1PL model. This is an important issue that test developers would need to keep in mind, particularly if they anticipate use of the instrument primarily with higher math ability examinees.

In order to get a sense for how all of the items, and the scale as a whole, perform in the 2PL context, we can use the following commands to obtain the test information curve (Figure 9.14) and the IICs (Figure 9.15) for all the items in a single plot, just as we did for the other models.

```
plot(mathg6.2pl,type=c("IIC"), items=c(0))
plot(mathg6.2pl,type=c("IIC"))
```

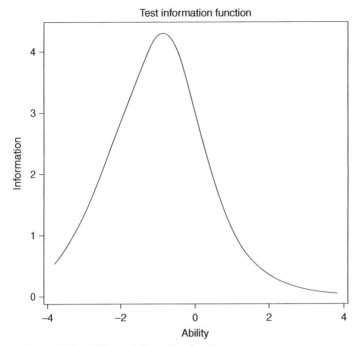

■ Figure 9.14: 2PL test information function curve

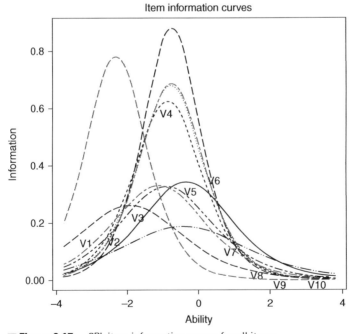

■ Figure 9.15: 2PL item information curves for all items

In terms of the instrument as a whole, maximum information was provided between θ of -1.5 and -1.0. In other words, the most precise estimates of the latent trait for the test as a whole would occur for those who have low math ability assessed by the measure. With respect to the individual items, we notice immediately that in the 2PL case the heights of the IICs are no longer uniform, as they were in the Rasch and 1PL cases. This fact is due to the differing item discrimination values. A closer examination of the IICs reveals that most of the items provide maximum information between θ of 0 and -2, with the notable exception of item 10, which peaked at approximately -2.5. None of the items had IIC peaks at levels of θ greater than 0, suggesting that they may not provide particularly precise latent trait estimates for those with above average mathematics ability; a result seen in the TIC itself.

The chi-square-based model-fit testing that we used in the Rasch and 1PL cases is not available in R for other models, including the 2PL and 3PL. Therefore, while we can compare the relative fit of these models with one another and with the Rasch and 1PL, we cannot explicitly test their fit to the data in R. However, we are still able to test the fit of the individual items for the more complex IRT models with the bootstrap test, using the `item.fit` command just as in the earlier examples.

```
item.fit(mathg6.2pl, simulate.p.value=TRUE)

Item-Fit Statistics and P-values

Call:
ltm(formula = mathg6 ~ z1)

Alternative: Items do not fit the model
Ability Categories: 10
Monte Carlo samples: 100

      X^2    Pr(>X^2)
V1   123.18 0.02
V2   129.45 0.01
V3   127.18 0.11
V4   157.80 0.34
V5   128.17 0.47
V6   161.19 0.54
V7   173.84 0.02
V8   185.19 0.18
V9   214.16 0.11
V10  170.41 0.03
```

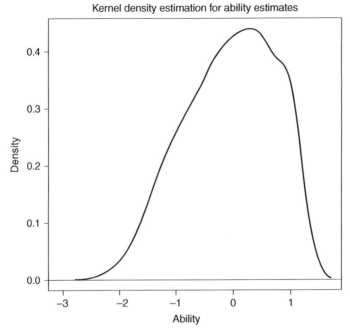

Kernel density estimation for ability estimates

■ **Figure 9.16:**   2PL distribution of theta estimates

Here we see that the 2PL model did not fit items 1, 7, or 10 well, but did provide adequate fit for the others. Thus, while we do not have a test for overall model fit, based on these results for the individual items, it does appear that the 2PL model may not provide adequate fit overall.

The plot and descriptive statistics for θ as estimated by the 2PL model appear below, along with the appropriate commands.

```
theta.2pl<-factor.scores(mathg6.2pl)
plot(theta.2pl)
```

The distribution of θ in the 2PL case, shown in Figure 9.16, is somewhat negatively skewed, as it was for the Rasch and 1PL models.

```
summary(theta.2pl$score.dat$z1)
    Min.  1st Qu. Median    Mean     3rd Qu. Max.
 -2.3480 -1.1030 -0.7494 -0.7633  -0.4109 0.9952
sqrt(var(theta.2pl$score.dat$z1))
[1] 0.5079626
```

The estimates of central tendency and standard deviation are also similar in value to those of the simpler models examined earlier.

Fitting the 3PL model in R

We will use a third function from the ltm library to fit the 3PL model, tpm. The key addition to the 3PL model, beyond the 2PL, is the inclusion of a **pseudo-chance** parameter (c). This value estimates the likelihood that an individual will endorse an item due solely to chance. For example, on our math test, it is possible that an examinee could answer an item correctly by guessing. Naively, we may assume that on a multiple choice exam with five options per item, the probability of correctly guessing would be 1/5 or 0.2. However, for most multiple choice items some incorrect response options are more appealing compared to others. Thus examinees who do not know the correct answer may be able to eliminate some options and thereby increase the likelihood of a correct guess. Conversely, some response options might be so attractive that they are more likely to be selected by individuals who do not know the correct answer than would be expected in the case of simple random guessing. Therefore, we should not expect c to equal 1 divided by the number of available response options. As a separate matter, including c is not appropriate for every situation involving dichotomous items. Indeed, only when an individual could realistically endorse an item solely due to chance would we want to use the 3PL model. The 3PL model is expressed as:

$$P\left(x_j = 1 \mid \theta, b_j\right) = c_i + \left(1 - c_i\right)\frac{e^{a_j\left(\theta, -b_j\right)}}{1 + e^{a_j\left(\theta, -b_j\right)}}. \tag{9.9}$$

Following is the R command for fitting it to the math achievement data and saving it to the object mathg6.3pl, followed by summary to obtain the item parameter estimates.

```
mathg6.3pl<-tpm(mathg6)
summary(mathg6.3pl)
Call:
tpm(data = mathg6)

Model Summary:
      log.Lik          AIC          BIC
-36393.34 72846.68 73052.84

Coefficients:
```

	Valu	std.err	z.vals
Gussng.V1	0.01	0.01	0.03
Gussng.V2	0.01	0.01	0.10
Gussng.V3	0.19	0.06	3.21
Gussng.V4	0.06	0.06	1.12
Gussng.V5	0.01	0.08	0.10
Gussng.V6	0.02	0.04	0.58
Gussng.V7	0.17	0.04	3.53
Gussng.V8	0.19	0.03	5.75
Gussng.V9	0.17	0.03	5.68
Gussng.V10	0.01	0.22	0.05
Dffclt.V1	-1.90	0.07	-25.23
Dffclt.V2	-1.10	0.04	-25.07
Dffclt.V3	-0.46	0.14	-3.20
Dffclt.V4	-0.73	0.10	-6.70
Dffclt.V5	-0.31	0.18	-1.76
Dffclt.V6	-0.73	0.08	-8.49
Dffclt.V7	0.06	0.13	0.45
Dffclt.V8	-0.40	0.06	-6.18
Dffclt.V9	-0.44	0.05	-8.06
Dffclt.V10	-2.32	0.23	-9.79
Dscrmn.V1	1.01	0.04	20.84
Dscrmn.V2	1.13	0.04	24.37
Dscrmn.V3	1.39	0.13	10.27
Dscrmn.V4	1.66	0.12	13.00
Dscrmn.V5	1.16	0.13	8.91
Dscrmn.V6	1.66	0.10	15.54
Dscrmn.V7	1.10	0.11	9.53
Dscrmn.V8	2.24	0.18	11.99
Dscrmn.V9	2.51	0.19	12.66
Dscrmn.V10	1.72	0.12	13.76

```
Integration:
method: Gauss-Hermite
quadrature points: 21

Optimization:
Optimizer: optim (BFGS)
Convergence: 0
max(|grad|): 0.086
```

In terms of fit, the 3PL model had a smaller value for AIC than did the 2PL, but a larger BIC. Thus, it is not clear which provides the best relative fit to the data based on these statistics. As mentioned previously, we will conclude this chapter by discussing methods for comparing model fit and deciding which may be optimal for a set of item response data. With respect to the item parameters, we may be particularly interested in the first set in the list, labeled Gussng, which are the estimates of c. There is a great deal of spread in these values across the items, with items 1, 2, and 5 having a very small likelihood of a correct response due solely to chance, and items 3, 7, 8, and 9 all having c values of just less than 0.2. Also of some interest are changes in the estimates for the other item parameters when c is included in the model. For example, items with low c values such as 1, 2, and 5 have very similar item difficulty and discrimination parameter estimates for the 3PL model as they did for the 2PL. On the other hand, items with larger c estimates such as 3, have markedly different difficulty estimates in the 3PL case (−0.4686 3PL versus −0.9092 2PL). Similar results are evident for the other items with large pseudo-chance estimates. The impact of including c in the model was not as great for the item discrimination parameter estimates.

We can obtain ICCs (Figure 9.17) and IICs (Figure 9.18) using the same plot command that we did for the other models.

```
plot(mathg6.3pl,type=c("ICC"), items=c(7,9))
plot(mathg6.3pl,type=c("IIC"), items=c(7,9))
```

The primary difference in the ICCs for these items when compared to the ICCs for the previous models excluding c is that the lower asymptote is not 0, but rather the value of c itself. In other words, the ICC for each item converges to the pseudo-chance value, which for these two items was approximately 0.17. The IICs for both items are shifted slightly up the ability continuum in the 3PL case, meaning that when the possibility of a correct item response due to chance is considered, each item provides maximum information for somewhat higher levels of math ability than is the case when such chance responding is ignored.

With respect to information, we see that for the instrument as a whole the 3PL model provides somewhat less information than did the 2PL, while yielding more information for the upper half of the ability distribution. Therefore, if our primary interest were examinees who are relatively good at math, the 3PL model would provide more information (i.e. more precise estimation of θ) than any of the other models that we have examined in this chapter.

```
information(mathg6.3pl, c(-10,10))

Call:
tpm(data = mathg6)

Total Information = 12.18
Information in (-10, 10) = 12.18 (100%)
```

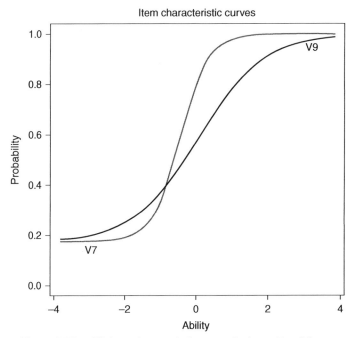

▩ **Figure 9.17:**   3PL item characteristic curves for items 7 and 9

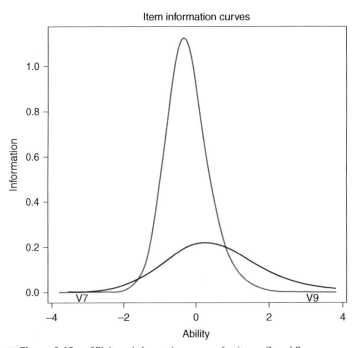

▩ **Figure 9.18:**   3PL item information curves for items 7 and 9

Based on all the items

```
information(mathg6.3pl, c(0,10))
```

```
Call:
tpm(data = mathg6)
```

```
Total Information = 12.18
Information in (0, 10) = 3.41 (27.97%)
Based on all the items
```

Finally, as with the other models, we can plot the TIC (Figure 9.19) and the IICs for all of the items simultaneously (Figure 9.20).

```
plot(mathg6.2pl,type=c("IIC"), items=c(0))
plot(mathg6.2pl,type=c("IIC"))
```

With R, we can also use the bootstrap χ^2 test to assess the fit of each item, though not the model as a whole.

```
item.fit(mathg6.3pl, simulate.p.value=TRUE)
Item-Fit Statistics and P-values
Call:
tpm(data = mathg6)
```

```
Alternative: Items do not fit the model
Ability Categories: 10
Monte Carlo samples: 100
```

	X^2	Pr(>X^2)
V1	136.23	0.01
V2	125.48	0.41
V3	122.90	0.06
V4	147.04	0.62
V5	97.85	0.76
V6	154.19	0.80
V7	94.97	0.40
V8	147.92	0.37
V9	150.07	0.90
V10	242.58	0.15

Only item 1 exhibited poor fit for the 3PL model. Thus, we might conclude that the 3PL is the optimal model for this data, given that only one of the items exhibited poor fit, and given that it had the lowest value for the AIC (though not the BIC). However, as we will see in the next section, there are other methods available for comparing model fit, and we should consider results from each of these before selecting the final model to use.

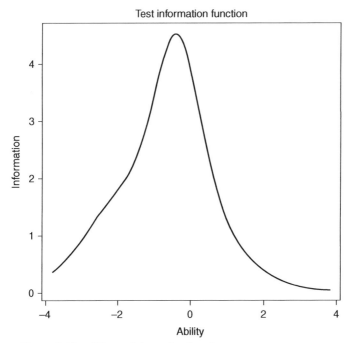

■ **Figure 9.19:**   3PL test information function curve

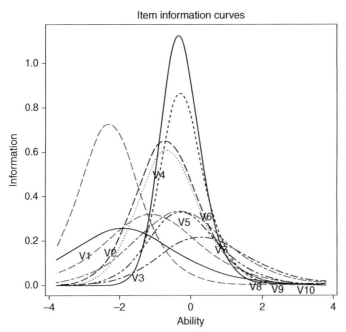

■ **Figure 9.20:**   3PL item information curves for all items

Finally, as with the other models we will look at the distribution of the latent trait for the 3PL model (see Figure 9.21).

```
theta.3pl<-factor.scores(mathg6.3pl)
plot(theta.3pl)
summary(theta.3pl$score.dat$z1)
    Min.   1st Qu. Median   Mean    3rd Qu. Max.
   -2.2300 -1.0550 -0.6926  -0.7287 -0.3677 0.9999
sqrt(var(theta.3pl$score.dat$z1))
[1] 0.5244587
```

Comparing fit for dichotomous IRT models

We have described one method for comparing the fit of IRT models, using the AIC and BIC indices. As we discussed previously, these are measures of the variation in the data not explained by the model, with a penalty for model complexity. Smaller values indicate relatively better fit, so that we would select the model with the lowest value. However, these statistics do not represent the only approach to comparing model fit, and as of the writing of this book, researchers have not identified a single method for this purpose that is definitively best in every case. Indeed, there

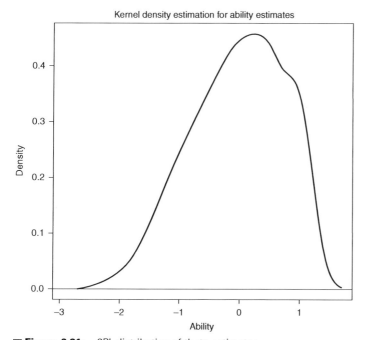

■ Figure 9.21: 3PL distribution of theta estimates

are several methods available to the researcher using R, and we will discuss each of these below, with an emphasis on their application and interpretation.

The first approach to model comparison that we will consider is **relative efficiency (RE)**. RE, (see Lord, 1980 for a more detailed discussion of RE for model selection) is simply the ratio of information available from a more complex versus from a less complex model. So, for example, we might assess the RE of the 2PL compared to the 1PL. We have already seen how to obtain model information for a given range of the latent trait using the `information` command in R. Therefore, if our interest is in calculating RE for the entire range of θ, we would use the following commands to obtain total information for the 1PL, 2PL, and 3PL models and then calculate RE for each pair of models.

```
information(mathg6.1pl, c(-10,10))    I₁ₚₗ = 13.02
information(mathg6.2pl, c(-10,10))    I₂ₚₗ = 13.72
information(mathg6.3pl, c(-10,10))    I₃ₚₗ = 12.18
```

$$\text{RE}_{1\text{PL},2\text{PL}} = \frac{I_{2\text{PL}}}{I_{1\text{PL}}} = \frac{13.72}{13.02} = 1.05$$

$$\text{RE}_{1\text{PL},3\text{PL}} = \frac{I_{3\text{PL}}}{I_{1\text{PL}}} = \frac{12.18}{13.02} = 0.94$$

$$\text{RE}_{2\text{PL},3\text{PL}} = \frac{I_{3\text{PL}}}{I_{2\text{PL}}} = \frac{12.18}{13.72} = 0.89$$

Based on these results, across the entire range of math ability the 2PL model provides roughly 5% more information than does the 1PL, while the 3PL provides only 94% and 89% as much information as the 1PL and 2PL, respectively. We would conclude, therefore, that based on the amount of information provided across the entire range of the latent trait, the 2PL model is optimal. Two caveats must be kept in mind, however. First, having more information does not mean that the 2PL model yields sufficient information, but simply that compared to the others it yields more information. Second, if the test will only be used with a subset of the total population such that not all levels of math ability are of interest, then we may not want to compare the models in terms of the total information that they yield. Instead, we may obtain the estimated information only for the portion of θ that is of interest and calculate RE based on this truncated region of the distribution. This can be completed easily in R, as we have already seen earlier in the chapter when we obtained information for the upper half of the θ distribution.

A second method for comparing the fit of nested models is with the **likelihood ratio test**. Models are nested when one is a simpler version of another. For example, the 1PL model is nested within the 2PL because the former constrains the item discrimination values to a single value while the latter releases this constraint. Similarly, the 2PL is nested within the 3PL because it constrains the pseudo-chance values to be 0 for all items, while the 3PL releases this constraint. Each IRT model has associated with it a $-2\ln(L)$, as we have seen. We can construct a statistical test of the null hypothesis of equal model fit by taking the difference in these values for the nested models. For comparing fit of the 1PL and 2PL models, the test statistic takes the form $G^2 = -2\ln(L_{1PL}) - (-2\ln(L_{2PL}))$. The test statistic is distributed as a chi-square, with degrees of freedom equal to the difference in the number of parameter estimates in the two models. So, for example, the degrees of freedom for the test comparing the 1PL and 2PL models is 9, because for the 1PL one discrimination parameter is estimated, while for the 2PL ten such parameters are estimated. Similarly, the degrees of freedom for the test comparing the 2PL and 3PL is 10 because the latter model has ten c parameter estimates, while the former has none. Both models provide equal numbers of item difficulty and discrimination parameter estimates.

We can obtain the likelihood ratio test using the anova command in the ltm library. Below are the results comparing the fit of the 1PL and 2PL, followed by the 2PL and 3PL.

```
anova(mathg6.1pl, mathg6.2pl)
```

Likelihood Ratio Table

	AIC	BIC	log.Lik	LRT	df	p.value
mathg6.1pl	73243.24	73318.83	-36610.62			
mathg6.2pl	72895.41	73032.86	-36427.71	365.83	9	<0.001

```
anova(mathg6.2pl, mathg6.3pl)
```

Likelihood Ratio Table

	AIC	BIC	log.Lik	LRT	df	p.value
mathg6.2pl	72895.41	73032.86	-36427.71			
mathg6.3pl	72846.68	73052.84	-36393.34	68.73	10	<0.001

The LRT column contains the test statistic, df contains the degrees of freedom, and p.value is the p-value for the test statistic. Once again, the null hypothesis is that the fit provided by the two models to the data does not differ. These results suggest that for both comparisons the null hypothesis of equivalent model fit should be rejected, given the p.value is less than 0.001 for both tests. Thus, we can conclude that the 2PL model provides significantly better fit than the 1PL, and the 3PL provides significantly better fit than the 2PL. Note that the anova command also provides a convenient juxtaposition of the AIC and BIC values for the models being compared.

A final method for assessing fit is to examine the relative reduction in the $-2\ln(L)$ values for two models using a statistic that is analogous to R^2 in regression analysis. A very helpful and thorough description of this methodology is provided by de Ayala (2009). In summary, we can take the difference in $-2\ln(L)$ for two nested models and divide it by the $-2\ln(L)$ for the simpler model in the hierarchy. For example, if we want to compare the 1PL and 2PL models, this value would be $R_\Delta^2 = \dfrac{36610.62 - 36427.71}{36610.62} = \dfrac{182.91}{36610.62} = .0050 = 0.50\%$, indicating that the 2PL model provides a 0.5% improvement in model fit when compared to the 1PL. For the 3PL versus 2PL comparison,

$R_\Delta^2 = \dfrac{36427.71 - 36393.34}{36427.71} = \dfrac{34.37}{36427.71} = .0009 = 0.09\%$. In other words, the 3PL improves model fit by 0.09% beyond that of the 2PL.

Of course, when making decisions regarding which model is optimal for a set of data, the researcher must consider not only relative fit, but also relative complexity. In other words, while the 3PL does improve fit somewhat, it is also a more complex model with more parameters to be estimated. The researcher would need to take this added complexity into account, along with the other model fit information, in order to decide which model, ultimately, should be selected. The results for this example do not necessarily provide a definitive answer to this question. Based on most of the measures, the 3PL would seem to provide the best fit to the data. It has the lowest AIC, provides a 0.09% better fit than the 2PL (which provides a better fit than the 1PL), and indeed its fit was significantly better than that of the 2PL. The 3PL also provides the best fit to the items, taken as a whole, with only item 1 exhibiting a significantly "bad" fit. At the same time, the 3PL has the lowest RE across the entire θ distribution, and has a higher BIC than the 2PL, which has the best RE of the models studied here. In addition, for approximately half of the items, the pseudo-chance value is very close to 0, indicating that it is largely unnecessary in those cases. Taken all together, we might prefer the 3PL model, if only slightly, because the preponderance of model fit evidence supported it. Also, the items were multiple choice format so modeling the guessing parameter makes practical sense from a theoretical perspective. This example demonstrates the importance of using the combination of empirical information and item format and content in selecting the best model to apply to estimate item and person parameters in IRT.

POLYTOMOUS ITEM RESPONSE THEORY MODELS

The previous set of models was designed for use with dichotomous item response data. Thus, they are ideal for situations in which items can be scored as correct (1) or incorrect (0), or cases where individuals are asked to agree or disagree with a statement. However, in many situations in psychology and education, item responses can take more than two values. For example, items may be based on a Likert-type scale with possible values being 1, 2, 3, 4, and 5, representing different levels of agreement with a statement. In other situations, an individual's performance on some task may be graded with possible scores of below basic (1), basic (2), proficient (3), or exemplary (4). In either of these situations, or others relying on items with more than two possible scores (polytomous items), the dichotomous item response models described above will not be appropriate.

As with the dichotomous item models, we have a choice of approaches for dealing with polytomous items, including models corresponding to Rasch, in which item discrimination parameters are set to 1, and models corresponding to the 2PL in which discrimination parameters are estimated for each item. There is not a polytomous item model corresponding to the 3PL, however, as pseudo-guessing is not typically seen as a viable scoring mechanism for such items. We will also see that the concept of item location (difficulty in the dichotomous item case) is somewhat different with polytomous items. We will first address the partial credit model, which corresponds to the Rasch model, and then turn our attention to two models that allow for separate discrimination parameters for each item, the generalized partial credit model and the graded response model.

Partial credit model (Rasch)

The **partial credit model (PCM)** expresses the relationship between a particular item response and the person and item locations on the latent trait being measured by the items. The PCM was described by Masters (1982), and is expressed as:

$$p\left(x_j = k \mid \theta, \delta_{jh}\right) = \frac{e^{\sum_{h=0}^{x_j}\left(\theta - \delta_{jh}\right)}}{e^{\sum_{h=0}^{m_j}\left(\theta - \delta_{jh}\right)}}, \tag{9.10}$$

where

x_j = Response x to item j

θ = Level of the latent trait being measured

δ_{jh} = Threshold parameter h for item j

m_j = Total number of possible response categories for item j.

The θ parameter holds the same meaning in polytomous item models that it does in the dichotomous case, as a measure of an individual's level of the latent trait being measured by the set of items. The δ_{jh} parameter measures location, but in this case it is the location of a particular item response rather than the item itself. More specifically, as stated by de Ayala (2009), δ_{jh} reflects the relative difficulty for an individual to select response option h versus $h-1$. Because it acts as a sort of demarcation between two adjacent item response categories, it is referred to as a **threshold**. There are $m-1$ thresholds for every item, and higher values of δ_{jh} indicate that an individual needs a higher value of θ to move from response $h-1$ to h. As an example, if an item has four response options (1, 2, 3, 4) then it will have three thresholds. The first threshold marks the transition from a response of 1 to a response of 2, whereas the second threshold marks the transition from a 2 to a 3, and the third threshold marks the transition from a 3 to a 4. Thus, if an item has δ_{jh} values of −1.5, 0, and 1, we would conclude that respondents with θ less than −1.5 are most likely to give a response of 1, those with θ between −1.5 and 0 are most likely to give a response of 2, those with θ between 0 and 1 are most likely to give a response of 3, and those with θ greater than 1 are most likely to give a response of 4. Finally, we should note that in the Rasch version of the PCM, the item discrimination parameter (a) is set equal to 1 for all items. There is a version of the PCM in which a common a is estimated for all of the items, just as with the 1PL for dichotomous items.

In order to explore using R to estimate polytomous IRT models, let's consider an example set of data taken from the Youth Risk Behavior Survey (YRBS). This survey is given to a sample of 15-year-old American high school students every two years, asking them questions about a variety of behaviors, including the composition of their diet, which is the focus of the following analyses. For the following examples, we will use a subsample ($N = 1000$) of the YRBS 2009 data (Centers for Disease Control and Prevention, 2009), and in particular the following items:

Q72	How many times fruit juice 7 days
Q73	How many times fruit 7 days
Q74	How many times green salad 7 days
Q75	How many times potatoes 7 days
Q76	How many times carrots 7 days
Q77	How many times other vegetables 7 days
Q79	How many glass of milk 7 days

Each item has the following response options:
1 = Never consume the food
2 = Consume 1–3 times in last 7 days
3 = Consume 4–6 times in last 7 days
4 = Consume 7+ times in last 7 days.

Together these items measure a latent trait associating with eating a healthy diet, such that higher values of θ indicate having a healthier diet.

To fit a Rasch version of the PCM where the discrimination parameter is set to 1 for each item and then obtain the output, we use the gpcm command from the ltm library. In this example, we only display the output for item Q72 in order to save space.

```
yrbsfoods1000.pcm<-gpcm(yrbsfoods1000,constraint="r
asch")
summary(yrbsfoods1000.pcm)

Call:
gpcm(data = yrbsfoods1000, constraint = "rasch")

Model Summary:
  log.Lik      AIC              BIC
-8354.85 16751.7 16854.76

Coefficients:
$Q72
                value    std.err z.value
Catgr.1 -1.008 0.100    -10.125
Catgr.2  0.661 0.101      6.556
Catgr.3 -0.035 0.106     -0.327
Dscrmn   1.000 NA                  NA
```

We can interpret the results for Q72 as a way to gain an understanding of what the threshold values mean. This item asks respondents how often they drink fruit juice each week. The first threshold is −1.008, indicating that it is at this level of θ that the likelihood of drinking no juice during the last 7 days becomes less likely than drinking juice 1–3 times during that period. The second δ_{jh} of 0.661 indicates that the transition from a response of 2 to 3 (4–6 times) occurs at a θ of 0.661, such that those with an ability value greater than 0.661 are more likely to give a response of 3 as opposed to 2. The final δ_{jh} is −0.035, meaning that the transition from a response of 3 to 4 (7+ times) occurs at a θ of -0.035. Thus, individuals with ability greater than -0.035 were more likely to indicate drinking juice 7+ times during the previous 7 days than drinking it 4–6 times. These results might appear to be somewhat confusing at first examination. However, when we study them further using the ICC below, they will become somewhat easier to understand. To complete explanation of the table, the z.value column contains the ratio of the threshold with its standard error, which can serve as a test of the null hypothesis that the threshold in the population is different from 0.

We need to say a brief word or two about what the latent trait in this example represents. When we worked with the math data earlier in the chapter, the notion of ability made intuitive sense: It represented an examinee's facility with math. However, with the food consumption data we are no longer investigating a cognitive trait using items that are answered correctly or not, but rather the propensity to eat healthy foods. Thus, the latent trait of interest is likelihood of eating a healthy diet (or at least reporting that you eat a healthy diet), so that θ now reflects the level of healthy eating exhibited by an individual. When working with polytomous data from questionnaires measuring attitude, mood, personality, and the like, such noncognitive latent traits are not at all uncommon.

As was true for dichotomous items, we can obtain the ICCs for the items using the plot command. However, whereas for dichotomous items there was a single ICC for each item, in the polytomous case there is a separate ICC for each possible item response. The plot command will produce separate ICCs for each item, but we have only included the plot for item Q72 in Figure 9.22 in the interest of saving space.

```
plot(yrbsfoods1000.pcm)
```

This ICC contains separate curves for each potential item response, so that we can see which response is most likely for a given value of θ. The points where the curves cross correspond to the threshold parameters described above. Thus, those with θ greater than approximately -1.008 (the point where the curves for responses 1 and 2 cross) are more likely to report drinking juice 1–3 times during the last 7 days, as opposed to never drinking it. A close examination of the ICCs leads to the following set of conclusions: (1) Individuals with θ less than -1.008 are unlikely to have consumed juice during the last 7 days, (2) those with θ between -1.008 and approximately 0.5 are most likely to report drinking fruit juice 1–3 times in the last week, and (3) respondents with θ greater than 0.5 are most likely to report drinking juice 7+ times during the last 7 days. Notice that category 3 (4–6 times) is never the most likely for any ability level.

Information curves can also be produced for polytomous items, yielding evidence about which items provide maximal information for which levels of the latent trait of interest. The following command produces the IICs for the seven items in our healthy diet scale (see Figure 9.23).

```
plot(yrbsfoods1000.pcm,type=c("IIC"))
```

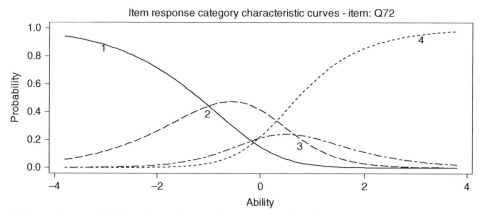

■ **Figure 9.22:**   PCM (Rasch) item characteristic curves for item 72

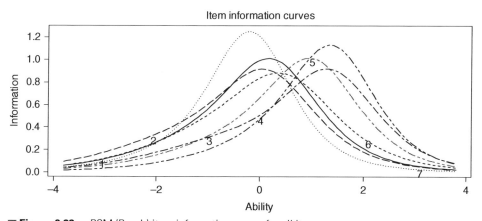

■ **Figure 9.23:**   PCM (Rasch) item information curves for all items

Here we see a curve for each item. In general, more information is obtained at θ values of 0 or higher, meaning that the items do not provide as much estimation accuracy for those who eat a relatively unhealthy diet. Item 7 ("How many times have you had milk during the last 7 days?") provides the greatest amount of information at the lowest level of θ, and item 5 ("How many times have you had carrots during the last 7 days?") provides the greatest amount of information at the highest level of θ. Just as with information in the context of dichotomous items, these values could be used to help construct or revise a scale depending upon who the respondents were most likely to be.

Finally, we assess goodness of fit in much the same way as we did for dichotomous item models. As we have already noted, the optimal approach currently available in R involves the bootstrap test for goodness of fit, which is essentially the same as for the dichotomous IRT models. The null hypothesis is that the model does fit the data. The command to test model fit for the PCM using the bootstrap appears below.

```
GoF.gpcm(yrbsfoods1000.pcm)
```

```
Parametric  Bootstrap  Approximation  to  Pearson  chi-squared
Goodness-of-Fit Measure

Call:
gpcm(data = yrbsfoods1000, constraint = "rasch")

Tobs: 48519.45
# data-sets: 100
p-value: 0.02
```

This result would suggest that the model does not fit the data, given the statistically significant hypothesis test. As with the dichotomous item response models, it will also be necessary to compare the fit of several models in order to determine which provides the optimal fit to the data.

Partial credit model (1PL)

Fitting the PCM in the 1PL context, where a single item discrimination parameter is estimated for all of the items (as opposed to constraining it to be 1 as in the previous model), is nearly identical in R to fitting the Rasch PCM. The 1PL PCM is expressed as:

$$p\left(x_j = k \mid \theta, a, \delta_{jh}\right) = \frac{e^{\sum_{h=0}^{x_j} a\left(\theta - \delta_{jh}\right)}}{e^{\sum_{h=0}^{m_j} a\left(\theta - \delta_{jh}\right)}}.$$

(9.11)

In equation (9.11) a common a parameter is estimated for all of the items on the scale, as opposed to being set equal to 1. In order to fit this model in R, we will use the gpcm command in the ltm library, as we did in the previous example. Note that the difference is in the constraint= subcommand where we specify "1PL" rather than "rasch". The commands to estimate and display the results appear below. Only results for item 72 are displayed in order to save space.

```
yrbsfoods1000.pcm1pl<-gpcm(yrbsfoods1000,constraint
="1PL")
summary(yrbsfoods1000.pcm1pl)

Call:
gpcm(data = yrbsfoods1000, constraint = "1PL")

Model Summary:
   log.Lik            AIC             BIC
-8298.132 16640.26 16748.23

Coefficients:
$Q72
         value std.err    z.value
Catgr.1 -1.327 0.148     -8.960
Catgr.2  1.005 0.153      6.548
Catgr.3 -0.241 0.157     -1.535
Dscrmn   0.657 0.027     24.466
```

Interpretation of the model parameter estimates is precisely the same as described above for the Rasch version of the PCM, and therefore we will not devote much more text to it here. However, it is important to note two things. First, the item discrimination value (Dscrmn) is no longer 1, but rather a common value of 0.657 was estimated for all of the items. This value is positive, which means that individuals with higher levels of the latent trait being measured (reporting a healthy diet) are more likely to provide higher responses to this item; i.e. are more likely to report consuming more juice during the last seven days. Second, notice that the estimates of δ_{jh} for this item are somewhat different, although the general pattern is similar to that of the Rasch PCM. The ICCs (Figure 9.24) and IICs (Figure 9.25) can be obtained using the plot command in conjunction with the proper type option, as below.

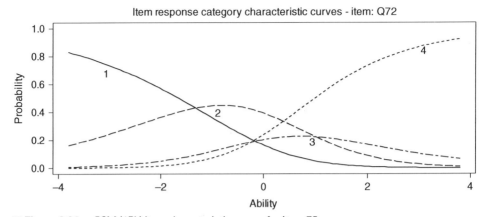

■ **Figure 9.24:** PCM (1PL) item characteristic curves for item 72

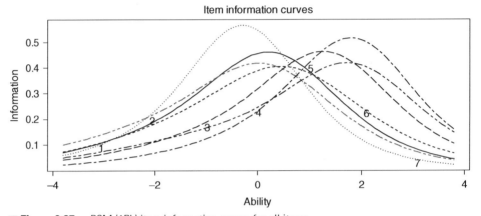

■ **Figure 9.25:** PCM (1PL) item information curves for all items

```
plot(yrbsfoods1000.pcm1pl,type=c("ICC"))
plot(yrbsfoods1000.pcm1pl,type=c("IIC"))
```

Model fit is also tested using the bootstrap as with the PCM Rasch model.

```
GoF.gpcm(yrbsfoods1000.pcm1pl)
```

Parametric Bootstrap Approximation to Pearson chi-squared Goodness-of-Fit Measure

Call:
gpcm(data = yrbsfoods1000, constraint = "1PL")

Tobs: 27142.84
data-sets: 100
p-value: 0.01

As was true with the previous model, the null hypothesis of good model fit to the data is rejected, given that the p-value (0.01) is less than 0.05. At the end of this chapter, we will address comparison of fit for polytomous IRT models. In general, it is very similar to comparing fit for dichotomous models, which we addressed earlier in the chapter. Prior to dealing with the issue of comparing fit, we will discuss two additional models that can be used with polytomous item response data, the generalized partial credit model and the graded response model.

Generalized partial credit model

The **generalized partial credit model (GPCM)** is simply an extension of the PCM in which each item has an individual discrimination parameter estimate, a_j. The model is written as:

$$p\left(x_j = k \mid \theta, a_j, \delta_{jh}\right) = \frac{e^{\sum_{h=0}^{x_j} a_j\left(\theta - \delta_{jh}\right)}}{e^{\sum_{h=0}^{m_j} a_j\left(\theta - \delta_{jh}\right)}}. \tag{9.12}$$

We can fit the GPCM in R using the gpcm command in the ltm library, with the constraint="gpcm" subcommand. The following gives the commands, with the output for Q72.

```
yrbsfoods1000.gpcm<-gpcm(yrbsfoods1000,constraint="
gpcm")
summary(yrbsfoods1000.gpcm)

Call:
gpcm(data = yrbsfoods1000, constraint = "gpcm")
Model Summary:
   log.Lik    AIC       BIC
-8244.734   16545.47  16682.88

Coefficients:
$Q72
           value   std.err   z.value
Catgr.1 -1.513    0.206     -7.341
Catgr.2 1.324     0.238      5.562
Catgr.3 -0.515    0.231     -2.226
Dscrmn   0.503    0.054      9.323
```

From these results, we see that the discrimination parameter is estimated to be 0.503 for this item, and the item thresholds follow a similar pattern to those for the PCMs, though the values have changed with the estimation of unique item

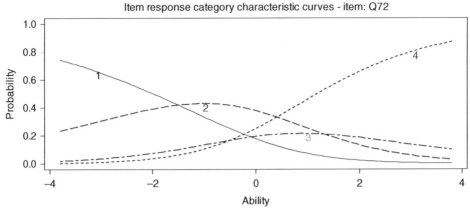

Figure 9.26: GPCM item characteristic curves for item 72

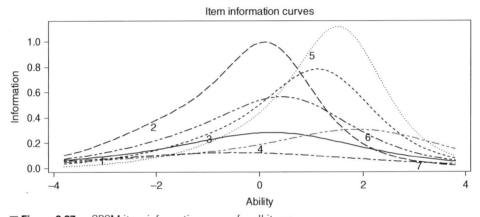

Figure 9.27: GPCM item information curves for all items

discrimination parameters. The ICC (Figure 9.26) and IIC (Figure 9.27) plots are obtained in the usual fashion. Once again ICC results are shown only for item Q72 in order to save space.

```
plot(yrbsfoods1000.gpcm)
plot(yrbsfoods1000.gpcm,type=c("IIC"))
```

One interesting point to note is that when individual discrimination values are estimated for each item, the shapes of the IICs are dramatically impacted. In particular, the curve for item 7 (Q79) is nearly flat, indicating that it provides very little information across the entire spectrum of the ability scale. Its item parameter estimates appear below, including the discrimination value, which is quite low at 0.296. This result demonstrates the fact that items with low discrimination values provide relatively little in the way of information when compared with those items that have high discrimination values.

```
$Q79
value std.err z.value
Catgr.1 -0.863 0.330 -2.612
Catgr.2 1.656 0.434 3.819
Catgr.3 -3.415 0.601 -5.680
Dscrmn 0.296 0.039 7.493
```

Finally, model fit is assessed using the bootstrapped chi-square test, as with the other models.

```
GoF.gpcm(yrbsfoods1000.gpcm)

Parametric  Bootstrap  Approximation  to  Pearson  chi-squared
Goodness-of-Fit Measure

Call:
gpcm(data = yrbsfoods1000, constraint = "gpcm")

Tobs: 27017.83
# data-sets: 100
p-value: 0.01
```

The results of the hypothesis test indicate that the GPCM does not provide a good fit to the data, given the statistically significant result ($p = 0.01$).

Graded response model

The final model for polytomous data that we will examine here is the **graded response model (GRM)** developed by Samejima (1969). As with the GPCM, the GRM provides unique parameter estimates for each item, as well as estimates for item discrimination parameters. However, the models differ in regard to how they conceptualize the transitions from one response option to another. With the GPCM these transitions are seen as occurring in a binary fashion. In other words, GPCM models the likelihood of responding with a 1 versus a 2, or a 2 versus a 3, or a 3 versus a 4. On the other hand, the GRM expresses the transition in terms of the likelihood of an individual selecting a particular response option or higher, versus responding with a lower option. In this framework, a response of 2 or higher is modeled against a response of 1, and a response of 3 or higher is modeled against a response of 1 or 2. The model itself is expressed as:

$$p\left(x_j = k \mid \theta, a, \delta_{jh}\right) = \frac{e^{a_j\left(\theta - \delta_{jh}\right)}}{1 + e^{a_j\left(\theta - \delta_{jh}\right)}}.$$ (9.13)

The parameters in equation (9.13) are similar to those in (9.12), though the interpretation of δ_{jh} is somewhat different, given that it provides information about cumulative transitions in item response likelihoods, rather than dichotomous transitions. In addition, unlike with the GPCM, the δ_{jh} from the GRM will always be in ascending order, reflecting this cumulative transition.

We can fit the GRM using the grm command in the ltm library.

```
yrbsfoods1000.grm<-grm(yrbsfoods1000)
summary(yrbsfoods1000.grm)
Call:
grm(data = yrbsfoods1000)

Model Summary:
   log.Lik           AIC        BIC
-8233.082 16522.16 16659.58

Coefficients:
$Q72
             value
Extrmt1 -1.721
Extrmt2  0.209
Extrmt3  1.173
Dscrmn   0.948
```

Here we see that the values of the thresholds for the GRM are -1.721, 0.209, and 1.173. Thus, the transition point from a response of 1 (Never drink juice in last 7 days) to 2 or higher is at a θ value of -1.721. Likewise, the transition from a response of 1 or 2 versus 3 or 4 occurs at a θ of 0.209. The ICCs (Figure 9.28) and IICs (Figure 9.29) for the GRM are obtained in the usual way. Their interpretation is the same as that for the GPCM.

```
plot(yrbsfoods1000.grm,type=c("ICC"))
plot(yrbsfoods1000.grm,type=c("IIC"))
```

As of this writing, there is not a function in R to conduct the goodness of fit test for the GRM.

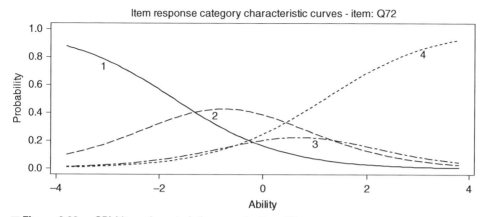

■ **Figure 9.28:**   GRM item characteristic curves for item 72

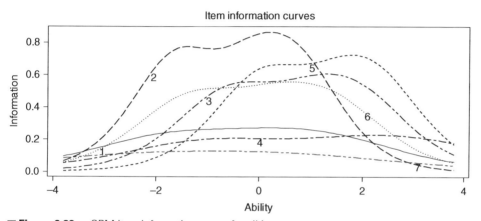

■ **Figure 9.29:**   GRM item information curves for all items

Comparing model fit for the polytomous item response models

We have just investigated the healthy diet items using a number of polytomous item response models. The results were generally similar across these models, though by no means identical, leading to the natural question regarding which model is to be preferred. Comparing the fit across models is done in much the same fashion as it was for dichotomous items, as we shall see. For comparing the fit of the PCM and GPCM, we can use the likelihood ratio test that we employed with the dichotomous item models. In this case, the PCM is nested within the GPCM. This test can be carried out using the anova command in R.

```
anova.gpcm(yrbsfoods1000.pcm,yrbsfoods1000.gpcm)
```

```
Likelihood Ratio Table
```

```
                            AIC       BIC       log.Lik LRT     df p.value
yrbsfoods1000.pcm   16751.70 16854.76 -8354.85              21
yrbsfoods1000.gpcm  16545.47 16682.88 -8244.73 220.23 28 <0.001
```

The results of the test are statistically significant ($p < 0.001$), leading to the rejection of the null hypothesis of equivalent model fit. We can also compare the fit of the models using the AIC and BIC, which also appear in the likelihood ratio results table. The lower values, indicating superior fit, belong to the GPCM. Thus, taking these results together, we would conclude that the GPCM provides significantly better fit to the data than does the PCM. In other words, estimating individual discrimination values for the items improves model fit.

It is not possible to directly compare the fit of the GRM with either the PCM or GPCM using the likelihood ratio test because these models are not nested in one another. However, their fit can be compared by examining their relative efficiency (RE) with one another. Recall that RE is the ratio of test information provided by each of the models, across the latent trait space. RE can be calculated for essentially the entire range of θ, or for a subset of θ that is of some interest to the researcher. In this case, we are interested in the RE across essentially all possible values of θ, which we define as between -10 and 10.

```
information(yrbsfoods1000.gpcm,c(-10,10))

Call:
gpcm(data = yrbsfoods1000, constraint = "gpcm")

Total Information = 15.36
Information in (-10, 10) = 15.36 (100%)
Based on all the items
information(yrbsfoods1000.grm,c(-10,10))

Call:
grm(data = yrbsfoods1000)

Total Information = 16.83
Information in (-10, 10) = 16.83 (100%)
Based on all the items
```

Using the item information values, we can then calculate the RE as:

$$RE_{GPCM,GRM} = \frac{15.36}{16.83} = 0.913.$$

This result indicates that the GPCM provides 91.3% as much information as the GRM. Put another way, the GRM provides more information about the latent trait, propensity to report eating a healthy diet, making it preferable to the GPCM when the goal is to estimate the latent trait. Finally, the AIC/BIC of the models can be compared with one another to ascertain relative model fit. In this case, the AIC and BIC of the GRM (16522.16 and 16659.58, respectively) are lower than those of the GPCM (16545.47 and 16682.88, respectively), also supporting that the GRM fits the data somewhat better than the GPCM.

SUMMARY

In this chapter we have focused on the estimation of IRT model parameters using R. In particular, we learned how to fit models for dichotomous and ordered polytomous items, as well as how to compare the fit of such models, and how to interpret them using the parameter estimates as well as ICCs and IICs. We found that there are a number of such models available to the researcher, and several ways in which their fit can be compared in order to identify the optimal model for a set of data. When selecting the optimal model, it is important for the researcher applying IRT to be cognizant not only of the statistical aspects of parameter estimation and model fit, but also the conceptual basis upon which the scale was developed. Such conceptual issues will inform the initial selection of potential candidate models to be fit in the first place.

FURTHER READING

de Ayala, R.J. (2009). *The Theory and Practice of Item Response Theory*. New York: The Guilford Press.

Embretson, S.E., & Reise, S.P. (2000). *Item Response Theory for Psychologists*. Mahwah, NJ: Lawrence Erlbaum and Associates, Publishers.

Hambleton, R.K., Swaminathan, H., & Rogers, H.J. (1991). *Fundamentals of Item Response Theory*. Thousand Oaks, CA: Sage.

McDonald, R.P. (1999). *Test Theory: A Unified Treatment*. Mahwah, NJ: Lawrence Erlbaum and Associates, Publishers.

Nering, M.L., & Ostini, R. (2010). *Handbook of Polytomous Item Response Theory Models*. New York: Routledge.

REFERENCES

Centers for Disease Control and Prevention. (2009). Youth Risk Behavior Survey. Available at: www.cdc.gov/yrbs. Accessed on 08/22/14.

SUMMARY
9

FURTHER
READING
9

REFERENCES
9

de Ayala, R.J. (2009). *The Theory and Practice of Item Response Theory.* New York: The Guilford Press.

Ebel, R.L. (1969). Expected reliability as a function of choices per item. *Educational and Psychological Measurement*, 19, 171–9.

Hambleton, R.K., Swaminathan, H., & Rogers, H.J. (1991). *Fundamentals of Item Response Theory.* Thousand Oaks, CA: Sage.

Lord, F.M. (1980). *Applications of Item Response Theory to Practical Testing Problems.* Hillsdale, NJ: Erlbaum.

Lord, F.M., & Novick, M.R. (1968). *Statistical Theories of Mental Test Scores.* Reading, MA: Addison-Wesley Publishing Company, Inc.

Masters, G.N. (1982). A Rasch model for partial credit scoring. *Psychometrika*, 47, 149–74.

Muthén, B., & Lehman. J. (1985). Multiple-group IRT modeling: Applications to item bias analysis. *Journal of Educational Statistics*, 10, 133–42.

Nunnally, J.C., & Bernstein, I.H. (1994). *PsychometricTheory.* New York: McGraw-Hill.

Samejima, F. (1969). Estimation of latent ability using a response pattern of graded scores. *Psychometrika Monograph Supplement*, 17.

Tam, H.P., & Li, Y.H. (1997). *Is the use of the difference likelihood ratio chi-square statistic for comparing nested IRT models justifiable?* Paper presented at the Annual Meeting of the American Educational Research Association, Chicago, IL, April 1997.

Thissen, D.J., Steinberg, L., & Wainer, H. (1993). Detection of differential item functioning using the parameters of item response theory models. In P.W. Holland, & H. Wainer (eds), *Differential Item Functioning* (pp. 67–113). Hillsdale, NJ: Erlbaum.

## Chapter 10

FURTHER TOPICS IN ITEM RESPONSE THEORY

INTRODUCTION

In the previous chapter we learned how to fit a variety of item response theory (IRT) models for dichotomous and polytomous data, including the Rasch, 1PL, 2PL, 3PL, PCM, GPCM, and GRM. These models rested on three primary assumptions about the data: (1) The function relating the latent trait, θ, and the item response was monotonically increasing, (2) the latent trait was unidimensional, and (3) conditioning on the latent trait, the item responses were independent of one another (local independence). In addition, there is an assumption made that the item parameter estimates are equivalent across subgroups in the population. The focus of this chapter is on models and methods for dealing with item response data that do not conform to these assumptions, and on the assessment of certain of these using R. We will begin by examining how to assess the unidimensionality and local independence assumptions, and then turn our attention to fitting multidimensional IRT models in R. We will then investigate methods for testing whether IRT model parameters are equivalent across groups, after which we will finish the chapter by learning about a nonparametric approach to IRT for use when it is not reasonable to assume a particular model form underlying the item responses.

ASSESSING UNIDIMENSIONALITY

A primary assumption underlying both dichotomous and polytomous IRT models is that there is only one latent trait being measured by the set of items, also known as unidimensionality. When this assumption is violated, estimation of both person and item parameters can be compromised (Reckase *et al.* 1986; Reckase, 1985; Ansley & Forsyth, 1985). Therefore, it is important for researchers using the models described in Chapter 9 to be sure that they are in fact dealing with a unidimensional construct. There are several approaches for assessing the unidimensionality assumption, two of which are available using R, and will therefore be described here. We do want to emphasize that while these methods are both proven, there do exist other methods that are not available in R, but which have also been shown to be effective tools in dimensionality assessment, chief among these being the conditional-covariance-based methods DETECT and DIMTEST (Stout *et al.* 1996). The approaches that we will examine here are exploratory factor analysis (EFA) especially designed for item response data, and the bootstrap modified parallel analysis test (BMPAT), which is based on the parallel analysis methodology for EFA described in Chapter 2.

In order to demonstrate the use of EFA for item response data, we will focus on the sixth-grade math test data that we fit with IRT models in Chapter 9. Recall that this test consisted of ten dichotomously scored items. The approach we use here is very closely associated with the EFA methodology described in Chapter 2. However, in that case the observed data were assumed to be continuous in nature (and multivariate normal when using the maximum likelihood approach). However, clearly item response data are not continuous, and cannot be assumed to be multivariate normal. Indeed, researchers have found that using continuous data EFA with dichotomous item response data will result in the identification of spurious factors, leading to incorrect conclusions regarding data dimensionality (Hattie, 1985). Therefore, we will need to make use of an alternative approach for fitting EFA models to the dichotomous item data in the math examination. We fit such models using the mirt command in the mirt library in R. Below, we fit one- and two-factor EFA models to the math data using the full information maximum likelihood expectation maximization (EM) algorithm of Bock and Aitkin (1981). The researcher can also use the Metropolis–Hastings approach for this purpose outlined by Cai (2010). The fit of the models can then be compared using the AIC and BIC as well as a likelihood ratio test, all of which have been described in previous chapters. If the two-factor model is found to provide a superior fit to the one-factor, then we would conclude that the data are not unidimensional. We could then further explore the nature of the multidimensionality through an examination of factor loadings, much as we did in Chapter 2 for EFA with continuous observed variables. The R commands to fit the one- and two-factor models to the math data, and then to conduct the likelihood ratio test, appear below, followed by the output for the hypothesis test.

```
library(mirt)
attach(mathg6)

efa.math.1factor<-mirt(mathg6,1)
efa.math.2factor<-mirt(mathg6,2)
```

```
anova(efa.math.1factor, efa.math.2factor)
Model 1: mirt(data = mathg6, model = 1)
Model 2: mirt(data = mathg6, model = 2)
```

	AIC	AICc	SABIC	BIC	logLik	X2	df	p
1	72895.26	72895.37	72969.14	73032.7	−36427.63	NaN	NaN	NaN
2	72777.81	72778.06	72884.95	72977.1	−36359.91	135.443	9	0

The statistically significant results ($p < 0.05$), along with the lower values for the information indces (AIC, BIC, AICc, and SABIC) suggest that the two-factor model fits the data better than the one-factor model. Therefore, we would conclude that the assumption of unidimensionality has not been met, and that in fact multiple latent traits underlie the responses to the ten math items. If we were interested in learning more about the nature of these latent traits, we could assess whether a third factor is necessary; i.e. does a three-factor model fit the data better than a two-factor model? Once we decide on the optimal model, we can examine the factor loadings to ascertain which items appear to group together. Interpretation of these factors would then proceed much as with EFA using continuous variables, through an examination of item content in order to determine the nature of the factors (dimensions) themselves. The R code and model fit comparison results for the three-factor model appear below.

```
anova(efa.math.2factor, efa.math.3factor)

Model 1: mirt(data = mathg6, model = 2)
Model 2: mirt(data = mathg6, model = 3)
```

	AIC	AICc	SABIC	BIC	logLik	X2	df	p
1	72777.81	72778.06	72884.95	72977.10	−36359.91	NaN	NaN	NaN
2	72771.92	72772.31	72908.61	73026.18	−36348.96	21.894	8	0.0051

While the likelihood ratio is statistically significant, indicating a difference in model fit, the information indices provide a more mixed picture, with AIC and AICc indicating better fit (lower values) for the three-factor model, but the SABIC and BIC indicating better fit for the two-factor model. Given this mixed result, we should consider the interpretability of the factors and the goal of retaining the most parsimonious solution possible when deciding on the optimal model. In order to obtain the factor loadings for each solution, we would use the following commands.

```
summary(efa.math.2factor)

Rotation: oblimin

Rotated factor loadings:
```

```
        F_1   F_2   h2
v1   -0.066 0.642 0.358
v2    0.010 0.625 0.400
v3    0.160 0.453 0.331
v4    0.472 0.253 0.451
v5    0.304 0.302 0.311
v6    0.366 0.384 0.475
v7    0.245 0.242 0.201
v8    0.591 0.151 0.495
v9    0.888 -0.078 0.699
v10  0.414 0.361 0.507

Rotated SS loadings: 1.848 1.529

Factor correlations:

     F_1   F_2
F_1 1.000 0.691
F_2 0.691 1.000

summary(efa.math.3factor)

Rotation: oblimin

Rotated factor loadings:

        F_1     F_2     F_3    h2
v1   -0.087  0.623  -0.086 0.365
v2   -0.009  0.593  -0.102 0.399
v3    0.135  0.428  -0.102 0.332
v4    0.451  0.265  -0.040 0.457
v5    0.270  0.284  -0.105 0.313
v6    0.342  0.389  -0.057 0.481
v7    0.106  0.079  -0.566 0.430
v8    0.551  0.144  -0.101 0.497
v9    0.862 -0.070  -0.056 0.707
v10   0.432  0.449   0.153 0.564

Rotated SS loadings: 1.664 1.459 0.401

Factor correlations:

        F_1   F_2     F_3
F_1   1.000 0.666  -0.408
```

```
F_2   0.666 1.000 -0.373
F_3  -0.408 -0.373 1.000
```

We could use the item content in an attempt to better understand the nature of the factors, and attempt to make interpretive sense of the results. This in turn would allow us to decide which factor solution might be optimal. However, as to the larger question of whether the assumption of unidimensionality holds, we can conclude from these results that it does not.

A second approach for assessing the assumption of unidimensionality is to use the **bootstrap modified parallel analysis test** (BMPAT; Finch & Monahan, 2008). The BMPAT is an extension of modified parallel analysis (Budescu, Cohen, & Ben-Simon, 1997), which itself is based on Horn's (1965) parallel analysis method for determining the number of factors that was described in Chapter 2. The BMPAT works using the following steps:

Step 1. Estimate a unidimensional IRT model for the data.
Step 2. Conduct an item factor analysis as described above, and save the eigenvalues.
Step 3. Simulate θ for N examinees based on the θ distribution for the actual data.
Step 4. Simulate unidimensional item responses using the θ values from step 3 and the item parameters from step 1.
Step 5. Conduct item EFA on the data simulated in step 4, and save the eigenvalues.
Step 6. Repeat steps 3–5 many (e.g. 1000) times.
Step 7. Compare the eigenvalues for each factor from the original data (step 2) with the distributions of eigenvalues for each factor created in steps 3–5. If the observed eigenvalue for a given factor is greater than or equal to the 95th percentile of the simulated eigenvalue distribution, then we conclude that the observed factor is present in the data.
Step 8. Repeat step 7 until the observed eigenvalue does not exceed the 95th percentile for a given factor.

If our primary goal is to test the null hypothesis of unidimensionality, then we need only concern ourselves with the test of the second eigenvalue. If it is statistically significant, then we conclude that the data are multidimensional, whereas if it is not then we conclude that the data are unidimensional. The function to conduct this test, unidimTest, is part of the ltm library. Therefore, we need to make sure that we have loaded it prior to conducting the analysis.

```
library(ltm)
unidimTest(mathg6.3pl,mathg6)
```

Unidimensionality Check using Modified Parallel Analysis

```
Call:
tpm(data = mathg6)
```

```
Matrix of tertachoric correlations
      v1     v2     v3     v4     v5     v6     v7     v8     v9     v10
v1  1.0000 0.3737 0.2881 0.3175 0.2920 0.3763 0.2448 0.2942 0.2723 0.3858
v2  0.3737 1.0000 0.3965 0.3348 0.3024 0.4005 0.2664 0.3759 0.3484 0.3655
v3  0.2881 0.3965 1.0000 0.3861 0.3168 0.3726 0.2703 0.3435 0.3826 0.3359
v4  0.3175 0.3348 0.3861 1.0000 0.4146 0.4797 0.2966 0.4218 0.5302 0.4383
v5  0.2920 0.3024 0.3168 0.4146 1.0000 0.3860 0.2823 0.4017 0.3969 0.3601
v6  0.3763 0.4005 0.3726 0.4797 0.3860 1.0000 0.3093 0.4683 0.5069 0.4403
v7  0.2448 0.2664 0.2703 0.2966 0.2823 0.3093 1.0000 0.3354 0.3453 0.1932
v8  0.2942 0.3759 0.3435 0.4218 0.4017 0.4683 0.3354 1.0000 0.5771 0.4764
v9  0.2723 0.3484 0.3826 0.5302 0.3969 0.5069 0.3453 0.5771 1.0000 0.4734
v10 0.3858 0.3655 0.3359 0.4383 0.3601 0.4403 0.1932 0.4764 0.4734 1.0000
```

```
Alternative hypothesis: the second eigenvalue of the observed
data is substantially larger than the second eigenvalue of data
under the assumed IRT model
```

```
Second eigenvalue in the observed data: 0.4498
Average of second eigenvalues in Monte Carlo samples: 0.3215
Monte Carlo samples: 100
p-value: 0.0099
```

In this case, we selected the 3PL model for simulating the data, based upon results in Chapter 9 that suggested the 3PL may be optimal for these data. The results of the BMPAT were statistically significant for the second eigenvalue ($p = 0.0099$), meaning that the data are not unidimensional. This result matches what we found using the likelihood ratio test. In addition to the hypothesis test, this function also provides the tetrachoric correlations among the items.

ASSESSING LOCAL INDEPENDENCE

A second assumption underlying the use of standard IRT models is that, conditioning on the latent trait being measured, item responses are independent of one another. This assumption can also be expressed by saying that any correlations among item responses are due to the common latent trait that they are measuring. There are a number of methods available for scrutinizing the assumption of local independence. Kim, de Ayala, Ferdous, and Nering (2011) provide an excellent review of these indices, as well as reporting the results of a simulation study comparing their performance for dichotomous items. The results of their study suggest that one of the best methods for assessing the local independence assumption remains **Yen's Q_3 statistic** (Yen, 1984; 1993). This approach is relatively easy to carry out, and has consistently been shown to be perhaps the most effective method available for this purpose. Q_3 is simply the correlation between residuals for pairs of items, based on the appropriate IRT model. In order to calculate Q_3, the researcher would first determine which IRT model fits the data best. Once the optimal model is decided upon, it is then used to predict item response values for each individual in the sample. The residual for each item is then calculated as the difference between the actual item response (coded as 1 or 0 in the dichotomous case) and the model-predicted item response. This residual represents the portion of the item response that is not associated with the underlying IRT model. Therefore, the correlation between the residuals for a pair of items represents the relationship between the portion of the items that is not associated with the latent trait being measured or the underlying model. If local independence holds, this correlation should be near zero. Yen (1993) suggested a cut value of 0.2 such that values greater than this suggest a violation of the local independence assumption. Other cut values and approaches for using Q_3 have been suggested (e.g. Chen & Thissen, 1997), but the 0.2 value has persisted and been shown to provide reasonable accuracy for correctly detecting violations of local independence (Kim, *et al.*, 2011).

In order to estimate Q_3 for a pair of items using R, the following command sequence can be used. Note that in the example, we focus on the items 1 and 2 pair, so that similar code would need to be used for each item pair of interest. It is also important to note that, as of the writing of this book, the R library `sirt` does have a function to estimate Q_3 for all pairs of items automatically, assuming the correctness of a Rasch model for the data. However, given the importance of selecting the correct model to the performance of Q_3 (Yen, 1993), we believe that it may be preferable at this time to use the following commands in R unless the Rasch model is determined to be optimal. In the following set of commands, we assume that 3PL is the optimal model for the sixth-grade math data, based on the results we presented in Chapter 9. The first step prior to employing the techniques described below is for the researcher to ascertain the optimal model and then fit that model to the data. The following commands are then used after the model is fit.

```
library(boot)
prob1<-0
prob2<-0
resid1<-0
resid2<-0
```

```
mathg6.3pl.thetas<-factor.scores(mathg6.3pl)
for (i in 1:673){
prob1[i]<-0.01+(1-.01)*(1/(1+exp(-
1.7*(1.01)*(mathg6.3pl.thetas$score.dat[i,13]-(-1.90))))))
prob2[i]<-0.01+(1-.01)*(1/(1+exp(-
1.7*(1.13)*(mathg6.3pl.thetas$score.dat[i,13]-(-1.1))))))
resid1[i]<-mathg6.3pl.thetas$score.dat[i,1]-prob1[i]
resid2[i]<-mathg6.3pl.thetas$score.dat[i,2]-prob2[i]
}
items12<-cbind(resid1,resid2)
weights<-mathg6.3pl.thetas$score.dat[,11]
corr(items12, w=weights)
```

We will need to load the **boot** library because some of its functions will be referenced indirectly in the other commands. We then initialize the variables `prob1`, `prob2`, `resid1`, and `resid2`, corresponding to the predicted and residual values for the first two items in the instrument. In the next line, the estimated latent trait values for each individual in the sample, based on the 3PL model, are created using the `factor.scores` command as applied to the 3PL model estimates for the sixth-grade math data. Again, this code presupposes that the appropriate model (3PL) was already fit to the data and saved in the object `mathg6.3pl`. Next, we calculate the probability of a correct item response (`prob1` and `prob2`) for each item, based on the 3PL model parameters and the estimated value of the latent trait for each individual. The item parameter values are taken directly from the output for the 3PL model that appears in Chapter 9. The latent trait estimates themselves are in the following object: `mathg6.3pl.thetas$score.dat[i,13]`.

Note that the index `i` refers to each row containing a unique value of θ, of which there are 673. In addition, the 13 following the `i` refers to the column in the output from the `factor.scores` command that contains the actual values of θ.

To further clarify how we obtained these values to put into the program, let us first see how the number of unique thetas can be ascertained from R. The object `mathg6.3pl.thetas$score.dat` contains the actual estimates of the latent trait, so that, using the `nrow` command as follows, we can find out how many unique such values there are.

```
nrow(mathg6.3pl.thetas$score.dat)
[1] 673
```

In order to see which column contains the actual estimates themselves, we can simply print out the results using the following command. Only the first 3 of the 673 rows are displayed below in order to save space.

```
mathg6.3pl.thetas$score.dat
  v1 v2 v3 v4 v5 v6 v7 v8 v9 v10 Obs Exp    z1      se.z1
1 0 0 0 0 0 0 0 0 0 0  17 17.560  -2.2299873435 0.5684779
2 0 0 0 0 0 0 0 0 0 1  32 29.311  -1.7335187372 0.5089021
3 0 0 0 0 0 0 0 0 1 0   5  4.239  -2.1749562506 0.6014286
```

We can see that the first ten columns correspond to the actual item response values, followed by a column containing the number of individuals with that item response pattern. Therefore, there were 17 respondents who missed all 10 items on the test, 32 individuals who missed items 1–9, but got item 10 correct, and 5 who missed items 1–8 and 10 but got item 9 correct. The Exp column contains the expected (predicted) number of individuals with each score pattern, assuming the correctness of the model. The z1 column includes the estimates of θ for each item response pattern, and the se.z1 column includes the standard error for each of these. Thus, if we had 20 items, rather than 10, the object mathg6.3pl.thetas$score.dat[i,13] would instead look like mathg6.3pl.thetas$score.dat[i,23], reflecting that the latent trait estimates appear in the z1 column, which will always be three columns after the last item response value. After the predicted item responses are calculated, the residuals for each item are then determined by subtracting the actual item response (e.g. for mathg6.3pl.thetas$score.dat[i,1] item 1) from the model-predicted value. Finally, the number of individuals with each response pattern are saved in a vector we call weights, which is then used in the next line to weight the residual values appropriately, reflecting the number of individuals with each response pattern. The resulting correlation is 0.01398912, which is well below the cutoff of 0.2, indicating that conditioning on the latent trait and 3PL model, the local independence assumption holds for items 1 and 2. In order to assess this assumption for the entire scale, we would need to replicate the previous code for all item pairs.

FITTING MULTIDIMENSIONAL MODELS IN R

When data are known to be multidimensional in nature, such that the items measure more than one latent trait, we will want to fit a model appropriate to this reality. In this section, we consider two common **multidimensional item response theory (MIRT) models**. In many respects, MIRT models are similar in form to the CFA models that we discussed in Chapter 3, with multiple indicators (items in the case of MIRT) associated with each latent trait, and typically no indicator associated with more than one trait. The first model that we will examine is the standard compensatory 2PL MIRT model, which can be expressed as:

$$P\left(u_i = 1 \mid \underline{\theta_i}\right) = \frac{e^{\sum_{k=1}^{K} a_{ik}\left(\theta_{jk} + d_i\right)}}{1 + e^{\sum_{k=1}^{K} a_{ik}\left(\theta_{jk} + d_i\right)}}, \tag{10.1}$$

where

a_{ik} = Discrimination for item i on latent trait k

θ_{jk} = Level of latent trait k for person j

d_i = Difficulty for item i.

The interpretation of the item and person parameters is much as in the unidimensional case, with the exception that there are multiple latent traits of interest so that we have more than one item discrimination value and more than one θ estimate for each individual in the sample. This model is known as compensatory MIRT because the impact of the latent traits is summative, so that deficits on one can be at least partially offset by higher values on the other.

In addition to the standard item discrimination and difficulty parameters, it is also possible to obtain multidimensional discrimination and difficulty parameter estimates from the MIRT model. These statistics provide overall measures of item characteristics, in contrast to the unidimensional information contained in the a_{ik} and d_i parameters of (10.1). These multidimensional item parameters are calculated as follows:

$$\text{MDISC} = \sqrt{\sum_{K=1}^{k} a_{ik}^2} \tag{10.2}$$

$$\text{MDIFF} = \frac{-d_i}{\sqrt{\text{MDISC}}} \tag{10.3}$$

As the motivating example for fitting the standard compensatory MIRT model, we will use a dataset containing 32 items from the law school admissions test (LSAT). Based on the test map, there should exist three underlying latent traits, each associated with a different paragraph that examinees are asked to read and about which they are presented with multiple items. We will estimate the compensatory

MIRT model, assuming that the proposed structure is correctly specified. The data (`fulldata`) are coded as 0 (incorrect) or 1 (correct), and the R code necessary to fit the model appears below. Note that the items are simply referred to by their number, and are associated with the appropriate latent trait (F1, F2, F3) following the = and separated by commas. We name the model `model.10.1`, and specify it using the `mirt.model` command. The SE=TRUE subcommand requests the estimation of standard errors for the item parameters, which are then used to construct their 95% confidence intervals.

```
library(mirt)
model.10.1<-mirt.model('
F1=7,9,10,11,13,15,17,18,21,22,24,27,31
F2=1,3,6,8,16,29,32
F3=2,4,5,12,14,19,20,23,25,26,28,30')

model.10.1.fit<-mirt(fulldata, model.10.1, SE=TRUE)
```

In order to obtain the model parameter estimates in the context of factor analysis (i.e. factor loadings), we use the following command:

```
summary(mod1)

Factor loadings metric:
          F1    F2    F3    h2
Item.1  0.000 0.557 0.000 0.3100
Item.2  0.000 0.000 0.680 0.4621
Item.3  0.000 0.464 0.000 0.2154
Item.4  0.000 0.000 0.378 0.1425
Item.5  0.000 0.000 0.542 0.2940
Item.6  0.000 0.653 0.000 0.4270
Item.7  0.569 0.000 0.000 0.3233
Item.8  0.000 0.449 0.000 0.2017
Item.9  0.358 0.000 0.000 0.1280
Item.10 0.519 0.000 0.000 0.2691
Item.11 0.690 0.000 0.000 0.4755
Item.12 0.000 0.000 0.144 0.0209
Item.13 0.555 0.000 0.000 0.3076
Item.14 0.000 0.000 0.622 0.3869
Item.15 0.660 0.000 0.000 0.4351
Item.16 0.000 0.488 0.000 0.2378
Item.17 0.687 0.000 0.000 0.4722
Item.18 0.683 0.000 0.000 0.4662
Item.19 0.000 0.000 0.378 0.1431
Item.20 0.000 0.000 0.639 0.4078
Item.21 0.388 0.000 0.000 0.1505
```

```
Item.22 0.660 0.000 0.000 0.4360
Item.23 0.000 0.000 0.412 0.1696
Item.24 0.615 0.000 0.000 0.3779
Item.25 0.000 0.000 0.500 0.2498
Item.26 0.000 0.000 0.664 0.4408
Item.27 0.703 0.000 0.000 0.4944
Item.28 0.000 0.000 0.469 0.2199
Item.29 0.000 0.611 0.000 0.3729
Item.30 0.000 0.000 0.188 0.0353
Item.31 0.696 0.000 0.000 0.4839
Item.32 0.000 0.101 0.000 0.0103

SS loadings: 4.82 1.775 2.973

Factor covariance:

   F1 F2 F3
F1 1 0  0
F2 0 1  0
F3 0 0  1
```

The resulting output includes the factor loadings, and the proportion of variance in the item explained by the factor solution (h2), known as the communality. This value is equal to the sum of the squared factor loadings.

The parameters produced by the standard MIRT model are in the metric common to factor analysis, so that the values above are factor loadings and not item discrimination and difficulty values. However, when working with item response data, we may prefer having the estimates in the metrics of item discrimination and difficulty. McDonald (1999) shows how these factor analysis parameters are directly linked to the IRT parameters that we are familiar with from Chapters 9 and 10. In order to obtain these from R, we simply use the coef command as below.

```
coef(model.10.1)
$Item.1
        a1    a2     a3   d      g  u
par     0     1.162  0    -1.157 0  1
CI_2.5  NA    0.740  NA   -1.428 NA NA
CI_97.5 NA    1.584  NA   -0.885 NA NA
```

Only the results for item 1 are displayed here, in order to save space. The resulting output includes a discrimination parameter estimate for each item on each factor (a1, a2, and a3), the item difficulty estimate (d), and the 95% confidence intervals for each. The g and u columns include the possible item responses, 0 and 1. For item 1, the discrimination parameter estimate is 1.162, with a 95% confidence interval of 0.740 to 1.584. The item difficulty estimate is −1.157 with a 95% confidence interval of −1.428 to −0.885.

BIFACTOR MODEL

A second very common way in which MIRT models can be specified is as a **bifactor model.** With the bifactor model, each item is associated with a general factor, and with what is called a specific factor. There is only a single general factor with which all items are associated, and then multiple general factors with which subsets of the items are associated. As an example, rather than conceive of each of the 32 LSAT items as being uniquely associated with a single latent trait based on the paragraph to which it refers, we might think of each item as being associated with the single general trait of aptitude for practicing law, and also associated with a unique paragraph-based latent trait. Thus, the item would have two factor loadings/discrimination parameters, one for the general latent trait and one for the specific latent trait. This model differs from the general compensatory MIRT model in that for the bifactor model, each item is associated with two dimensions. However, at a more basic level, it also represents a different way in which we might view the mechanism underlying item responses. Researchers deciding which approach to use should consider what they believe to be the underlying item response mechanism, and make decisions regarding which is optimal accordingly.

In order to fit the bifactor model to the 32 items of the LSAT described previously, we would use the following commands. There is an implicit assumption that each item is associated with the general factor. However, we must explicitly indicate which items belong to which of the specific factors. This is done by creating an object called specific, followed by a listing of which items are expected to be associated with which specific factors, by number. Thus, the first item is associated with specific factor 2, the second item with specific factor 3, and so on. We then use the bifactor command to fit the data, indicating which dataset to use (fulldata), the name of the list containing the link between items and the specific factors (specific), and whether we would like to obtain standard errors for the estimates, which we do.

```
specific <- c(2,3,2,3,3,2,1,2,1,1,1,3,1,3,1,2,1,1,3,3
,1,1,3,1,3,3,1,3,2,3,1,2)
lsat.bifactor <- bfactor(fulldata, specific, SE=TRUE)
summary(lsat.bifactor)
coef(lsat.bifactor)
```

The resulting output appears below. Note that the IRT parameter estimates are only presented for item 1 in order to save space.

```
Factor loadings metric:
         G      S1      S2      S3     h2
Item.1  0.4081 0.0000 0.2297 0.0000 0.21932
Item.2  0.6201 0.0000 0.0000 0.3383 0.49892
Item.3  0.5575 0.0000-0.0742 0.0000 0.31632
Item.4  0.2815 0.0000 0.0000 0.3102 0.17546
Item.5  0.4782 0.0000 0.0000 0.2536 0.29305
Item.6  0.5349 0.0000 0.2740 0.0000 0.36115
Item.7  0.4699 0.4307 0.0000 0.0000 0.40629
Item.8  0.3536 0.0000 0.2752 0.0000 0.20076
Item.9  0.2171 0.5197 0.0000 0.0000 0.31726
Item.10 0.4834 0.3725 0.0000 0.0000 0.37236
Item.11 0.6390 0.3456 0.0000 0.0000 0.52768
Item.12 0.0707 0.0000 0.0000 0.1578 0.02992
Item.13 0.5197 0.2793 0.0000 0.0000 0.34815
Item.14 0.4804 0.0000 0.0000 0.4553 0.43813
Item.15 0.5947 0.2548 0.0000 0.0000 0.41858
Item.16 0.3891 0.0000 0.2063 0.0000 0.19393
Item.17 0.6607 0.1323 0.0000 0.0000 0.45406
Item.18 0.7161 0.0786 0.0000 0.0000 0.51903
Item.19 0.4529 0.0000 0.0000 0.0172 0.20541
Item.20 0.6589 0.0000 0.0000 0.1762 0.46515
Item.21 0.2759 0.3557 0.0000 0.0000 0.20265
Item.22 0.7010-0.0139 0.0000 0.0000 0.49162
Item.23 0.3249 0.0000 0.0000 0.2638 0.17513
Item.24 0.5824 0.1151 0.0000 0.0000 0.35240
Item.25 0.3748 0.0000 0.0000 0.3274 0.24765
Item.26 0.6440 0.0000 0.0000 0.2099 0.45881
Item.27 0.7362 0.1605 0.0000 0.0000 0.56770
Item.28 0.5262 0.0000 0.0000 0.0741 0.28239
Item.29 0.4195 0.0000 0.6970 0.0000 0.66180
Item.30 0.2460 0.0000 0.0000-0.0982 0.07018
Item.31 0.8325-0.0753 0.0000 0.0000 0.69867
Item.32 0.0777 0.0000 0.0172 0.0000 0.00633

SS loadings: 8.412 1.052 0.738 0.775

Factor covariance:
  F1 F2 F3 F4
F1 1 0  0  0
F2 0 1  0  0
```

```
F3 0 0    1   0
F4 0 0    0   1
$Item.1
         a1      a2 a3    a4   d      g  u
par      0.786   0  0.443 0   -1.073  0  1
CI_2.5 0.516    NA 0.010 NA  -1.312 NA NA
CI_97. 5 1.056  NA 0.875 NA  -0.834 NA NA
```

These results for the bifactor model are interpreted just as they were for the compensatory MIRT model above, with the addition of the general factor, factor loadings and discrimination parameters for which appear in the first column of the tables.

DIFFERENTIAL ITEM FUNCTIONING

A primary assumption of developers and users of psychological and educational tests alike is that specific items provide the same information for individuals within different subgroups within the population (Camilli & Shepard, 1994). More specifically, if a test is being used to assess mathematics aptitude for sixth-grade students, teachers and administrators assume that the items provide the same quality of information regarding math achievement for both boys and girls in the population. However, this assumption may not always be met, such that a particular item behaves differently (i.e. has different item discrimination or difficulty parameter values) for members of different groups (e.g. males and females). Such differential item performance threatens the validity of the assessment, and any conclusions drawn from it about the latent trait being measured. In the context of psychometrics, such differential performance is referred to as **differential item functioning (DIF)**. An alternative definition of DIF is that it occurs when the probability of a given item response (e.g. correct) differs for members of two distinct groups, when members of the groups are matched on the latent trait being measured. DIF is generally categorized into one of two types:

(1) **Uniform DIF** – item difficulty parameters differ between the groups
(2) **Nonuniform DIF** – item discrimination parameters differ between the groups.

These types of DIF can also be seen graphically, as in Figures 10.1 and 10.2.

Many researchers have devoted much time to the development of methods for detecting each type of DIF (e.g. Thissen, 2001; Li & Stout, 1996; Camilli & Shepard, 1994; Narayanan & Swaminathan, 1994; 1996; Shealy & Stout, 1993; Holland & Thayer, 1988; Thissen, Steinberg, & Wainer, 1988). Indeed, given the

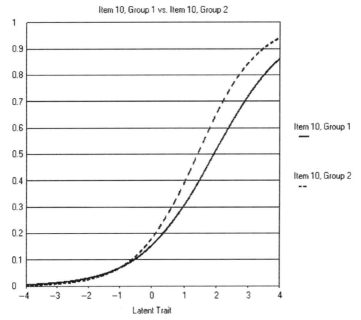

▪ **Figure 10.1:** Group ICCs for uniform DIF

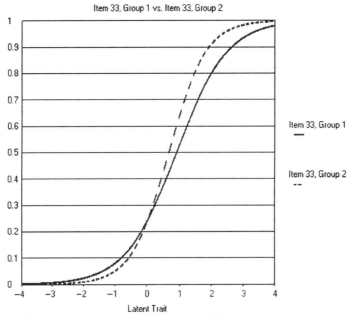

▪ **Figure 10.2:** Group ICCs for nonuniform DIF

many excellent works describing the various methods, we will forego the technical details of those here, and instead focus on implementing several of them using R. However, we strongly recommend that researchers interested in using one or more of the methods that we demonstrate below refer to the associated references to learn more about how the methods work, and under what conditions they are most appropriate. In the following, we will describe how to use a number of these methods for detecting DIF using R.

Within R, the difR library contains a number of functions to test for the presence of uniform and nonuniform DIF. In order to demonstrate these functions, we will use a dataset within the difR package itself, containing 24 items measuring verbal aggression on 316 individuals (females = 243). The items measure verbal responses to potentially frustrating situations and are coded as 1 (Yes, I would do this) or 0 (No, I would not do this). The dataset contains 26 columns, with the first 24 including the individual item responses, the 25th including a measure of trait anger, and the 26th containing gender (0 = female, 1 = male). The four frustrating situations appear below:

S1: A bus fails to stop for me.
S2: I miss a train because a clerk gave me faulty information.
S3: The grocery store closes just as I am about to enter.
S4: The operator disconnects me when I had used up my last ten cents for a call.

Respondents are asked whether they would want to or would actually do each of the following verbal responses: curse, scold, or shout. So, as an example, one item would be: If a bus fails to stop for me I would want to curse. A second item would be: If a bus fails to stop for me I would curse, and so on. Our interest is in determining whether there is evidence of either uniform or nonuniform DIF for any of these items, with respect to respondent gender.

In order to access the verbal anger dataset from difR, we simply type data(verbal). We will next remove the anger trait score from the dataset because we won't be using it in the DIF analyses. The command to do this is:

```
verbal.noanger<-verbal[colnames(verbal)!="Anger"]
```

Next, we will review several of the methods for DIF detection available through difR, each using the same dataset. As mentioned above, our focus will be on the use of the computer to carry out these analyses, leaving the technical details to the associated references.

Mantel–Haenszel statistic for DIF detection

The Mantel–Haenszel statistic (MH) is a very popular and well proven method for use in detecting uniform DIF (e.g. Roussos & Stout, 1996; Narayanan & Swaminathan, 1994). Essentially, individuals are grouped based upon their total scores on the scale of interest, in this case their propensity to be verbally aggressive. Within each of these score groups, the relationship between group membership (e.g. gender) and item response (e.g. yes or no) is assessed. In addition to providing a test of the null hypothesis that an item displays uniform DIF, the MH procedure also yields an effect size measure known as the Educational Testing Service (ETS) Δ, with associated guidelines for interpretation, which is utilized by difR. The following set of commands request the MH DIF detection procedure. Prior to reading through the resulting output, we should note a few aspects of the code itself. The function used, difMH, requires that the dataset appear first, followed by the name of the grouping variable, in this case **Gender**. One of the genders must be identified as the focal group. We selected males (coded as 1 in the data), though generally speaking such designations are not particularly important in most instances. Finally, we requested that the matching scale scores be purified. This means that an iterative process is used so that the final score on which individuals are matched, as described above, does not contain items exhibiting DIF (see Clauser, Mazor, & Hambleton, 1993; French & Maller, 2007; Woods, 2009 for a description of methods for item purification, and its importance in DIF analysis). When nonpurified items are included in the matching score, the accuracy of DIF detection can be greatly diminished. Following the commands to carry out this analysis, the resulting output appears, interspersed with explanatory text.

```
mh.out<-difMH(verbal.noanger,group="Gender",focal.
name=1,purify=TRUE)
mh.out


Detection   of   Differential   Item   Functioning   using
Mantel-Haenszel method
with continuity correction and with item purification

Convergence reached after 6 iterations

Mantel-Haenszel Chi-square statistic:

            Stat.   P-value
S1wantCurse 0.0069  0.9336
S1WantScold 0.0376  0.8462
S1WantShout 0.0087  0.9256
```

```
S2WantCurse 0.8881 0.3460
S2WantScold 0.1112 0.7388
S2WantShout 4.2680 0.0388 *
S3WantCurse 0.0987 0.7534
S3WantScold 4.3724 0.0365 *
S3WantShout 0.3454 0.5567
S4WantCurse 0.1406 0.7077
S4WantScold 1.6853 0.1942
S4WantShout 1.0766 0.2995
S1DoCurse 2.0959 0.1477
S1DoScold 6.2736 0.0123 *
S1DoShout 0.0172 0.8957
S2DoCurse 9.6672 0.0019 **
S2DoScold 11.9436 0.0005 ***
S2DoShout 0.6997 0.4029
S3DoCurse 9.4644 0.0021 **
S3DoScold 6.4356 0.0112 *
S3DoShout 1.4190 0.2336
S4DoCurse 3.9323 0.0474 *
S4DoScold 5.7987 0.0160 *
S4DoShout 0.3223 0.5702


Signif. codes: 0 '***' 0.001 '**' 0.01 '*' 0.05 '.' 0.1 ' ' 1

Detection threshold: 3.8415 (significance level: 0.05)
```

The previous table includes the results of the test of the null hypothesis of no DIF for each item. We can see that several of the items, denoted by *, were found to have statistically significant results. In the table below, R lists for us all items that did in fact have significant MH results.

```
Items detected as DIF items:

  S2WantShout
  S3WantScold
  S1DoScold
  S2DoCurse
  S2DoScold
  S3DoCurse
  S3DoScold
  S4DoCurse
  S4DoScold
```

Next, we see the log of the odds ratio for each item (alphaMH) as well as the ETS Δ mentioned previously (deltaMH). For each item, the ETS effect designation based upon the value of Δ and the hypothesis test for DIF is provided. The actual guide-lines associated with A, B, and C DIF appear below the table.

```
Effect size (ETS Delta scale):

Effect size code:
'A': negligible effect
'B': moderate effect
'C': large effect

             alphaMH deltaMH
S1wantCurse 1.1054 -0.2355 A
S1WantScold 1.1357 -0.2990 A
S1WantShout 1.0919 -0.2066 A
S2WantCurse 1.5998 -1.1042 B
S2WantScold 1.1994 -0.4272 A
S2WantShout 2.2088 -1.8623 C
S3WantCurse 0.8584  0.3588 A
S3WantScold 0.4593  1.8283 C
S3WantShout 1.3348 -0.6786 A
S4WantCurse 1.2183 -0.4639 A
S4WantScold 0.6322  1.0776 B
S4WantShout 1.5764 -1.0696 B
S1DoCurse   0.5481  1.4130 B
S1DoScold   0.3832  2.2540 C
S1DoShout   0.9822  0.0421 A
S2DoCurse   0.2658  3.1134 C
S2DoScold   0.3014  2.8186 C
S2DoShout   0.6832  0.8954 A
S3DoCurse   0.3713  2.3284 C
S3DoScold   0.4079  2.1075 C
S3DoShout   0.4654  1.7974 C
S4DoCurse   0.4744  1.7526 C
S4DoScold   0.4148  2.0681 C
S4DoShout   1.4040 -0.7974 A

Effect size codes: 0 'A' 1.0 'B' 1.5 'C'
(for absolute values of 'deltaMH')

Output was not captured!
```

In order to better interpret the DIF testing results it will be helpful for us to have access to the item parameter estimates for males and females. These are eas-ily obtained using the following R code. In the first two lines, we use the subset command to create two datasets, one containing only the males' item responses (data.focal), and the other containing only those for the females (data.reference). We then use the itemParEst command to estimate 2PL model parameters for each group, and combine the results together into a single output object called item.2PL, using the rbind command. We can then simply type the name of the file and see the item discrimination and difficulty parameter estimates, along with their standard errors and the covariance between them, for each item.

```
data.reference<-subset(verbal.noanger, Gender==0)
data.focal<-subset(verbal.noanger, Gender==1)
item.2PL<-rbind(itemParEst(data.reference,
model="2PL"),
+ itemParEst(data.focal, model="2PL"))
item.2PL
```

	a	b	se(a)	se(b)	cov(a,b)
S1wantCurse	1.3751404	-0.890398670	0.2533944	0.2150148	2.271969e-02
S1WantScold	1.4480268	-0.395712843	0.2484962	0.1931135	9.312153e-03
S1WantShout	1.4784641	-0.059799928	0.2495372	0.1879887	9.311578e-05
S2WantCurse	1.4311676	-1.285397399	0.2827679	0.2627901	4.252736e-02
S2WantScold	1.4866904	-0.503917199	0.2558274	0.2009432	1.337700e-02
S2WantShout	1.4669586	-0.106999352	0.2500314	0.1874361	7.325601e-04
S3WantCurse	1.0037349	-0.418543506	0.1964815	0.1631414	4.303084e-03
S3WantScold	1.4539596	0.616452450	0.2555397	0.2039838	-1.854605e-02
S3WantShout	1.0770071	1.256426154	0.2194030	0.2012634	-1.955766e-02
S4WantCurse	1.0641982	-0.937334564	0.2128826	0.1832396	1.251707e-02
S4WantScold	1.7317921	0.291092583	0.2858142	0.2100267	-1.322940e-02
S4WantShout	1.0425129	0.844563060	0.2059799	0.1779645	-1.189451e-02
S1DoCurse	1.5251349	-0.732622563	0.2642338	0.2148510	1.947300e-02
S1DoScold	2.3723094	-0.085146013	0.3893721	0.2512950	1.238948e-03
S1DoShout	1.4623938	0.631625269	0.2568890	0.2056529	-1.927797e-02
S2DoCurse	1.4515612	-0.411512969	0.2474084	0.1933409	9.054556e-03
S2DoScold	2.1759413	0.210908083	0.3600816	0.2395500	-1.611536e-02
S2DoShout	1.9323012	0.974952493	0.3540456	0.2997595	-6.546907e-02
S3DoCurse	1.1506980	0.403762984	0.2119211	0.1725803	-7.426363e-03
S3DoScold	1.5126454	1.228986018	0.2867437	0.2655540	-4.489451e-02
S3DoShout	1.0985191	2.646445638	0.2917295	0.3492785	-6.745756e-02
S4DoCurse	1.2440183	-0.397758767	0.2219998	0.1780211	6.008851e-03
S4DoScold	1.3668066	0.430607462	0.2384043	0.1877564	-1.060185e-02
S4DoShout	1.2264532	1.548729086	0.2540674	0.2498690	-3.648979e-02
S1wantCurse	1.5054416	-0.791244298	0.5376630	0.3745879	1.057522e-01
S1WantScold	2.0650798	-0.329153773	0.6660526	0.3862399	1.132790e-01
S1WantShout	1.1332384	-0.002651252	0.3942832	0.2815317	1.310719e-02
S2WantCurse	2.0006530	-0.896886477	0.6990654	0.5071774	2.429038e-01

S2WantScold	2.1799469	-0.366664329	0.7057947	0.4106348	1.449472e-01
S2WantShout	1.1534042	0.417113519	0.4033181	0.2887341	-4.879597e-03
S3WantCurse	0.5385692	-0.949858962	0.3113108	0.2555407	1.302319e-02
S3WantScold	1.3159486	0.098440522	0.4357383	0.2948216	1.003959e-02
S3WantShout	0.5881629	2.444598724	0.3378217	0.3164515	-2.952536e-02
S4WantCurse	1.5803341	-0.664420732	0.5356126	0.3660187	9.625200e-02
S4WantScold	1.2522397	0.048240302	0.4231542	0.2899155	1.237572e-02
S4WantShout	1.0421490	1.179004101	0.3875797	0.3262056	-3.771389e-02
S1DoCurse	2.5894365	-0.913719752	0.9175456	0.6883654	4.941956e-01
S1DoScold	2.1071178	-0.681862968	0.7002567	0.4564146	1.956320e-01
S1DoShout	.5898798	0.537168532	0.4985641	0.3429407	-3.537131e-02
S2DoCurse	1.6685012	-1.227422666	0.6310416	0.5178026	2.283467e-01
S2DoScold	1.5998886	-0.608523169	0.5307346	0.3598136	8.915498e-02
S2DoShout	1.0351811	1.025321276	0.3832656	0.3113654	-2.913596e-02
S3DoCurse	0.8897546	-0.638338811	0.3653413	0.2785331	2.680091e-02
S3DoScold	0.9339865	0.715844292	0.3563488	0.2824033	-1.403553e-02
S3DoShout	1.1759222	2.036827591	0.4740622	0.5045030	-1.355312e-01
S4DoCurse	2.1054231	-0.777883006	0.7122519	0.4928755	2.333088e-01
S4DoScold	1.8041116	-0.160966140	0.5619060	0.3424882	5.755250e-02
S4DoShout	1.2915878	1.588461020	0.4822645	0.4565156	-1.173072e-01

The results are stacked so that the reference group (females) item parameters come first, followed by those of the focal group (males). As an example of how these values will aid with interpretation, we see from the MH results that S2WantShout has a high level of DIF. The difficulty estimate for this item for females is −0.106999352, whereas for males it is 0.417113519. Therefore, we can conclude that it is somewhat easier for females to endorse wanting to shout when they miss a train due to being given faulty information by the clerk. The item S2DoCurse also displayed large DIF. In this case, the item difficulty estimate for women was −0.411512969, and that for men was −1.227422666. Thus, men were more likely to endorse actually cursing when they missed a train due to a clerk's error than were women. We can use a similar approach to characterize all of the items that displayed DIF in this analysis.

Finally, it is easy to obtain a graphical display for the MH chi-square test results, which provides an easy-to-interpret visual display. Using the command plot(mh. out), we obtain the graph shown in Figure 10.3. Note that the reference line appears at the critical value for the test statistic, and item numbers above this line were found to be statistically significant.

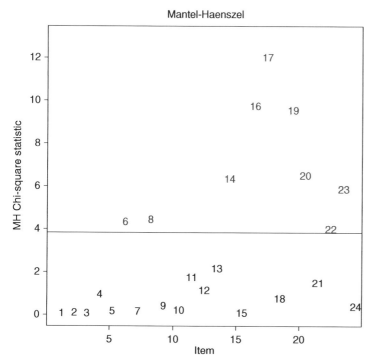

■ Figure 10.3: MH chi-square statistics by item

Logistic regression for DIF detection

A second popular and highly effective method for investigating a set of item responses for DIF is logistic regression (LR). As with MH, LR is a general-use statistical method that has been adopted by psychometricians for use in DIF assessment (Zumbo, 1999; Narayanan & Swaminathan, 1996). It has an advantage over MH when the researcher is interested in checking the data for both uniform and nonuniform DIF, as it can easily be adapted for both. The basic LR model for DIF testing can be expressed as:

$$\ln\left[\frac{p_i}{1-p_i}\right] = \beta_0 + \beta_1\left(Score_i\right) + \beta_2\left(group\right) + \beta_3\left(group \times Score_i\right). \qquad \textbf{(10.4)}$$

In this case, p_i is the probability of endorsing the item, or a correct response, $Score_i$ is the score on the total scale leaving out the item being assessed for DIF, and *group* is the grouping variable (e.g. gender). The coefficient β_2 provides the estimate of uniform DIF, and when significantly different from zero indicates the presence of such. Likewise, β_3 is the estimate of nonuniform DIF. Zumbo (1999) provides a very nice description of how LR can be used for assessing DIF, and the reader interested in more detail is strongly encouraged to refer to this work. Using difLogistic in the difR package, we will first check for uniform DIF. We indicate this with the subcommand type="udif". As with MH, we request a purified scale for matching, and use males as the focal group.

```
lr.uniform.out<-difLogistic(verbal.
noanger,group="Gender",focal.name=1,purify=TRUE,typ
e="udif")
```

```
lr.out
```

```
Detection of uniform Differential Item Functioning
using Logistic regression method, with item purification
and with LRT DIF statistic
```

```
Convergence reached after 3 iterations
```

```
Logistic regression DIF statistic:
```

	Stat.	P-value	
S1wantCurse	0.1325	0.7159	
S1WantScold	0.0517	0.8202	
S1WantShout	0.1342	0.7141	
S2WantCurse	1.2510	0.2634	
S2WantScold	0.2865	0.5924	
S2WantShout	4.9649	0.0259	*
S3WantCurse	0.2793	0.5972	
S3WantScold	4.8580	0.0275	*
S3WantShout	0.6754	0.4112	
S4WantCurse	0.2098	0.6469	
S4WantScold	1.4648	0.2262	
S4WantShout	1.4513	0.2283	
S1DoCurse	2.8616	0.0907	.
S1DoScold	9.2442	0.0024	**
S1DoShout	0.0201	0.8873	
S2DoCurse	11.9225	0.0006	***
S2DoScold	14.6969	0.0001	***
S2DoShout	1.6116	0.2043	
S3DoCurse	11.1076	0.0009	***
S3DoScold	7.5135	0.0061	**
S3DoShout	1.4899	0.2222	
S4DoCurse	4.9448	0.0262	*
S4DoScold	5.5109	0.0189	*
S4DoShout	0.1366	0.7117	

```
Signif. codes: 0 '***' 0.001 '**' 0.01 '*' 0.05 '.' 0.1 ' ' 1

Detection threshold: 3.8415 (significance level: 0.05)

Items detected as uniform DIF items:

    S2WantShout
    S3WantScold
    S1DoScold
    S2DoCurse
    S2DoScold
    S3DoCurse
    S3DoScold
    S4DoCurse
    S4DoScold
```

As with MH, R provides a list of the hypothesis test results for each item, as well as a list of the items that were found to exhibit uniform DIF. With LR, the uniform DIF effect size is the change in the proportion of variation accounted for in the item response that is associated with the addition of the group variable to model (10.4). There are currently two sets of guidelines for interpreting these, and both are provided by difR under the ZT and JG columns. Based on these results, only the items S2DoCurse, S2DoScold, and S3DoCurse demonstrated high levels of uniform DIF, according to LR.

```
Effect size (Nagelkerke's R^2):

Effect size code:
'A': negligible effect
'B': moderate effect
'C': large effect

            R^2    ZT JG
S1wantCurse 0.0008 A A
S1WantScold 0.0003 A A
S1WantShout 0.0007 A A
S2WantCurse 0.0078 A A
S2WantScold 0.0015 A A
S2WantShout 0.0245 A A
S3WantCurse 0.0023 A A
S3WantScold 0.0282 A A
S3WantShout 0.0071 A A
S4WantCurse 0.0014 A A
S4WantScold 0.0084 A A
```

```
S4WantShout 0.0113 A A
S1DoCurse   0.0251 A A
S1DoScold   0.0437 A B
S1DoShout   0.0001 A A
S2DoCurse   0.0849 A C
S2DoScold   0.0763 A C
S2DoShout   0.0099 A A
S3DoCurse   0.0829 A C
S3DoScold   0.0682 A B
S3DoShout   0.0189 A A
S4DoCurse   0.0368 A B
S4DoScold   0.0362 A B
S4DoShout   0.0013 A A


Effect size codes:
Zumbo & Thomas (ZT): 0 'A' 0.13 'B' 0.26 'C' 1
Jodoign & Gierl (JG): 0 'A' 0.035 'B' 0.07 'C' 1

Output was not captured!
```

We can use a very similar command sequence to assess the items for nonuniform DIF, with the only change being the inclusion of the subcommand type="nudif".

```
lr.nonuniform.out<-difLogistic(verbal.
noanger,group="Gender",focal.name=1,purify=TRUE,typ
e="nudif")
lr.nonuniform.out

Detection of nonuniform Differential Item Functioning
using Logistic regression method, with item purification
and with LRT DIF statistic

Convergence reached after 0 iteration

Logistic regression DIF statistic:

              Stat.  P-value
S1wantCurse 0.0016 0.9686
S1WantScold 1.4476 0.2289
S1WantShout 0.3136 0.5755
S2WantCurse 0.4658 0.4949
S2WantScold 1.2367 0.2661
S2WantShout 0.1080 0.7425
S3WantCurse 1.5106 0.2190
```

```
S3WantScold 0.0071 0.9330
S3WantShout 0.5592 0.4546
S4WantCurse 0.4983 0.4802
S4WantScold 2.0955 0.1477
S4WantShout 0.0386 0.8442
S1DoCurse   0.7962 0.3722
S1DoScold   0.6335 0.4261
S1DoShout   0.3293 0.5661
S2DoCurse   0.0563 0.8124
S2DoScold   1.1221 0.2895
S2DoShout   1.6088 0.2047
S3DoCurse   0.0945 0.7585
S3DoScold   1.2184 0.2697
S3DoShout   0.7505 0.3863
S4DoCurse   1.1182 0.2903
S4DoScold   0.3039 0.5815
S4DoShout   0.2947 0.5872


Signif. codes: 0 '***' 0.001 '**' 0.01 '*' 0.05 '.' 0.1 ' ' 1


Detection threshold: 3.8415 (significance level: 0.05)


Items detected as DIF items: No DIF item detected


Effect size (Nagelkerke's R^2):
Effect size code:
'A': negligible effect
'B': moderate effect
'C': large effect


            R^2    ZT JG
S1wantCurse 0.0000 A  A
S1WantScold 0.0085 A  A
S1WantShout 0.0018 A  A
S2WantCurse 0.0035 A  A
S2WantScold 0.0070 A  A
S2WantShout 0.0006 A  A
S3WantCurse 0.0132 A  A
S3WantScold 0.0000 A  A
S3WantShout 0.0057 A  A
S4WantCurse 0.0039 A  A
S4WantScold 0.0104 A  A
S4WantShout 0.0003 A  A
S1DoCurse   0.0045 A  A
```

```
S1DoScold    0.0027 A A
S1DoShout    0.0020 A A
S2DoCurse    0.0003 A A
S2DoScold    0.0050 A A
S2DoShout    0.0098 A A
S3DoCurse    0.0006 A A
S3DoScold    0.0089 A A
S3DoShout    0.0087 A A
S4DoCurse    0.0070 A A
S4DoScold    0.0020 A A
S4DoShout    0.0028 A A


Effect size codes:
  Zumbo & Thomas (ZT): 0 'A' 0.13 'B' 0.26 'C' 1
  Jodoign & Gierl (JG): 0 'A' 0.035 'B' 0.07 'C' 1

Output was not captured!
```

None of the items exhibited statistically significant nonuniform DIF, and all had effect size values of A, indicating negligible nonuniform DIF.

As with the MH, it is possible to obtain the hypothesis test results graphically, with a reference line at the critical value, using the `plot` command. Figure 10.4 shows the plot for the LR uniform DIF results. A similar graph can be obtained for LR nonuniform DIF.

Raju's area method for detecting DIF

Raju (1988; 1990) proposed a method for assessing a set of items for DIF by comparing the area between the ICCs for two groups of examinees. Essentially, an IRT model is fit to each group's item responses and then the unsigned area between the resulting functions, as represented by the individual ICCs, is calculated. The z statistic tests the null hypothesis that there is not DIF for the item. In this case, we will fit the 2PL model for each group using the `model="2PL"` command.

```
raju.out<-
difRaju(verbal.noanger,group="Gender",focal.name=1,purify=TRUE,model="
2PL")
raju.out

    Detection of Differential Item Functioning using Raju's method
    with 2PL model and with item purification
```

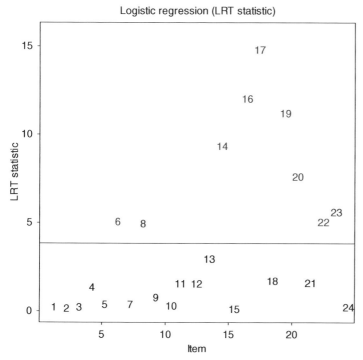

■ Figure 10.4: LR likelihood ratio test statistics by item

Type of Raju's Z statistic: based on unsigned area

Engine 'ltm' for item parameter estimation

Convergence reached after 3 iterations

Raju's statistic:

	Stat.	P-value	
S1wantCurse	0.2687	0.7882	
S1WantScold	1.1258	0.2603	
S1WantShout	-0.6110	0.5412	
S2WantCurse	1.0415	0.2976	
S2WantScold	1.1761	0.2395	
S2WantShout	-1.1961	0.2317	
S3WantCurse	-0.8300	0.4066	
S3WantScold	-2.3441	0.0191	*
S3WantShout	-0.7801	0.4353	
S4WantCurse	1.0969	0.2727	
S4WantScold	-1.5172	0.1292	

```
S4WantShout   0.4270 0.6693
S1DoCurse     2.5971 0.0094 **
S1DoScold    -3.1485 0.0016 **
S1DoShout     0.7107 0.4773
S2DoCurse     2.5459 0.0109 *
S2DoScold    -3.7406 0.0002 ***
S2DoShout    -1.2640 0.2062
S3DoCurse    -2.9092 0.0036 **
S3DoScold    -2.5417 0.0110 *
S3DoShout     0.8674 0.3857
S4DoCurse     3.1291 0.0018 **
S4DoScold     3.0961 0.0020 **
S4DoShout     0.1714 0.8639


Signif. codes: 0 '***' 0.001 '**' 0.01 '*' 0.05 '.' 0.1 ' ' 1

Detection thresholds: -1.96 and 1.96 (significance level: 0.05)

Items detected as DIF items:

  S3WantScold
  S1DoCurse
  S1DoScold
  S2DoCurse
  S2DoScold
  S3DoCurse
  S3DoScold
  S4DoCurse
  S4DoScold


Output was not captured!
```

Here we can see that nine items were found to exhibit DIF based on Raju's measure. As with MH and LR, we can plot these results as well (see Figure 10.5).

```
plot(raju.out)
```

Lord's chi-square test for DIF detection

Finally, we will examine a method for DIF assessment based on work by Lord (1980), directly comparing IRT item parameter estimates between groups under a given IRT model (e.g. 2PL). The null hypothesis of no DIF is tested using a

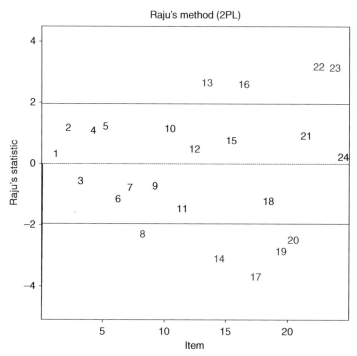

■ Figure 10.5: Raju's area test statistic by item

chi-square with degrees of freedom equal to the number of item parameters estimated. The null hypothesis for this test is that there is not uniform or nonuniform DIF.

```
lord.out<-difLord(verbal.noanger,group="Gender",focal.name=1,p
urify=TRUE,model="2PL")
lord.out
Detection of Differential Item Functioning using Lord's method

with 2PL model and with item purification

Engine 'ltm' for item parameter estimation

Convergence reached after 4 iterations

Lord's chi-square statistic:
```

```
               Stat.   P-value
S1wantCurse 0.0874 0.9573
S1WantScold 0.8609 0.6502
S1WantShout 0.4333 0.8052
S2WantCurse 1.3994 0.4967
S2WantScold 1.0388 0.5949
S2WantShout 2.2989 0.3168
S3WantCurse 1.4446 0.4856
S3WantScold 5.2992 0.0707 .
S3WantShout 1.4133 0.4933
S4WantCurse 1.0386 0.5949
S4WantScold 2.4471 0.2942
S4WantShout 0.6664 0.7166
S1DoCurse   4.1495 0.1256
S1DoScold   9.2635 0.0097 **
S1DoShout   0.3305 0.8477
S2DoCurse  13.1620 0.0014 **
S2DoScol   12.5660 0.0019 **
S2DoShout   4.7176 0.0945 .
S3DoCurse   8.4738 0.0145 *
S3DoScold   8.8319 0.0121 *
S3DoShout   1.7397 0.4190
S4DoCurse   7.5247 0.0232 *
S4DoScold   8.2736 0.0160 *
S4DoShout   0.0395 0.9805


Signif. codes: 0 '***' 0.001 '**' 0.01 '*' 0.05 '.' 0.1 ' ' 1

Detection threshold: 5.9915 (significance level: 0.05)

Items detected as DIF items:

S1DoScold
S2DoCurse
S2DoScold
S3DoCurse
S3DoScold
S4DoCurse
S4DoScold

Output was not captured!
```

These results show that seven items displayed DIF based on Lord's test. As with the other methods, it is possible to plot the results from Lord's test for DIF. We can

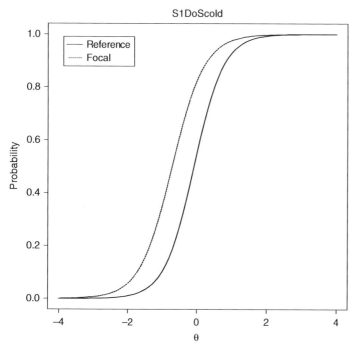

■ Figure 10.6: ICCs for S1DoScold for males and females

plot the test statistics for all of the items, as we did with the other methods, using the `plot(lord.out)` command for this example. We can also plot the reference and focal group ICCs using the command `plot(lord.out, plot="itemCurve", item=14)`. In this case, we selected item 14 as it was found to contain DIF.

Figure 10.6 shows that the item was somewhat easier for the focal group (males) to endorse than it was for the reference group (females), which matches the individual item difficulties presented above.

MOKKEN SCALING AND NONPARAMETRIC IRT MODELING

The IRT models that we studied in Chapter 9 rested on an assumption that underlying item responses is a logistic model relating the latent trait being measured with the item response. However, this model structure is not likely to fit every scale that a researcher uses. In addition, IRT model estimation typically requires fairly large samples, which are not always possible to obtain in practice (Meijer & Baneke, 2004). For these reasons, alternative methods for characterizing items and scales are needed on some occasions. One approach for investigating item properties and identifying an optimal set of items for making up a scale that can be useful when the standard IRT models may not fit the data is **Mokken scaling** (Mokken, 1971). There are a number of well-written papers and an excellent book on this topic (Sijtsma & Molenaar, 2002). Of particular utility to the applied researcher is the manuscript by Meijer and Baneke (2004). Given the excellent work in this area, we will not describe many of the technical details of Mokken scaling here. However, we will show how it can be carried out using R in order to investigate the properties of a scale.

For the purposes of finding homogeneous clusters of items, and identifying sets of items that provide what Meijer and Baneke (2004) termed "sensitive measurement" of the trait of interest, Mokken scaling based on the scalability coefficient has been shown to be quite effective. For any item pair (x_i, x_j) we can define the scalability coefficient as:

$$H_{i,j} = \frac{Cov(x_i, x_j)}{MaxCov(x_i, x_j)}.$$

(10.5)

Here $Cov(x_i, x_j)$ is the observed covariance between items i and j, and $MaxCov(x_i, x_j)$ is the maximum possible such covariance. Thus, $H_{i,j}$ is the normalized covariance between the item responses, and will be positive for items belonging to the same scale. It is also possible to calculate a scalability coefficient for each item individually:

$$H_i = \frac{Cov(x_i, R_{-i})}{MaxCov(x_i, R_{-i})}.$$

(10.6)

Here, R_{-i} is the score on the total scale excluding item i, so that H_i is the normalized covariance for item i. Finally, the scale as a whole can also have a scalability coefficient, H, which is calculated as:

$$H = \frac{\sum_{i=1}^{I-1}\sum_{j=i+1}^{I} Cov(x_i, x_j)}{\sum_{i=1}^{I-1}\sum_{j=i+1}^{I} MaxCov(x_i, x_j)}.$$

(10.7)

Mokken (1971) suggested that scales could be characterized as weak, medium, or strong based upon their values of H. Below are his specific guidelines in this regard:

$0.3 \leq H < 0.4$ = Weak scale

$0.4 \leq H < 0.5$ = Medium scale

$0.5 \geq H$ = Strong scale.

Thus, we can use the scalability coefficients and these guidelines to ascertain the strength of our scale, and to identify clusters of items that might serve as potentially more optimal scales based upon the relationships of items with one another.

We will apply Mokken scaling to the "purpose in life" data that we examined in Chapter 8. As a quick reminder, a researcher administered a purpose in life survey to a group of 374 middle school students. The 17 items were answered as either yes (1) or no (0). Below are the individual purposes to which the subjects responded. In addition to these items, the researcher also collected scores on a meaning in life scale, where higher scores indicated that the respondent viewed life as having more meaning.

1. Help others
2. Serve God
3. Make the world better
4. Change the way people think
5. Create something new
6. Make things beautiful
7. Fulfill duties
8. Do the right thing
9. Live life to the fullest
10. Make money
11. Discover new things
12. Earn the respect of others
13. Support family/friends
14. Serve country
15. Have fun
16. Be successful
17. Have good career.

Prior to requesting the scalability coefficient for these data, we must first remove missing data, which we do using the following command:

```
purpose.nomiss<-na.omit(purpose)
```

We can then obtain the three types of scalability coefficients using the `coefH` command, which is a part of the `mokken` library.

```
library(mokken)
coefH(purpose.nomiss)
```

$Hij

Correlation matrix (columns v1–v9), with standard errors in parentheses:

	v1	v2	v3	v4	v5	v6	v7	v8	v9
v1									
v2	0.772 (0.104)								
v3	0.568 (0.104)	0.457 (0.107)							
v4	0.743 (0.117)	0.179 (0.062)	0.715 (0.096)						
v5	0.412 (0.154)	0.052 (0.063)	0.254 (0.125)	0.263 (0.054)					
v6	0.586 (0.131)	0.003 (0.055)	0.587 (0.103)	0.274 (0.059)	0.546 (0.058)				
v7	0.534 (0.112)	0.452 (0.082)	0.380 (0.089)	0.281 (0.094)	0.215 (0.096)	0.337 (0.087)			
v8	0.418 (0.102)	0.523 (0.127)	0.438 (0.102)	0.284 (0.151)	0.150 (0.155)	0.505 (0.096)	0.525 (0.108)		
v9	0.247 (0.094)	-0.039 (0.119)	0.214 (0.119)	0.221 (0.089)	0.037 (0.094)	0.538 (0.132)	0.314 (0.125)	0.301 (0.108)	
v10	-0.027 (0.154)	0.097 (0.062)	-0.140 (0.116)	0.098 (0.052)	0.048 (0.053)	0.019 (0.052)	0.152 (0.058)	0.165 (0.094)	0.276 (0.152)
v11	0.388 (0.125)	0.080 (0.065)	0.288 (0.097)	0.274 (0.076)	0.427 (0.075)	0.247 (0.070)	0.143 (0.070)	0.242 (0.071)	0.204 (0.119)
v12	0.410 (0.112)	0.167 (0.089)	0.223 (0.081)	0.385 (0.100)	0.254 (0.103)	0.217 (0.094)	0.299 (0.072)	0.326 (0.072)	0.371 (0.106)
v13	0.463 (0.131)	0.536 (0.169)	0.368 (0.097)	0.374 (0.198)	0.256 (0.207)	0.519 (0.176)	0.395 (0.148)	0.595 (0.148)	0.388 (0.129)
v14	0.560 (0.154)	0.421 (0.154)	0.348 (0.135)	0.160 (0.061)	0.157 (0.059)	0.141 (0.067)	0.589 (0.092)	0.591 (0.092)	0.046 (0.145)
v15	0.114 (0.081)	-0.079 (0.111)	0.081 (0.071)	0.039 (0.137)	0.021 (0.137)	0.114 (0.126)	0.266 (0.098)	0.177 (0.085)	0.342 (0.085)
v16	0.350 (0.105)	0.187 (0.107)	0.176 (0.072)	0.245 (0.121)	0.150 (0.121)	0.047 (0.108)	0.308 (0.087)	0.236 (0.095)	0.324 (0.095)
v17	0.324 (0.109)	0.029 (0.088)	0.114 (0.073)	0.211 (0.104)	0.227 (0.106)	0.133 (0.095)	0.208 (0.071)	0.246 (0.101)	0.257 (0.101)

Correlation matrix (columns v10–v17), with standard errors in parentheses:

	v10	v11	v12	v13	v14	v15	v16	v17
v1	-0.027 (0.094)	0.388 (0.154)	0.410 (0.125)	0.463 (0.131)	0.560 (0.154)	0.114 (0.081)	0.350 (0.105)	0.324 (0.109)
v2	0.097 (0.119)	0.080 (0.062)	0.167 (0.065)	0.536 (0.169)	0.421 (0.069)	-0.079 (0.111)	0.187 (0.107)	0.029 (0.088)
v3	-0.140 (0.089)	0.288 (0.116)	0.223 (0.097)	0.368 (0.097)	0.348 (0.135)	0.081 (0.071)	0.176 (0.072)	0.114 (0.073)
v4	0.098 (0.146)	0.274 (0.052)	0.385 (0.076)	0.374 (0.100)	0.160 (0.061)	0.039 (0.137)	0.245 (0.121)	0.211 (0.104)
v5	0.048 (0.147)	0.427 (0.053)	0.254 (0.075)	0.256 (0.198)	0.157 (0.207)	0.021 (0.176)	0.150 (0.124)	0.227 (0.104)
v6	0.019 (0.125)	0.247 (0.058)	0.217 (0.070)	0.519 (0.059)	0.141 (0.067)	0.114 (0.092)	0.047 (0.145)	0.133 (0.167)
v7	0.152 (0.105)	0.143 (0.094)	0.299 (0.072)	0.395 (0.140)	0.589 (0.141)	0.266 (0.148)	0.308 (0.085)	0.208 (0.093)
v8	0.165 (0.094)	0.242 (0.105)	0.326 (0.072)	0.595 (0.124)	0.591 (0.126)	0.177 (0.098)	0.236 (0.095)	0.246 (0.096)
v9	0.276 (0.145)	0.204 (0.152)	0.371 (0.106)	0.388 (0.132)	0.046 (0.167)	0.342 (0.145)	0.324 (0.098)	0.257 (0.082)
v10		0.256 (0.145)	0.561 (0.145)	0.478 (0.190)	0.160 (0.061)	0.747 (0.102)	0.801 (0.082)	0.696 (0.084)

	v11	v12	v13	v14	v15	v16	v17
v11 (0.113)	0.256 (0.076)						
v12 (0.103)	0.561 (0.093)	0.325 (0.081)					
v13 (0.132)	0.478 (0.190)	0.337 (0.162)	0.484 (0.143)				
v14 (0.167)	0.160 (0.061)	0.233 (0.086)	0.330 (0.113)	0.404 (0.217)			
v15 (0.093)	0.747 (0.102)	0.437 (0.110)	0.499 (0.098)	0.383 (0.133)	0.422 (0.147)		
v16 (0.096)	0.801 (0.082)	0.368 (0.096)	0.551 (0.084)	0.437 (0.138)	0.409 (0.130)	0.624 (0.090)	
v17 (0.098)	0.696 (0.084)	0.204 (0.080)	0.378 (0.073)	0.560 (0.140)	0.480 (0.109)	0.467 (0.097)	0.665 (0.079)

```
$Hi
    Item H se
v1  0.418 (0.059)
v2  0.186 (0.039)
v3  0.304 (0.049)
v4  0.249 (0.037)
v5  0.225 (0.039)
v6  0.245 (0.036)
v7  0.319 (0.039)
v8  0.349 (0.061)
v9  0.260 (0.060)
v10 0.200 (0.038)
v11 0.263 (0.038)
v12 0.351 (0.038)
v13 0.440 (0.078)
v14 0.278 (0.041)
v15 0.296 (0.049)
v16 0.371 (0.044)
v17 0.310 (0.042)


$H
  Scale H se
     0.281 (0.028)
```

Let's study each of these sets of statistics individually. The vast majority of the $H_{i,j}$ are positive, though not all of them are. This would seem to make sense, given that these values are normalized covariances and therefore should be positive if the items belong to the same scale. Moving to the next table of output, 9 of the 17 items have H_i values below the minimally acceptable cutoff of 0.3, suggesting that they are not particularly scalable. Finally, the overall H is below the 0.3 value as well, suggesting that it is not even a "weak" scale. Taken together, we would have to conclude that the set of 17 items does not make a particularly useful scale.

In order to investigate the possibility of identifying subsets of items that might yield more statistically coherent scales, we can use the `search.normal` command that is part of the `mokken` library. This function initiates a search algorithm designed to identify subsets of items that maximize the H_i statistic, thereby creating subscales that, statistically speaking, hold together. This tool may prove particularly useful for researchers engaged in scale development. Below is an example of the command in use.

```
purpose.scale<-search.normal(purpose.nomiss)
```

SCALE 1

```
Item: v16                          Scale 1 H = 0.8
Item: v10                          Scale 1 H = 0.8
Item: v15                          Scale 1 H = 0.72
Item: v17                          Scale 1 H = 0.66
Item: v13                          Scale 1 H = 0.61
Item: v12                          Scale 1 H = 0.56
Item: v9                           Scale 1 H = 0.5
Scale 1 is completed. No items left such that Hi > 0.3 .


SCALE 2


Item: v2                           Scale 2 H = 0.77
Item: v1                           Scale 2 H = 0.77
Item: v3                           Scale 2 H = 0.58
Item: v8                           Scale 2 H = 0.52
Item: v7                           Scale 2 H = 0.49
Item: v14                          Scale 2 H = 0.49
Scale 2 is completed. No items left such that Hi > 0.3 .


SCALE 3


Item: v6                           Scale 3 H = 0.55
Item: v5                           Scale 3 H = 0.55
Item: v11                          Scale 3 H = 0.42
Scale 3 is completed. No items left such that Hi > 0.3 .


SCALE 4


Less than two items left. PROCEDURE STOPS
```

The Mokken scaling analysis yielded three potential scales based on the H_i statistic. Much as with EFA (Chapter 2), we must examine the content of the items that have been grouped together in order to determine whether the groupings make conceptual sense for the purposes of creating subscales. As an example, the first proposed scale includes the items "Be successful", "Make money", "Have fun", "Have a good career", "Support family/friends", "Earn the respect of others", and "Live life to fullest". These items might be seen as representing purposes tied to the self and those close to the self. Similar examinations of the other scales can be conducted. Certainly one conclusion to be drawn from this analysis is that the purpose scale does not appear to be unidimensional in nature.

KERNEL SMOOTHING IRT

The final topic that we will address in this chapter is the **kernel smoothing** of item response data. As we noted previously, standard parameteric IRT models rest on several assumptions about the nature of the data. However, frequently such assumptions are not tenable, and/or the sample size is not sufficiently large for standard IRT estimation techniques to be appropriately used. In such instances, a nonparametric approach based on work by Ramsay (1997) may be preferable for researchers who would like to characterize the underlying response function to an item, or set of items. This nonparametric approach links the item response to an estimate of the latent trait using a kernel density estimator. Essentially, this estimator is a locally weighted average such that observations with latent trait estimates closer to those of an individual receive more weight than do those observations with latent trait estimates further away (Simonoff, 1996). Because the kernel smoothing approach relies on locally weighted averages, it is not parametric in nature and does not presume the existence of a particular underlying item response model. This approach is particularly useful for providing graphical information about the relationship between an item response and the underlying ability that is measured by the scale, as we shall see below.

We will use the R package KernSmoothIRT to apply kernel smoothing to the data. In this case, we will use the purpose data to demonstrate some of the tools available in the realm of kernel smoothing. We want to emphasize that we are showing only some of the very basic tools in order to provide the reader with a basic idea of how this methodology might be applied in R, and some of the basic information that it will provide. However, we would strongly urge the interested reader who feels that this methodology may be appropriate for their research scenario to refer to the references listed above, as well as to Mazza, Punzo, and McGuire (2014), which provides a more in-depth description of the R code. Nonetheless, we hope that the following examples will provide the interested reader with sufficient information to carry out some basic kernel smoothing IRT analyses.

In order to kernel smooth the purpose data in the context of IRT, we would use the following commands:

```
Library(KernSmoothIRT)
purpose.key<-1
purpose.ksIRT<-ksIRT(purpose, key=purpose.key, format=1)
```

In order to use the kernel-smoothed approach with dichotomous items, we must provide a key. In this case, the key indicates what constitutes item endorsement, which is 1 for all of the items in this example. Therefore, we need only create a

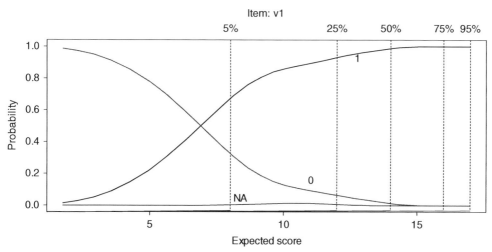

■ Figure 10.7: OCC for item 1

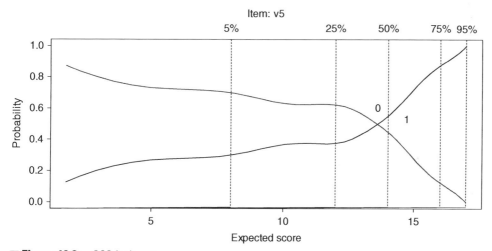

■ Figure 10.8: OCC for item 5

single scalar that applies to all items. However, if we had a situation in which different item responses indicated endorsement, or a correct response, as with multiple choice items, then the key would be a vector containing a separate value for each item. Once we have saved the kernel-smoothed results in the object `purpose.ksIRT`, we can obtain some useful plots that will provide us with information about the relationship of each individual item response with the trait being measured by the items as a whole. For example, we can see how the item responses relate to the total score on the instrument using the option characteristic curve (OCC). In this case, the total score is a measure of an individual's sense of purpose, so that higher scores indicate a greater sense of purpose. To obtain the OCC

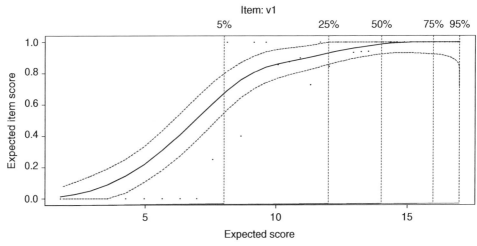

for specific items (e.g. items 1 and 5; see Figures 10.7 and 10.8), we use the `plot` command.

```
plot(purpose.ksIRT, plottype="OCC", item=c(1, 5))
```

These graphs provide us with information about the response probabilities for individuals in the sample for each item. For example, for both items 1 and 5 the relationship between the probability of item endorsement and the total score is monotonically increasing. In addition, given its much steeper curve, item 1 appears to be better at discriminating among people with different levels of purpose than item 5, particularly for lower scores (i.e. those with a lower sense of purpose). Also note that item 1 had some missing data, which is represented by the line hovering near the zero probability value across scores, and which is denoted by the NA label very close to the vertical line at 5%. Inclusion of missing data as an option may provide useful information about which types of individuals are more likely not to respond to an item. In this case, there does not appear to be any such relationship.

In addition to the OCC, we can also obtain the expected item score (EIS) across levels of the total score on the scale, with a 95% confidence interval included. The width of the interval can be adjusted using the `alpha` option in the `plot` command. The observed average scores appear as dots in Figures 10.9 and 10.10 for items 1 and 5 respectively. The primary utility of this graph is to provide the researcher with confidence intervals for the endorsed (or correct) item response.

```
plot(purpose.ksIRT, plottype="EIS", item=c(1, 5))
```

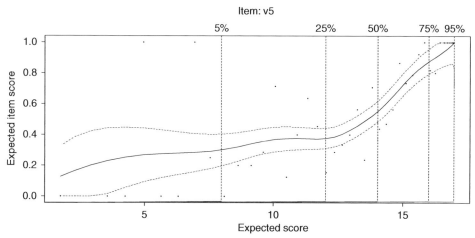

As we noted previously, the purpose of this section of the chapter is not to provide a thorough treatment of kernel smoothing IRT analysis. Rather, we hope that it gives the reader some basic tools that they can use when they would like information regarding items and their relationships with the total score on the scale when the use of standard parametric IRT models may not be appropriate for one reason or another. The tools we have examined here, and the many others available in the KernSmoothIRT package, can provide the researcher with information regarding the quality of their items, particularly with respect to whether they are monotonically related to the total scale score.

SUMMARY

This chapter focused on three broad topics: the examination of assumptions underlying standard IRT models, the investigation of situations in which items do not behave the same way for all examinees, and alternatives to the standard IRT models described in Chapter 9. In each case, the purpose of the techniques described in Chapter 10 was to provide researchers with greater clarity and information regarding the nature of the item response data at hand. Indeed, quite often the analyses demonstrated here, such as MIRT modeling, factor analysis of item response data, DIF analysis, and use of nonparametric methods can be the end goal of a study. In other words, while they may be supportive of a standard IRT analysis, they do not need to be so. In addition, the reader should note that these areas, particularly DIF and nonparametric IRT modelling, are areas of very active research, with many changes occurring frequently. Thus, it is important to keep abreast of such changes when working with these methods.

SUMMARY
10

FURTHER READING

Emgretson, S.E., & Hershberger, S.L. (eds) (1999). *The New Rules of Measurement: What Every Psychologist and Educator Should Know*. Mahwah, NJ: Lawrence Erlbaum Associates, Publishers.

Holland, P.W., & Wainer, H. (1993). *Differential Item Functioning*. Hillsdale, NJ: Lawrence Erlbaum Associates, Publishers.

Millsap, R.E. (2011). *Statistical Approaches to Measurement Invariance*. New York: Routledge.

Rao, C.R., & Sinharay, S. (2007). *Handbook of Statistics, 26: Psychometrics*. Amsterdam: Elsevier.

REFERENCES

Ansley, R.A., & Forsyth, T.N. (1985). An examination of the characteristics of unidimensional IRT parameter estimates derived from two-dimensional data. *Applied Psychological Measurement*, 9, 37–48.

Bock, R.D., & Aitkin, M. (1981). Marginal maximum likelihood estimation of item parameters: Application of an EM algorithm. *Psychometrika*, 46(4), 443–59.

Budescu, D.V., Cohen, Y., & Ben-Simon, A. (1997). A revised modified parallel analysis for the construction of unidimensional item pools. *Applied Psychological Measurement*, 21(3), 233–52.

Cai, L. (2010). High-dimensional exploratory item factor analysis by a Metropolis–Hastings Robbins–Monro algorithm. *Psychometrika*, 75, 33–57.

Camilli, G., & Shepard, L.A. (1994). *Methods for Identifying Biased Test Items*. Thousand Oaks, CA: Sage.

Chen, W-H., & Thissen, D. (1997). Local dependence indexes for item pairs using item response theory. *Journal of Educational and Behavioral Statistics*, 22(3), 265–89.

Clauser, B., Mazor, K., & Hambleton, R K. (1993). The effects of purification of the matching criterion on the identification of DIF using the Mantel–Haenszel procedure. *Applied Measurement in Education*, 6, 269–79.

Finch, H., & Monahan, P. (2008). A bootstrap generalization of modified parallel analysis for IRT dimensionality assessment. *Applied Measurement in Education*, 21, 119–40.

French, B.F., & Maller, S.J. (2007). Iterative purification and effect size use with logistic regression for DIF detection. *Educational and Psychological Measurement*, 67, 373–93.

Hattie, J. (1985). Methodology review: Assessing unidimensionality of tests and items. *Applied Psychological Measurement*, 9(2), 139–64.

Holland, P.W., & Thayer, D.T. (1988). Differential item performance and the Mantel–Haenszel procedure. In H. Holland & H.I. Braun (eds), *Test Validity* (pp. 129–45). Hillsdale, NJ: Erlbaum.

Horn, J.L. (1965). A rationale and test for the number of factors in factor analysis. *Psychometrika*, 30, 179–85.

Kim, D., de Ayala, R.J., Ferdous, A.A., & Nering, M.L. (2011). The comparative performance of conditional independence indices. *Applied Psychological Measurement*, 35(6), 447–71.

Li, H-H., & Stout, W. (1996). A new procedure for detection of crossing DIF. *Psychometrika*, 61(4), 647–77.

Lord, F.M. (1980). *Applications of Item Response Theory to Practical Testing Problems*. Hillsdale, NJ: Erlbaum.

McDonald, R.P. (1999). *Test Theory: A Unified Treatment*. Mahwah, NJ: Lawrence Erlbaum and Associates, Publishers.

Mazza, A., Punzo, A., & McGuire, B. (2014). KernSmoothIRT: An R package for kernel smoothing in item response theory. arXiv:1211.1183v2. Retrieved 07/14/14.

Meijer, R.R., & Baneke, J.J. (2004). Analyzing psychopathology items: A case for nonparametric item response theory modeling. *Psychological Methods*, 9(3), 354–68.

Mokken, R.J. (1971). *A Theory and Procedure of Scale Analysis*. The Hague: Mouton.

Narayanan, P., & Swaminathan, H. (1994). Performance of the Mantel–Haenszel and simultaneous item bias procedures for detecting differential item functioning. *Applied Psychological Measurement*, 18, 315–28.

Narayanan, P., & Swaminathan, H. (1996). Identification of items that show non-uniform DIF. *Applied Psychological Measurement*, 20, 257–74.

Raju, N.S. (1988). The area between two item characteristic curves. *Psychometrika*, 53, 495–502.

Raju, N.S. (1990). Determining the significance of estimated signed and unsigned areas between two item response functions. *Applied Psychological Measurement*, 14, 197–207.

Ramsay, J.O. (1997). A functional approach to modeling test data. In W.J. van der Linden & R.K. Hambleton (eds), *Handbook of Modern Item Response Theory* (pp. 381–94). New York: Springer.

Reckase. M.D. (1985). The difficulty of test items that measure more than one ability. *Applied Psychological Measurement*, 9(4), 401–12.

Reckase, M.D., Carlson, J.E., Ackerman, T.A., & Spray, J.A. (1986). The interpretation of unidimensional IRT parameters when estimated from multidimensional data. Paper presented at the Annual Meeting of the Psychometric Society.

Roussos, L., & Stout, W. (1996). A multidimensionality-based DIF analysis paradigm. *Applied Psychological Measurement*, 20(4), 355–71.

Shealy, R., & Stout, W.F. (1993b). A model-based standardization approach that separates true bias/DIF from group differences and detects test bias/DTF as well as item bias/DIF. *Psychometrika*, 58, 159–94.

Sijtsma, K. & Molenaar, I.W. (2002). *Introduction to Nonparametric Item Response Theory*. Thousand Oaks, CA: Sage.

Simonoff, J.S. (1996). *Smoothing Methods in Statistics*. New York: Springer.

Stout, W.F., Habing, B., Douglas, J., Kim, H.R., Roussos, L., & Zhang, J. (1996). Conditional covariance-based nonparametric multidimensionality assessment. *Applied Psychological Measurement*, 19(4), 331–54.

Thissen, D. (June, 2001). *IRTLRDIF v.2.0b: Software for the Computation of the Statistics Involved in Item Response Theory Likelihood Ratio Tests for Differential Item Functioning*. Unpublished manual from the L.L. Thurstone Psychometric Laboratory: University of North Carolina at Chapel Hill.

Thissen, D., Steinberg, L., & Wainer, H. (1988). Use of item response theory in the study of group differences in trace lines. In H. Wainer & P.W. Holland (eds), *Test Validity* (pp. 147–69). Hillsdale, NJ: Erlbaum.

Woods, C. (2009). Empirical selection of anchors for tests of differential item functioning, *Applied Psychological Measurement*, 33, 42–57.

Yen, W.M. (1984). Effects of local item dependence on the fit and equating performance of the three-parameter logistic model. *Applied Psychological Measurement*, 8(2), 125–45.

Yen, W.M. (1993). Scaling performance assessments: Strategies for managing local item dependence. *Journal of Educational Measurement*, 30, 187–213.

Zumbo, B.D. (1999). *A Handbook on the Theory and Methods of Differential Item Functioning (DIF): Logistic Regression Modeling as a Unitary Framework for Binary and Likert-Type (Ordinal) Item Scores*. Ottowa, ON: Directorate of Human Resources Research and Evaluation, Department of National Defense.

Chapter 11

DATA SIMULATION FOR LATENT VARIABLE MODELING IN R

INTRODUCTION

Monte Carlo simulations are a major component in statistical research. Statisticians often use the simulation of data in order to test statistical tests and modeling procedures (e.g. Bandalos & Leite, 2013), and other researchers can use simulation as a tool for sample size planning (Muthén & Muthén, 2002). For both applications, the goal of simulation is to generate data that mirror those we would expect to see in actual practice, and to then use that data to assess the performance of some statistical analysis of interest. When examination of a method's performance is the focus of the simulation study, researchers typically focus on parameter estimation accuracy, variability in the estimates in the population, and overall model fit. Statisticians will use these performance indicators to ascertain when a given procedure is likely to work well, and when it will not. When sample size determination is the primary goal of the simulation study, the researcher will focus his attention on the parameter estimation accuracy, variation in parameter estimates, and power of statistical tests for various sample sizes, under conditions that are expected to be present in the actual data once it is collected. In this chapter, we will describe tools in R that the researcher can use to simulate data for either of these purposes for SEMs, IRT models, and latent class/mixture models. The purpose of this chapter is not intended to be exhaustive with regards to the simulation of data. The number of variations and applications are simply too many for that. However, we do intend to provide readers with an initial set of tools for simulation that they can then expand and customize for their own purposes. The remainder of the chapter is organized into three sections for simulation of SEM, IRT, and LCA data, respectively.

SIMULATIONS FOR SEM

In this section, we will describe a relatively simple set of R code for simulating data associated with a specific SEM. For this example, we will simulate the model associated with Figure 11.1, in which we have three latent variables, with phi serving as the endogenous, or dependent variable, and eta and theta as the exogenous, or independent variables. Each latent variable has associated with it five observed indicators.

We will simulate the indicators, the errors, and the latent variables to be from the standard normal distribution. The figure shows that the loadings in this simulation are all equal to 1, and the coefficients linking eta, theta, and phi are 1.5 and 1.2, respectively. Below is the full set of R code to simulate this model, and then analyze the simulated data using `lavaan`. Following the full set of commands, we describe the individual components and their roles in simulating the data. We finish this section by examining the results of the simulation.

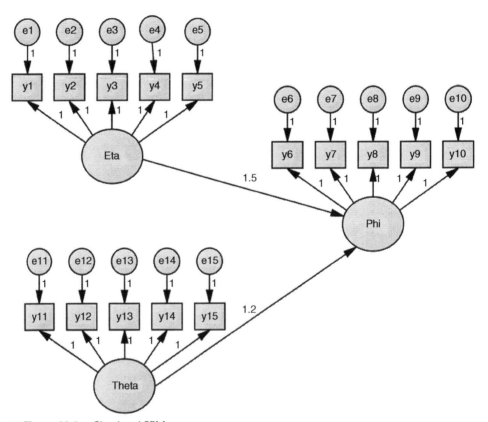

■ **Figure 11.1:** Simulated SEM

```
##Simulate Structural Equation Model

simulation.sem.results<-NULL

# Define Population parameters
n <- 500 # sample size
J <- 5 # number of replications
lambda.1 <- 1
lambda.2 <- 1
lambda.3 <- 1
lambda.4 <- 1
lambda.5 <- 1

lambda.6 <- 1
lambda.7 <- 1
lambda.8 <- 1
lambda.9 <- 1
lambda.10 <- 1

lambda.11 <- 1
lambda.12 <- 1
lambda.13 <- 1
lambda.14 <- 1
lambda.15 <- 1

sigma.eta <- 1 # Variance for eta
sigma.phi <- 1 # Variance for phi
sigma.theta <- 1 # Variance for theta
sigma.ey <- 1 # Variance for error term of y

# define relationships among latent variables
f1<-function (x, y) {1.5*x+1.2*y}
# simulate eta and phi, the latent factors
set.seed (451)
eta <- rnorm (n, 0, sigma.eta)
phi <- rnorm (n, 0, sigma.phi)
theta <- rnorm(n, 0, sigma.theta)
#Define relationship between eta and phi.
phi [1: n] <- f1 (eta, theta [1:n])

# DATASETS do not include eta and phi columns
ContArray  <-  BinArray  <-  matrix(NA,  nrow=(n),
ncol=(15*J))
dim(ContArray) <- dim(BinArray) <- c((n), 15, J)
```

```
dimnames(ContArray)<-dimnames(BinArray)<-list(NULL,
c("y1","y2","y3","y4","y5","y6","y7","y8","y9","y10
","y11","y12","y13","y14","y15"),1:J)

# DATASETS include eta and phi columns
ContArray2  <-  BinArray2  <-  matrix(NA,  nrow=(n),
ncol=(18*J))
dim(ContArray2) <- dim(BinArray2) <- c((n), 18, J)
dimnames(ContArray2)      <-      dimnames(BinArray2)<-
list(NULL,
c("y1","y2","y3","y4","y5","y6","y7","y8","y9","y
10","y11","y12","y13","y14","y15",   "ETA",   "PHI",
"THETA"),1:J)

# SIMULATION
for (j in 1:J){
# simulate y1 to y5
e1 <- rnorm (n, 0, sigma.ey)
y1 <- lambda.1 * eta + e1
e2 <- rnorm (n, 0, sigma.ey)
y2 <- lambda.2 * eta + e2
e3 <- rnorm (n, 0, sigma.ey)
y3 <- lambda.3 * eta + e3
e4 <- rnorm (n, 0, sigma.ey)
y4 <- lambda.4 * eta + e4
e5 <- rnorm (n, 0, sigma.ey)
y5 <- lambda.5 * eta + e5

# simulate y6 to y10
e6 <- rnorm (n, 0, sigma.ey)
y6 <- lambda.6 * phi + e6
e7 <- rnorm (n, 0, sigma.ey)
y7 <- lambda.7 * phi + e7
e8 <- rnorm (n, 0, sigma.ey)
y8 <- lambda.8 * phi + e8
e9 <- rnorm (n, 0, sigma.ey)
y9 <- lambda.9 * phi + e9
e10 <- rnorm (n, 0, sigma.ey)
y10 <- lambda.10 * phi + e10

# simulate y11 to y15
e11 <- rnorm (n, 0, sigma.ey)
y11 <- lambda.11 * theta + e11
e12 <- rnorm (n, 0, sigma.ey)
```

```
y12 <- lambda.12 * theta + e12
e13 <- rnorm (n, 0, sigma.ey)
y13 <- lambda.13 * theta + e13
e14 <- rnorm (n, 0, sigma.ey)
y14 <- lambda.14 * theta + e14
e15 <- rnorm (n, 0, sigma.ey)
y15 <- lambda.15 * theta + e15

ContArray[,,j] <- cbind (y1, y2, y3, y4, y5, y6, y7,
y8, y9, y10, y11, y12, y13, y14, y15)
ContArray2[,,j] <- cbind (y1, y2, y3, y4, y5, y6, y7,
y8, y9, y10, y11, y12, y13, y14, y15, eta, phi, theta)

sem.simulated.data<-round(data.
frame(j,ContArray[,,j]),3)

library(lavaan)
simulated.model<-'
    eta=~y1+y2+y3+y4+y5
    phi=~y6+y7+y8+y9+y10
    theta=~y11+y12+y13+y14+y15
    phi~eta+theta
'
simulated.model.fit<-sem(simulated.model,    data=sem.
simulated.data, estimator="WLSMV")
simulated.estimates<-coef(simulated.model.fit)

sim.sem.output<-data.frame(simulated.
estimates, n, j)

#Combining results from each replication
simulation.sem.results<-rbind(simulation.sem.
results, sim.sem.output)
}
```

One R programming convention to note is the use of # as a marker for comment lines. Comment, or remark, lines are simply segments of computer code that the computer ignores and are included to provide documentation about specific aspects of the program for ourselves later, and for others who might use the code. The first line simply serves as a title explaining the purpose of the following code, namely to simulate a structural equation model. The following lines of code initialize specific variables and conditions that we would like to simulate, including the total sample size, the number of simulated replications, the values of each factor loading, and the variances of the latent variables and the error terms.

```
simulation.sem.results<-NULL

# Define Population parameters
n <- 500 # sample size
J <- 5 # number of replications
lambda.1 <- 1
lambda.2 <- 1
lambda.3 <- 1
lambda.4 <- 1
lambda.5 <- 1

lambda.6 <- 1
lambda.7 <- 1
lambda.8 <- 1
lambda.9 <- 1
lambda.10 <- 1

lambda.11 <- 1
lambda.12 <- 1
lambda.13 <- 1
lambda.14 <- 1
lambda.15 <- 1

sigma.eta <- 1 # Variance for eta
sigma.phi <- 1 # Variance for phi
sigma.theta <- 1 # Variance for theta
sigma.ey <- 1 # Variance for error term of y
```

The data frame that will be used to store the results of the simulation is called `simulate.sem.results`, and must be initialized at the beginning of the code before its first use. After initializing the variables and the output data frame, we then create a small R function that will be used later in the code to simulate the relationships among the latent variables.

```
# define relationships among latent variables
f1<-function (x, y) {1.5*x+1.2*y}
```

Note that we use generic variable names x and y, rather than the specific names of the factors. This makes the code more general so that we can use it in a variety of contexts.

We complete the preparations for simulating the data with the following commands.

```
# simulate eta and phi, the latent factors
set.seed (451)
eta <- rnorm (n, 0, sigma.eta)
phi <- rnorm (n, 0, sigma.phi)
theta <- rnorm(n, 0, sigma.theta)
#Define relationship between eta and phi.
phi [1: n] <- f1 (eta, theta [1:n])

# DATASETS do not include eta and phi columns
ContArray   <-   BinArray   <-   matrix(NA,   nrow=(n),
ncol=(15*J))
dim(ContArray) <- dim(BinArray) <- c((n), 15, J)
dimnames(ContArray)<-dimnames(BinArray)<-list(NULL,
c("y1","y2","y3","y4","y5","y6","y7","y8","y9","y10
","y11","y12","y13","y14","y15"),1:J)

# DATASETS include eta and phi columns
ContArray2  <-  BinArray2  <-  matrix(NA,  nrow=(n),
ncol=(18*J))
dim(ContArray2) <- dim(BinArray2) <- c((n), 18, J)
dimnames(ContArray2)     <-     dimnames(BinArray2)<-
list(NULL,
c("y1","y2","y3","y4","y5","y6","y7","y8","y9","y
10","y11","y12","y13","y14","y15",   "ETA",   "PHI",
"THETA"),1:J)
```

First we set the random number generating seed, which can be any integer. If we did not use such a seed, R would use the computer clock as the initial random number for generating the data. By using a specific number, however, we have the capability of recreating this particular simulation run any time that we would like to. Each time we run this simulation we will want to change the seed, perhaps by adding 1 to it. Next, we generate an initial set of latent variable values from the normal distribution with a mean of zero and variance equal to that defined previously in the program. We use the previously defined sample size (n) to indicate how many individuals we would like in the sample. Once the initial set of random values has been simulated, the value of the endogenous variable, phi, is adjusted through the relationship expressed in function f1. Note that when we call the function, we replace x and y with eta and theta. We must also indicate to R that we would like this relationship to apply to members of the sample from 1 to n; i.e. each of the simulated data points.

Once the data are simulated, we must create arrays that will contain the values of the observed indicator variables for each of the simulated datasets. One set of these will accommodate only the 15 indicators (`ContArray`), while the other will accommodate the 15 indicators as well as the 3 latent variables (`ContArray2`). We are now ready to actually conduct the simulation itself. First we must set up the iterative counter, using the line:

```
for (j in 1:J){
```

The { is matched at the very end of the program with a } to indicate the beginning and ending of the iterated code. We have requested the simulation be run J times, where we set J earlier in the program, in this case to 5. The next step is to generate the values for the observed indicators and their associated error terms.

```
# simulate y1 to y5
e1 <- rnorm (n, 0, sigma.ey)
y1 <- lambda.1 * eta + e1
e2 <- rnorm (n, 0, sigma.ey)
y2 <- lambda.2 * eta + e2
e3 <- rnorm (n, 0, sigma.ey)
y3 <- lambda.3 * eta + e3
e4 <- rnorm (n, 0, sigma.ey)
y4 <- lambda.4 * eta + e4
e5 <- rnorm (n, 0, sigma.ey)
y5 <- lambda.5 * eta + e5

# simulate y6 to y10
e6 <- rnorm (n, 0, sigma.ey)
y6 <- lambda.6 * phi + e6
e7 <- rnorm (n, 0, sigma.ey)
y7 <- lambda.7 * phi + e7
e8 <- rnorm (n, 0, sigma.ey)
y8 <- lambda.8 * phi + e8
e9 <- rnorm (n, 0, sigma.ey)
y9 <- lambda.9 * phi + e9
e10 <- rnorm (n, 0, sigma.ey)
y10 <- lambda.10 * phi + e10

# simulate y11 to y15
e11 <- rnorm (n, 0, sigma.ey)
y11 <- lambda.11 * theta + e11
e12 <- rnorm (n, 0, sigma.ey)
y12 <- lambda.12 * theta + e12
e13 <- rnorm (n, 0, sigma.ey)
y13 <- lambda.13 * theta + e13
e14 <- rnorm (n, 0, sigma.ey)
```

```
y14 <- lambda.14 * theta + e14
e15 <- rnorm (n, 0, sigma.ey)
y15 <- lambda.15 * theta + e15
```

The error terms are generated from the normal distribution with a mean of zero, a variance of `sigma.ey`, and a sample size of `n`. The indicators are a function of the factor loadings, the latent variable value, and the error term. These individual variables are then placed into the arrays that we defined above, which are in turn converted to the dataframe `sem.simulated.data` for use with `lavaan`.

```
ContArray[,,j] <- cbind (y1, y2, y3, y4, y5, y6, y7,
y8, y9, y10, y11, y12, y13, y14, y15)
ContArray2[,,j] <- cbind (y1, y2, y3, y4, y5, y6, y7,
y8, y9, y10, y11, y12, y13, y14, y15, eta, phi, theta)
sem.simulated.data<-round(data.
frame(j,ContArray[,,j]),3)
```

We have now simulated the data and are ready to call the `lavaan` library and run the analysis of interest.

```
library(lavaan)
simulated.model<-'
        eta=~y1+y2+y3+y4+y5
        phi=~y6+y7+y8+y9+y10
        theta=~y11+y12+y13+y14+y15

        phi~eta+theta
'
simulated.model.fit<-sem(simulated.model,   data=sem.
simulated.data, estimator="WLSMV")
simulated.estimates<-coef(simulated.model.fit)
```

These uses of `lavaan` in the simulation study are similar to what we saw in Chapter 4, and serve to specify and fit the model. The last line takes the model coefficients and saves them to the output object `simulated.estimates`. Finally, we save the output from a single replication into another output object called `sim.sem.output`, as below.

```
sim.sem.output<-data.frame(simulated.
estimates, n, j)
```

In this case, we save the parameter estimates, the sample size, and the replication number. Finally, below we combine the results of the simulation using the `rbind` command.

```
#Combining results from each replication
simulation.sem.results<-rbind(simulation.sem.
results, sim.sem.output)
```

When running this simulation, we would type and save these commands into a script window in the R console, or we could keep it in a word processing program, such as Notepad in Windows or TextEdit in Apple Mac OS. In either case, we would copy and paste all of the code at once into the R command window and let it run. By typing in the name of the output file, `simulation.sem.results`, we can see the results across the replications. Below are the results for the first of the five replications here.

	simulated.estimates	n	j
eta=~y2	0.998884616	500	1
eta=~y3	1.014209356	500	1
eta=~y4	0.982010278	500	1
eta=~y5	1.024187409	500	1
phi=~y7	0.985864181	500	1
phi=~y8	1.014049416	500	1
phi=~y9	1.033526525	500	1
phi=~y10	1.021590376	500	1
theta=~y12	0.958297904	500	1
theta=~y13	1.030955440	500	1
theta=~y14	1.060478144	500	1
theta=~y15	1.043321056	500	1
phi~eta	1.570213204	500	1
phi~theta	1.360284698	500	1
y1~~y1	1.047446846	500	1
y2~~y2	0.969322234	500	1
y3~~y3	1.050192200	500	1
y4~~y4	0.970011236	500	1
y5~~y5	1.039474999	500	1
y6~~y6	1.049240458	500	1
y7~~y7	1.033575545	500	1
y8~~y8	0.852609836	500	1
y9~~y9	1.056960103	500	1
y10~~y10	0.998457930	500	1
y11~~y11	0.955260557	500	1
y12~~y12	1.078710062	500	1
y13~~y13	0.923864179	500	1
y14~~y14	0.994478829	500	1
y15~~y15	1.045036955	500	1
eta~~eta	0.877605906	500	1

```
phi~~phi          -0.471870561 500 1
theta~~theta       0.985717277 500 1
eta~~theta         0.046960698 500 1
y1~1               0.070858000 500 1
y2~1               0.080642000 500 1
y3~1               0.019194000 500 1
y4~1               0.060394000 500 1
y5~1               0.045226000 500 1
y6~1               0.039192000 500 1
y7~1              -0.035386000 500 1
y8~1               0.018828000 500 1
y9~1               0.051584000 500 1
y10~1              0.057132000 500 1
y11~1             -0.012096000 500 1
y12~1             -0.086642000 500 1
y13~1             -0.032478000 500 1
y14~1              0.000318000 500 1
y15~1              0.005826000 500 1
```

We can see that these are generally very close to the data generating values, suggesting that the model we requested does a good job of fitting the data. If we were interested in determining the sample size that might be required for a future study, we would try several values and compare the parameter estimation accuracy across values of n.

SIMULATIONS FOR IRT

In principle, the simulation of IRT data in R is very closely related to simulation of SEM data. However, whereas we used our own program in the case of SEM, we will be able to use an R library, catIrt, for item response data. The existence of the catIrt library does not preclude us from writing our own data simulation code if we would like. Indeed, there may be cases where we are interested in simulating data for particular IRT models that are not available in the library. In that case, our code would be similar to that for SEM, though with important differences allowing us to create categorical variables. However, for many routine IRT data simulation applications, catIrt will be more than sufficient. The code for simulating data from a Rasch model and then obtaining item parameter estimates appears below. Note that the conventions and order of code is very similar to that described previously for simulating SEM data. Therefore, we will focus on aspects of IRT simulation with catIrt that are unique and that have not been previously described.

```
library(catIrt)
library(ltm)

##Simulate Rasch Model Data

set.seed(190731)

#Sample size
n=1000

#Population Item parameters
sim.params <- cbind(a = c(1, 1, 1, 1, 1, 1, 1, 1, 1,
1, 1, 1, 1, 1, 1, 1, 1, 1), b = c(0.0, -1.45,
-0.04, -0.54, 0.98, -3, 1.97, 0.90, -1.20, -0.6, 0,
-1.45, -0.04, -0.54, 0.98, -3, 1.97, 0.90, -1.20,
-0.6), c = 0)

simulation.rasch.results<-NULL

for(z in 1:5) {

#Generation of theta
sim.theta<-rnorm(n)

#Generate item response data for each group separately.
sim.data<-simIrt(theta=sim.theta, params=sim.params,
mod="brm")

#Combine item responses for the two groups into
one file.
sim.data.resp<-sim.data$resp

sim.rasch<-rasch(sim.data.resp,
constraint=cbind(ncol(sim.data.resp)+1, 1))

#Save coefficients from Rasch model
sim.rasch.coefs<-coef(sim.rasch)

#Combining results from each replication
sim.rasch.output<-data.frame(sim.rasch.coefs, n, z)

simulation.rasch.results<-rbind(simulation.rasch.
results, sim.rasch.output)
}
```

As with the simulation of SEM data, we begin the IRT simulation program by initializing the variables and the data frame that we will use.

```
library(catIrt)
library(ltm)

##Simulate Rasch Model Data
set.seed(190731)

#Sample size
n=1000

#Population Item parameters
sim.params <- cbind(a = c(1, 1, 1, 1, 1, 1, 1, 1, 1,
1, 1, 1, 1, 1, 1, 1, 1, 1, 1, 1), b = c(0.0, -1.45,
-0.04, -0.54, 0.98, -3, 1.97, 0.90, -1.20, -0.6, 0,
-1.45, -0.04, -0.54, 0.98, -3, 1.97, 0.90, -1.20,
-0.6), c = 0)

simulation.rasch.results<-NULL
```

We first call the `catIrt` and `ltm` libraries, as we will use functions from them to generate and analyze the data. We then set the random generating seed and the sample size. Next, we must specify the model parameters, which will be saved in the matrix `sim.params`. We will take three vectors, a (item discrimination), b (item difficulty), and c (item pseudo-chance), and combine them into a single matrix using the `cbind` command. In this case, we will simulate data for 20 items, meaning that each must have a value for a, b, and c. Here there are unique values of a for each item, though they are all assigned the value 1 because we are simulating data for the Rasch model. We could also have simply put a=1, just as we have c=0 to indicate that all items have a pseudo-guessing value of 0. Each item has a unique item difficulty value, and we finish this section of code by initializing the data frame that will contain the item parameter estimation results, `simulation.rasch.results`.

After the initialization portion of the program, we are ready to simulate and analyze the data. As in the previous program, we must set up the counter to keep track of the replications, after which we generate the values of theta from the standard normal distribution for each of the n individuals in the sample. We then use the function `simIrt` from the `catIrt` library to actually simulate the item responses.

```
for(z in 1:5) {

#Generation of theta
sim.theta<-rnorm(n)
```

```
#Generate item response data for each group separately.
sim.data<-simIrt(theta=sim.theta, params=sim.params,
mod="brm")
```

The mod="brm" subcommand indicates to R that we are interested in simulating binary item responses. Were we interested in simulating ordinal data from the graded responses model, this subcommand would be mod="grm". In the simIrt function call, we must indicate in which objects theta and the item parameters are kept. The object sim.data contains the item responses, the item parameter values, and the values of theta. In order to analyze the data, we must next extract the actual item responses:

```
sim.data.resp<-sim.data$resp
```

These data are then submitted to the rasch function in the ltm library as described in Chapter 9. The model parameter estimates are then obtained and accumulated across replications in the data frame simulation.rasch.results using the following commands. This is very similar in format to the simulation code for SEM, including marking the end of the simulation with }.

```
sim.rasch<-rasch(sim.data.resp,
constraint=cbind(ncol(sim.data.resp)+1, 1))

#Save coefficients from Rasch model
sim.rasch.coefs<-coef(sim.rasch)

#Combining results from each replication
sim.rasch.output<-data.frame(sim.rasch.coefs, n, z)

simulation.rasch.results<-rbind(simulation.rasch.
results, sim.rasch.output)
}
```

The parameter estimates for the first replication in the simulation appear below.

```
simulation.rasch.results
          Dffclt Dscrmn   n z
1      0.027482035      1 1000 1
2     -1.423542507      1 1000 1
3     -0.025891484      1 1000 1
4     -0.491013580      1 1000 1
```

```
 5    0.935359735      1 1000 1
 6   -2.883654503      1 1000 1
 7    2.003887164      1 1000 1
 8    0.853865792      1 1000 1
 9   -1.175907737      1 1000 1
10   -0.647104004      1 1000 1
11   -0.005640077      1 1000 1
12   -1.422990610      1 1000 1
13   -0.096963970      1 1000 1
14   -0.551477853      1 1000 1
15    0.962907569      1 1000 1
16   -2.808975416      1 1000 1
17    1.995199813      1 1000 1
18    0.870031886      1 1000 1
19   -1.140698186      1 1000 1
20   -0.606198740      1 1000 1
```

Simulating data for a 3PL model can be done as easily using R as simulating Rasch model data, with the simIrt function. The code for doing so appears below, and is very similar to that used with the Rasch model, except that the values of a and c vary by item.

```
library(catIrt)
library(ltm)
##Simulate 3PL Model Data

set.seed(4109903)

#Sample size
n=1000

#Population Item parameters
sim.params <- cbind(a = c(1.3, .7, .91, 1.04, .51,
.99, 1.23, 1.56, 1.11, .74, .83, 1.01, .67, 1, 1.8,
2.3, .45, 1.77, 1.09, .88), b = c(0.0, -1.45, -0.04,
-0.54, 0.98, -3, 1.97, 0.90, -1.20, -0.6, 0, -1.45,
-0.04, -0.54, 0.98, -3, 1.97, 0.90, -1.20, -0.6),
c = c(.1, .13, .2, .14, .21, .23, .08, .12, .22, .19,
.09, .04, .11, .22, .2, .11, .12, .15, .2, .19))

simulation.3pl.results<-NULL

for(z in 1:5) {
```

```
#Generation of theta
sim.theta<-rnorm(n)

#Generate item response data for each group separately.
sim.data<-simIrt(theta=sim.theta, params=sim.params,
mod="brm")

#Combine item responses for the two groups into
one file.
sim.data.resp<-sim.data$resp
sim.3pl<-tpm(sim.data.resp)

#Save coefficients from 3PL model
sim.3pl.coefs<-coef(sim.3pl)

#Combining results from each replication
sim.3pl.output<-data.frame(sim.3pl.coefs, n, z)

simulation.3pl.results<-rbind(simulation.3pl.
results, sim.3pl.output)
}
```

The results for the first replication appear below.

```
simulation.3pl.results
          Gussng              Dffclt      Dscrmn      n z
Item 1    0.25860741091    0.48376528 1.4662426 1000 1
Item 2    0.60130064560    0.53185184 1.6348121 1000 1
Item 3    0.00979923779   -0.64825812 0.7741224 1000 1
Item 4    0.31568205133   -0.11962269 1.2473953 1000 1
Item 5    0.45095610279    1.46009026 3.1373198 1000 1
Item 6    0.86266651949   -0.28875226 5.7375101 1000 1
Item 7    0.01468697063    1.81820858 0.9289132 1000 1
Item 8    0.13572625215    0.81687910 1.5346676 1000 1
Item 9    0.00110620421   -1.70561609 0.9415825 1000 1
Item 10   0.00891449426   -1.34992479 0.6170357 1000 1
Item 11   0.00473403424   -0.23871637 0.6914646 1000 1
Item 12   0.00076944890   -1.30161947 1.1779966 1000 1
Item 13   0.21275495720    0.33121457 1.0690404 1000 1
Item 14   0.40530857911    0.03177534 1.3490317 1000 1
Item 15   0.10832886139    0.85397496 1.1685365 1000 1
Item 16   0.02064145301   -3.25688506 2.0013610 1000 1
Item 17   0.25139971382    2.43798329 0.7708148 1000 1
Item 18   0.08898803306    0.74749708 1.5278035 1000 1
Item 19   0.01511045799   -1.49761190 1.0156633 1000 1
Item 20   0.01829196374   -0.98186059 0.9084846 1000 1
```

SIMULATIONS FOR LCA

Just as with SEM and IRT, researchers in various areas may wish to simulate data for latent class models. Such simulations can easily be done using the poLCA. simdata function in the poLCA library. Below is the R code for simulating data for a model with three latent classes in the population, and five binary indicator variables.

```
library(poLCA)
set.seed (874)

probs<-list(
matrix(c(0.7,0.3, 0.3,0.7, 0.2,0.8),ncol=2,byrow=T),
matrix(c(0.7,0.3, 0.5,0.5, 0.2,0.8),ncol=2,byrow=T),
matrix(c(0.7,0.3, 0.3,0.7, 0.7,0.3),ncol=2,byrow=T),
matrix(c(0.7,0.3, 0.5,0.5, 0.7,0.3),ncol=2,byrow=T),
matrix(c(0.7,0.3, 0.3,0.7, 0.2,0.8),ncol=2,byrow=T))

classprop<-c(0.3,0.3,0.4)

n=1000

classes=3
simulated.lca.model<-poLCA.simdata(N=n, probs=probs,
p=classprop, nclass=classes, ndv=5)
simulated.lca.data<-simulated.lca.model$dat

f<-cbind(Y1,Y2,Y3,Y4,Y5)~1
simulated.lca.fit<-poLCA(f,simulated.lca.
data,nclass=3)
```

First, we must call the poLCA library, and set the seed value. Next, we specify the response probabilities for the five indicators for each of the three groups. These are kept in the R list probs, and appear as follows within R itself.

```
probs
[[1]]
        [,1] [,2]
[1,] 0.7 0.3
[2,] 0.3 0.7
[3,] 0.2 0.8
```

```
[[2]]
        [,1] [,2]
[1,] 0.7 0.3
[2,] 0.5 0.5
[3,] 0.2 0.8

[[3]]
        [,1] [,2]
[1,] 0.7 0.3
[2,] 0.3 0.7
[3,] 0.7 0.3

[[4]]
        [,1] [,2]
[1,] 0.7 0.3
[2,] 0.5 0.5
[3,] 0.7 0.3

[[5]]
        [,1] [,2]
[1,] 0.7 0.3
[2,] 0.3 0.7
[3,] 0.2 0.8
```

Each submatrix within the larger matrix corresponds to one of the indicators. Within each submatrix, the rows represent the latent classes and the columns the two item responses. These values are simply what we told R in the list command, and correspond to the item response patterns that we want to simulate from the population. We must also indicate the mixing proportions for the population (i.e. the proportion of individuals in each class), which is saved in the object classprop. Finally, we indicate the total sample size and the number of latent classes in the population.

The actual generation of the simulated data is done with poLCA.simdata, as mentioned above. The output object simulated.lca.model includes not only the simulated data, but also the true class to which each simulee belongs, along with the item response probabilities that we provided to the function, the number of responses for each item, and the observed mixing proportions. In order to extract the actual observed indicator response data for analysis, we use the following command:

```
simulated.lca.data<-simulated.lca.model$dat
```

The final two commands are taken directly from the examples in Chapter 8 for fitting the standard LCA model to the data. All of the diagnostic tools and model fit information that was described in that chapter are easily applied to the simulated data. In order to compare the model prediction with the known population values, for example, we can use the R `table` command as follows.

```
table(simulated.lca.model$trueclass, simulated.lca.
fit$predclass)
          1    2    3
1    49  87    189
2   189 200  49
3    40   182 15
```

The true latent classes appear in the rows, and the predicted classes in the columns. Recall from our discussion in Chapter 8 that the issue of label switching is one that we must take into account when interpreting results in LCA. As a reminder, label switching simply refers to the fact that numeric labels assigned to latent classes by the computer are arbitrary, meaning that the value we assigned to a class in our simulation may not be equivalent to the one that is assigned by the computer. From the results in the table, we might conclude that true class 1 corresponds to predicted class 3 because the majority of those in true class 1 were predicted to be in predicted class 3. Again, this is fine as the labels themselves are arbitrary. Likewise, true class 3 corresponds to predicted class 2. Interestingly, true class 2 is nearly equally divided between predicted classes 1 and 2, indicating a difficulty on the part of the LCA algorithm in differentiating these two latent classes.

SUMMARY

Chapter 11 is intended to serve as a basic introduction to the simulation of data for latent variable models. Obviously, this is an area that could be addressed in an entire book, as opposed to a single chapter. However, we are hopeful that this initial look at the issues surrounding data generation and analysis that are a primary component of any simulation study will serve as a useful tool in its own right, and a helpful introduction to those readers wanting to learn about data simulation in this context. In particular, we hope that by providing the basic tools for this type of work, the chapter will serve as a useful jumping-off point for further investigation on the part of interested readers into the methods and uses of data simulation, both of which are quite numerous.

SUMMARY
11

FURTHER READING

Bandalos, D.L., & Leite, W. (2013). Use of Monte Carlo studies in structural equation modeling research. In G.R. Hancock & R.O. Mueller (eds) *Structural Equation Modeling: A Second Course*. Charlotte, NC: Information Age Publishing.

Boomsma, A. (2013). Reporting Monte Carlo studies in structural equation modeling. *Structural Equation Modeling*, 20, 518–40.

Harwell, M., Stone, C.A., Hsu, T.C., & Kirisci, L. (1996). Monte Carlo studies in item response theory. *Applied Psychological Measurement*, 20, 101–25.

REFERENCES

Bandalos, D.L., & Leite, W. (2013). Use of Monte Carlo studies in structural equation modeling research. In G.R. Hancock & R.O. Mueller (eds) *Structural Equation Modeling: A Second Course*. Charlotte, NC: Information Age Publishing.

Muthén, L.K., & Muthén, B.O. (2002). How to use a Monte Carlo study to decide on sample size and determine power. *Structural Equation Modeling*, 9(4), 599–620.

KEY R COMMANDS

Chapter 2

Exploratory factor analysis

```
factanal(~VARIABLES TO BE FACTOR ANALYZED, factors=NUMBER OF
FACTORS, rotation="CHOICE OF ROTATION")

fa.parallel(DATA FRAME CONTAINING VARIABLES TO BE FACTOR
ANALYZED, fa="TYPE OF EXTRACTION FOR WHICH TO SHOW EIGENVALUES,
PC, FA, OR BOTH", fm="FACTOR EXTRACTION METHOD")

fa(DATA FRAME CONTAINING VARIABLES TO BE FACTOR ANALYZED,
nfactors=NUMBER OF FACTORS, residuals=TRUE, rotate="CHOICE OF
ROTATION", SMC=TRUE, fm="FACTOR EXTRACTION METHOD")
```

Principal components analysis

```
princomp(~VARIABLES TO BE INCLUDED IN THE PRINCIPAL COMPONENTS
ANALYSIS)
```

Chapter 3

Test for multivariate normality

```
mardia(DATA FRAME CONTAINING ONLY VARIABLES FOR WHICH
MULTIVARIATE NORMALITY SHOULD BE TESTED)
```

Confirmatory factor analysis

```
cfa(lavaan MODEL OBJECT, data=DATA FRAME CONTAINING VARIABLES
USED IN THE lavaan MODEL OBJECT, test="IF REQUESTED, THE CHOICE
OF ADJUSTMENT TO THE CHI-SQUARE GOODNESS OF FIT STATISTIC, AND
FIT INDICES DERIVED FROM IT", estimator="ESTIMATION ALGORITHM TO
BE USED")
summary(lavaan CFA OR SEM MODEL FIT OBJECT, fit.measures=T,
standardized=T)
```

Compare fit of structural equation models

```
anova(FIT OBJECT FOR MODEL 1, FIT OBJECT FOR MODEL 2)
```

Chapter 4

Structural equation models

```
sem(lavaan MODEL OBJECT, data= DATA FRAME CONTAINING VARIABLES
USED IN THE lavaan MODEL OBJECT, estimator="ESTIMATION ALGORITHM
TO BE USED")
summary(lavaan CFA OR SEM MODEL FIT OBJECT, fit.measures=T,
standardized=T)
```

Chapter 5

Fitting configural invariance model

```
cfa(lavaan MODEL OBJECT, data=DATA FRAME CONTAINING VARIABLES
USED IN THE lavaan MODEL OBJECT, test="IF REQUESTED, THE CHOICE
OF ADJUSTMENT TO THE CHI-SQUARE GOODNESS OF FIT STATISTIC, AND
FIT INDICES DERIVED FROM IT", group="NAME OF GROUPING VARIABLE",
estimator="ESTIMATION ALGORITHM TO BE USED")
summary(lavaan CFA OR SEM MODEL FIT OBJECT, fit.measures=T,
standardized=T)
```

Fitting fully invariant model

```
cfa(lavaan MODEL OBJECT, data=DATA FRAME CONTAINING VARIABLES
USED IN THE lavaan MODEL OBJECT, test="IF REQUESTED, THE CHOICE
OF ADJUSTMENT TO THE CHI-SQUARE GOODNESS OF FIT STATISTIC, AND
```

```
FIT INDICES DERIVED FROM IT", group="NAME OF GROUPING VARIABLE",
group.equal=c("loadings", "intercepts", "residuals", "lv.variances",
"lv.covariances"), estimator="ESTIMATION ALGORITHM TO BE USED")
```

Unconstraining equal factor loadings

```
cfa(lavaan MODEL OBJECT, data=DATA FRAME CONTAINING VARIABLES
USED IN THE lavaan MODEL OBJECT, test="IF REQUESTED, THE CHOICE
OF ADJUSTMENT TO THE CHI-SQUARE GOODNESS OF FIT STATISTIC, AND
FIT INDICES DERIVED FROM IT", group="NAME OF GROUPING VARIABLE",
group.equal=c("intercepts", "residuals", "lv.variances",
"lv.covariances"), estimator="ESTIMATION ALGORITHM TO BE USED")
```

Unconstraining equal factor intercepts

```
cfa(lavaan MODEL OBJECT, data=DATA FRAME CONTAINING VARIABLES
USED IN THE lavaan MODEL OBJECT, test="IF REQUESTED, THE CHOICE OF
ADJUSTMENT TO THE CHI-SQUARE GOODNESS OF FIT STATISTIC, AND FIT INDICES
DERIVED FROM IT", group="NAME OF GROUPING VARIABLE",
group.equal=c("loadings", "residuals", "lv.variances",
"lv.covariances"), estimator="ESTIMATION ALGORITHM TO BE USED")
```

Unconstraining equal error variances

```
cfa(lavaan MODEL OBJECT, data=DATA FRAME CONTAINING VARIABLES
USED IN THE lavaan MODEL OBJECT, test="IF REQUESTED, THE CHOICE
OF ADJUSTMENT TO THE CHI-SQUARE GOODNESS OF FIT STATISTIC, AND
FIT INDICES DERIVED FROM IT", group="NAME OF GROUPING VARIABLE",
group.equal=c("loadings", "intercepts", "lv.variances",
"lv.covariances"), estimator="ESTIMATION ALGORITHM TO BE USED")
```

Constrained equal factor means model

```
cfa(lavaan MODEL OBJECT, data=DATA FRAME CONTAINING VARIABLES
USED IN THE lavaan MODEL OBJECT, test="IF REQUESTED, THE CHOICE
OF ADJUSTMENT TO THE CHI-SQUARE GOODNESS OF FIT STATISTIC, AND
FIT INDICES DERIVED FROM IT", group="NAME OF GROUPING VARIABLE",
group.equal=c("loadings", "intercepts", "lv.variances", "means"),
estimator="ESTIMATION ALGORITHM TO BE USED")
```

Unconstrained factor means model

```
cfa(lavaan MODEL OBJECT, data=DATA FRAME CONTAINING VARIABLES
USED IN THE lavaan MODEL OBJECT, test="IF REQUESTED, THE CHOICE
OF ADJUSTMENT TO THE CHI-SQUARE GOODNESS OF FIT STATISTIC, AND
FIT INDICES DERIVED FROM IT", group="NAME OF GROUPING VARIABLE",
group.equal=c("loadings", "intercepts", "lv.variances", "means"),
estimator="ESTIMATION ALGORITHM TO BE USED")
```

Compare fit of structural equation models

```
anova(FIT OBJECT FOR MODEL 1, FIT OBJECT FOR MODEL 2)
```

Chapter 6

Fitting models using two-stage least squares

```
systemfit(EQUATION SYSTEM, method="2SLS", inst=list(~INSTRUMENTAL
VARIABLES))
summary(SYSTEM FIT OBJECT)
```

Chapter 7

Example linear growth curve model object

```
lang.growth.model1<-'
 i=~1*lf3+1*ls4+1*lf4+1*ls5+1*lf5+1*ls6
 s=~0*lf3+1*ls4+2*lf4+3*ls5+4*lf5+5*ls6
 '
```

Fitting linear growth curve model

```
growth(LINEAR GROWTH CURVE MODEL OBJECT, data= DATA FRAME
CONTAINING VARIABLES USED IN THE GROWTH CURVE MODEL OBJECT)
summary(GROWTH CURVE MODEL FIT OBJECT)
```

Example quadratic growth curve model object

```
lang.growth.model2<-'
i=~1*lf3+1*ls4+1*lf4+1*ls5+1*lf5+1*ls6
s=~0*lf3+1*ls4+2*lf4+3*ls5+4*lf5+5*ls6
q=~0*lf3+1*ls4+4*lf4+9*ls5+16*lf5+25*ls6
'
```

Fitting quadratic growth curve model

```
growth(QUADRATIC GROWTH CURVE MODEL OBJECT, data= DATA FRAME
CONTAINING VARIABLES USED IN THE GROWTH CURVE MODEL OBJECT)
```

Example linear growth curve model object with covariates

```
lang.growth.model1.mimic<-'
i=~1*lf3+1*ls4+1*lf4+1*ls5+1*lf5+1*ls6
s=~0*lf3+1*ls4+2*lf4+3*ls5+4*lf5+5*ls6
i~sex
s~sex
'
```

Fitting linear growth curve model with covariates

```
growth(LINEAR GROWTH CURVE MODEL WITH COVARIATES OBJECT, data=
DATA FRAME CONTAINING VARIABLES USED IN THE GROWTH CURVE MODEL
OBJECT)
```

Example linear growth curve model for two processes simultaneously

```
lang.growth.model3<-'
lang_i=~1*lf3+1*ls4+1*lf4+1*ls5+1*lf5+1*ls6
lang_s=~0*lf3+1*ls4+2*lf4+3*ls5+4*lf5+5*ls6
read_i=~1*rf3+1*rs4+1*rf4+1*rs5+1*rf5+1*rs6
read_s=~0*rf3+1*rs4+2*rf4+3*rs5+4*rf5+5*rs6
'
```

Fitting linear growth curve model for two processes simultaneously

```
growth(LINEAR GROWTH CURVE MODEL FOR TWO PROCESSES
SIMULTANEOUSLY, data= DATA FRAME CONTAINING VARIABLES USED IN THE
GROWTH CURVE MODEL OBJECT)
```

Chapter 8

Example mixture model object

```
f<-cbind(v1,v2,v3,v4,v5,v6,v7,v8,v9,v10,v11,v12,v13,v14,v15,v16,v17)~1
```

Fitting a mixture model

```
poLCA(MIXTURE MODEL OBJECT, DATA FRAME CONTAINING VARIABLES USED IN
THE MIXTURE MODEL OBJECT, nclass=NUMBER OF LATENT CLASSES)
```

Example mixture model object with covariates

```
f<-cbind(v1,v2,v3,v4,v5,v6,v7,v8,v9,v10,v11,v12,v13,v14,v15,v16,v17)
~meaning.score
```

Fitting a mixture model with covariates

```
poLCA(MIXTURE MODEL WITH COVARIATES OBJECT, DATA FRAME CONTAINING
VARIABLES USED IN THE MIXTURE MODEL WITH COVARIATES OBJECT,
nclass=NUMBER OF LATENT CLASSES)
```

Fitting a mixture regression model

```
flexmix(Y~X, data= DATA FRAME CONTAINING VARIABLES USED IN THE
MIXTURE REGRESSION MODEL, k=NUMBER OF LATENT CLASSES)
```

Chapter 9

Obtaining classical test theory item statistics, including item discrimination

```
item.exam(DATAFRAME CONTAINING ITEM RESPONSES, discrim=TRUE)
```

Obtaining Cronbach's alpha and associated confidence intervals

```
alpha(mathg6)
alpha.CI(0.7245, 10, 7130, level=0.95, onesided=FALSE)
```

Fitting Rasch model

```
rasch(DATAFRAME CONTAINING ITEM RESPONSES,
constraint=cbind(ncol(mathg6)+1, 1))
```

Producing item characteristic curves

```
plot(IRT MODEL OBJECT,type=c("ICC"), items=c(7,9))
```

Producing item information curves

```
plot(IRT MODEL OBJECT,type=c("IIC"), items=c(7,9))
```

Obtaining information for an IRT model

```
information(ITEM RESPONSE MODEL OBJECT, c(-10,10))
```

Obtaining IRT model fit statistics

```
item.fit(DATAFRAME CONTAINING ITEM RESPONSES,
simulate.p.value=TRUE)
```

Fitting 1 PL model

```
rasch(DATAFRAME CONTAINING ITEM RESPONSES)
```

Model goodness of fit test with bootstrapping

```
GoF.rasch(mathg6.1pl, B=1000)
```

Fitting 2 PL model

```
ltm(DATA FRAME CONTAINING ITEM RESPONSES~z1)
```

Fitting 3 PL model

```
tpm(DATA FRAME CONTAINING ITEM RESPONSES)
```

Compare fit of IRT models

```
anova(FIRST IRT MODEL, SECOND IRT MODEL)
```

Fitting generalized partial credit model with Rasch constraint

```
gpcm(DATA FRAME CONTAINING ITEM RESPONSES,constraint="rasch")
```

Fitting generalized partial credit model with 1PL constraint

```
gpcm(DATA FRAME CONTAINING ITEM RESPONSES,constraint="1PL")
```

Fitting generalized partial credit model

```
gpcm(DATA FRAME CONTAINING ITEM RESPONSES,constraint="gpcm")
```

Fitting graded response model

```
grm(DATA FRAME CONTAINING ITEM RESPONSES)
```

Chapter 10

Fitting exploratory factor IRT models

```
mirt(DATA FRAME CONTAINING ITEM RESPONSES,NUMBER OF DIMENSIONS)
```

Compare fit of exploratory factor IRT models

```
anova(MIRT MODEL OBJECT 1, MIRT MODEL OBJECT 2)
```

Calculate bootstrap test for unidimensionality

```
unidimTest(mathg6.3pl,mathg6)
```

Example confirmatory factor MIRT model object

```
model.10.1<-mirt.model('
F1=7,9,10,11,13,15,17,18,21,22,24,27,31
F2=1,3,6,8,16,29,32
F3=2,4,5,12,14,19,20,23,25,26,28,30')
```

Fitting confirmatory factor MIRT model

```
mirt(DATA FRAME CONTAINING ITEM RESPONSES, MODEL OBJECT, SE=TRUE)
```

Example bifactor model object

```
specific <- c(2,3,2,3,3,2,1,2,1,1,1,3,1,3,1,2,1,1,3,3,1,1,3,1,3,3,1,3
,2,3,1,2)
```

Fitting bifactor model

```
bfactor(DATA FRAME CONTAINING ITEM RESPONSES, BIFACTOR MODEL
OBJECT, SE=TRUE)
```

Mantel–Haenszel test for DIF

```
difMH(DATA FRAME CONTAINING ITEM RESPONSES,group="VARIABLE
CONTAINING GROUP INDICATORS",focal.name=INDICATOR VALUE FOR FOCAL
GROUP,purify=TRUE)
```

Logistic regression for DIF

```
difLogistic(DATA FRAME CONTAINING ITEM RESPONSES,group="VARIABLE
CONTAINING GROUP INDICATORS",focal.name=INDICATOR VALUE FOR FOCAL
GROUP,purify=TRUE,type="TYPE OF DIF TO BE ASSESSED")
```

Raju's area method for detecting DIF

```
difRaju(DATA FRAME CONTAINING ITEM RESPONSES,group="VARIABLE
CONTAINING GROUP INDICATORS",focal.name=INDICATOR VALUE FOR FOCAL
GROUP,purify=TRUE,model="IRT MODEL")
```

Lord's chi-square test for DIF

```
difLord(DATA FRAME CONTAINING ITEM RESPONSES,group="VARIABLE
CONTAINING GROUP
INDICATORS",focal.name=1,purify=TRUE,model="INDICATOR VALUE FOR
FOCAL GROUP")
```

Obtain Mokken scalability coefficients

```
coefH(DATA FRAME CONTAINING ITEM RESPONSES)
```

Identify optimal scale solution using Mokken scaling

```
search.normal(DATA FRAME CONTAINING ITEM RESPONSES)
```

Fitting kernel-smoothed item response curves

```
ksIRT(DATA FRAME CONTAINING ITEM RESPONSES, key=ITEM RESPONSE
KEY, format=1)
```

Chapter 11

Example Rasch model item parameter values for data simulation

```
sim.params <- cbind(a = c(1, 1, 1, 1, 1, 1, 1, 1, 1, 1, 1, 1, 1,
1, 1, 1, 1, 1, 1), b = c(0.0, -1.45, -0.04, -0.54, 0.98, -3,
1.97, 0.90, -1.20, -0.6, 0, -1.45, -0.04, -0.54, 0.98, -3, 1.97,
0.90, -1.20, -0.6), c = 0)
```

Example theta generation for data simulation

```
sim.theta<-rnorm(n)
```

Generate simulated item responses for Rasch model

```
sim.data<-simIrt(theta=sim.theta, params=sim.params, mod="brm")
```

Example 2PL model item parameter values for data simulation

```
sim.params <- cbind(a = c(1, 1, 1, 1, 1, 1, 1, 1, 1, 1, 1, 1, 1,
1, 1, 1, 1, 1, 1), b = c(0.0, -1.45, -0.04, -0.54, 0.98, -3,
1.97, 0.90, -1.20, -0.6, 0, -1.45, -0.04, -0.54, 0.98, -3, 1.97,
0.90, -1.20, -0.6), c = 0)
```

Generate simulated item responses for the 2PL model

```
sim.data<-simIrt(theta=sim.theta, params=sim.params, mod="brm")
```

Example 3PL model item parameter values for data simulation

```
sim.params <- cbind(a = c(1.3, .7, .91, 1.04, .51, .99, 1.23,
1.56, 1.11, .74, .83, 1.01, .67, 1, 1.8, 2.3, .45, 1.77, 1.09,
.88), b = c(0.0, -1.45, -0.04, -0.54, 0.98, -3, 1.97, 0.90,
-1.20, -0.6, 0, -1.45, -0.04, -0.54, 0.98, -3, 1.97, 0.90, -1.20,
-0.6), c = c(.1, .13, .2, .14, .21, .23, .08, .12, .22, .19, .09,
.04, .11, .22, .2, .11, .12, .15, .2, .19))
```

Generate simulated item responses for the 3PL model

```
sim.data<-simIrt(theta=sim.theta, params=sim.params, mod="brm")
```

Example R commands for simulating and extracting latent class data

```
probs<-list(
matrix(c(0.7,0.3,      0.3,0.7,      0.2,0.8),ncol=2,byrow=T),
matrix(c(0.7,0.3,      0.5,0.5,      0.2,0.8),ncol=2,byrow=T),
matrix(c(0.7,0.3,      0.3,0.7,      0.7,0.3),ncol=2,byrow=T),
matrix(c(0.7,0.3,      0.5,0.5,      0.7,0.3),ncol=2,byrow=T),
matrix(c(0.7,0.3,      0.3,0.7,      0.2,0.8),ncol=2,byrow=T))

classprop<-c(0.3, 0.3,0.4)

n=1000

classes=3

simulated.lca.model<-poLCA.simdata(N=n, probs=probs, p=classprop,
nclass=classes, ndv=5)
simulated.lca.data<-simulated.lca.model$dat
```

GLOSSARY

Akaike information criterion (AIC) Measure of relative model fit, reflecting the amount of variance in the observed indicators not explained by the model, with a penalty for model complexity.

Bayesian information criterion (BIC) Measure of relative model fit, reflecting the amount of variance in the observed indicators not explained by the model, with a penalty for model complexity.

Bifactor model A multidimensional IRT model in which all items are associated with a single general factor, and in addition, each item is associated with one of a small number of specific factors.

Bootstrap modified parallel analysis test Statistical method for testing the null hypothesis that a set of item responses are unidimensional.

Chi-square difference statistic Statistical test calculated as the difference between the chi-square goodness of fit statistics for nested models. The difference is itself distributed as a chi-square statistic, and can be used to test the null hypothesis that the fit of the two models is not different.

Chi-square goodness of fit test Statistical test assessing the null hypothesis that the model implied covariance matrix equals the observed covariance matrix.

Comparative fit index (CFI) Statistic used in assessing the fit of confirmatory factor and structural equation models. By convention, values of 0.95 or larger are assumed to signal good fit.

Configural invariance Overall latent structure (which indicators are associated with which factors) is the same across groups, but individual model parameters are allowed to vary from group to group.

Data frame An R data object, very much analogous to datasets in other software packages such as SPSS, Mplus, and SAS.

Diagonally weighted least squares An alternative parameter estimation method that can be used when the observed indicator variables violate the assumption of multivariate normality underlying maximum likelihood, and which does not require as large a sample as does standard weighted least squares.

Differential item functioning (DIF) The situation in which individuals in two or more groups are matched on the latent trait being measured by a scale, and the probability of a particular response to an item (e.g. correct) differs between/ among the groups.

Endogenous variable A variable in a linear equation that is predicted by (serves as the dependent variable to) other variables, known as exogenous variables.

Exogenous variable A variable in a linear equation that serves as the predictor of (independent variable to) one or more endogenous variables.

Factor analysis A statistical method using correlations among observed variables, such as subscales or items on an instrument, to estimate unobserved, or latent, variables and their relationships with the observed variables.

Factor invariance The case where the latent structure underlying observed indicators is equivalent across multiple groups. Factor invariance is a necessary requirement for researchers wishing to assume the comparability of the latent construct across groups.

Factor loadings A latent variable model parameter relating an observed indicator variable to a latent variable.

Factor rotation The statistical transformation of factor loadings in exploratory factor analysis to create simple structure, thereby making the loadings more interpretable.

Generalized partial credit model (GPCM) An IRT model for polytomous data in which the item thresholds and item discrimination values are freely estimated. Boundaries between categories are modeled as dichotomous choices between only those two categories.

Graded response model (GRM) An IRT model for polytomous data in which the item thresholds and item discrimination values are freely estimated. Boundaries between categories are modeled as choices between the lower category and all possible selections lower, and the higher category and all possible selections higher.

Growth curve models (GCMs) Use of the structural equation modeling framework with data measured for a group of individuals repeatedly over time in order to estimate linear and nonlinear growth.

Item characteristic curve (ICC) Graph associated with item response theory which plots the level of the latent trait for individuals on the x-axis, and the probability of a particular item response (e.g. correct) on the y-axis.

Item difficulty The location of an item on the latent trait being measured by a scale.

Item discrimination The ability of an item to differentiate among individuals with different levels of the latent trait being measured by the scale.

Item information A statistic used in item response theory to measure the degree to which an item reduces uncertainty in the estimation of the latent trait of interest.

Item response theory (IRT) Statistical modeling framework that links responses to items on a test or questionnaire with the latent trait that the items, collectively as a scale, are meant to measure.

Kernel smoothing A nonparametric method of estimating relationships between two (or more) variables. Kernel smoothing can be used in the context of IRT to estimate item response functions when the assumptions underlying standard IRT models may not hold.

Latent class analysis (LCA) Mixture model that identifies latent classes in the population based upon the values of observed variables. When the observed variables are categorical, the technique is referred to as latent class analysis, and when the variables are continuous it is sometimes referred to as latent profile analysis.

lavaan An R library designed to fit structural equation models.

Library A set of R functions written for a specific purpose; e.g. fitting structural equation models. Libraries can usually be found in and downloaded from the R repository using the LOAD PACKAGES menu command.

Likelihood ratio test Statistical test of the null hypothesis that two nested models provide the same fit to a set of data.

Local independence An assumption underlying standard IRT models which stipulates that when the latent trait being measured by a set of items is accounted for, there is no correlation between responses for any pair of items.

ltm R library that is used to fit standard IRT models for both dichotomous and polytomous data.

Mardia's test Statistical test of the null hypothesis that a set of variables are multivariate normally distributed.

Maximum likelihood The most popular technique for obtaining parameter estimates for confirmatory factor and structural equation models. Maximum likelihood is built on the assumption that the observed indicators are multivariate normally distributed.

Measurement invariance The situation in which factor loadings are equivalent across groups.

Measurement model The set of confirmatory factor models that precede the fitting of a structural equation model. The purpose of the measurement model is to ensure that each latent variable in the structural model fits the observed data.

Mixture models Statistical models used when it is believed that the population consists of subgroups, or mixtures, of cases that differ on the outcome of interest, whether that be a set of observed variables or the parameters of a model, such as regression.

Mixture regression models Mixture models that identify latent classes in the population based upon parameter estimates (e.g. slopes) from a regression analysis.

Mokken scaling Method based on inter-item covariances for identifying items that would constitute a statistically coherent scale.

Monotonicity Assumption underlying IRT models which stipulates that the relationship between the latent trait being measured and the item response is a monotonically increasing function.

Monte Carlo simulations The process of generating data for a specific model structure using random numbers, and hypothesized population parameter values. Monte Carlo simulations are frequently used by statisticians to test statistical methods, and to determine required sample size for a particular data analysis, such as structural equation modeling.

Multidimensional item response theory (MIRT) model Item response theory model allowing for multiple latent traits. The MIRT model is analogous to the confirmatory factor analysis model.

Multiple groups SEM Involves fitting a latent variable model to more than one group, allowing some parameter estimates to vary by group.

Multiple indicators multiple causes (MIMIC) model Structural equation model in which observed covariates serve as predictors of latent variables.

Nonrecursive structural equation models Structural equation models in which some of the relationships between the latent variables are bidirectional.

Nonuniform DIF The situation in which item discrimination parameters differ between/among two or more groups of individuals.

One-parameter logistic (1PL) model Item response theory model for dichotomous item response data in which a common discrimination value is estimated for all items, pseudo-chance is set to 0, and difficulty is freely estimated.

Partial credit model (PCM) An IRT model for polytomous data in which the item thresholds are freely estimated, but item discrimination is either set to 1, or a single discrimination value is estimated for all items. The PCM is analogous to the Rasch or 1PL models for dichotomous data.

Partially invariant The situation in which some, but not all, factor loadings are equivalent across groups.

poLCA R library and function used to fit latent class models.

Pseudo-chance The probability that an examinee will endorse an item (e.g. answer it correctly) due solely to chance.

R Commander A graphical user interface for use in R that makes running R code and reading in data from external files somewhat easier than doing so in the standard console window.

Rasch model Item response theory model in which discrimination is set to 1 for all items, pseudo-chance is set to 0, and difficulty is freely estimated.

Recursive structural equation models Structural equation model in which all of the relationships between the latent variables are unidirectional.

Relative efficiency (RE) The ratio of information provided by two different IRT models using the same data.

Root mean square error of approximation (RMSEA) Statistic used in assessing the fit of confirmatory factor and structural equation models. By convention, values of 0.05 or lower are assumed to signal good fit.

Rootogram Histogram featuring the posterior probability of latent class membership by the square root of the latent class size.

Sample-size-adjusted BIC Measure of relative model fit, reflecting the amount of variance in the observed indicators not explained by the model, with a penalty for model complexity.

Scalar invariance The situation in which factor model intercepts and factor loadings are equivalent across groups.

Standardized root mean square residual (SRMR) Statistic used in assessing the fit of confirmatory factor and structural equation models. By convention, values of 0.08 or smaller are assumed to signal good fit.

Strict factor invariance The situation in which individual indicator error variances, intercept variances, and factor loadings are equivalent across groups.

Structural model The portion of the structural equation model that links the latent variables with one another.

Three-parameter logistic (3PL) model Item response theory model for dichotomous item response data in which a unique discrimination value is estimated for each item, a unique pseudo-chance parameter is estimated for each item, and difficulty is freely estimated.

Threshold A parameter in polytomous IRT models marking the boundary between adjacent item responses.

Thurstone's simple structure The condition whereby each latent variable is associated with a subset of indicators with large factor loadings, and each indicator has a large loading for only one latent variable.

Tucker–Lewis index (TLI) Statistic used in assessing the fit of confirmatory factor and structural equation models. By convention, values of 0.95 or larger are assumed to signal good fit.

Two-parameter logistic model (2PL) Item response theory model for dichotomous item response data in which a unique discrimination value is estimated for each item, pseudo-chance is set to 0, and difficulty is freely estimated.

Two-stage least squares (2SLS) Method of model parameter estimation that is particularly useful for fitting nonrecursive models.

Unidimensionality An assumption underlying IRT models which stipulates that the set of items making up the scale measure a single latent variable.

Uniform DIF The situation in which item difficulty parameters differ between/among two or more groups of individuals.

Weighted least squares An alternative parameter estimation method that can be used when the observed indicator variables violate the assumption of multivariate normality underlying maximum likelihood. Weighted least squares can present problems with convergence when the sample is not large.

Yen's Q_3 statistic Statistic used to assess whether a pair of items are locally independent.

INDEX

absolute fit 189; assessing for Rasch model 189–91
academic frustration 117
Acceleration Factor approach 23–4
achievement goal scale (AGS) 10–11
AIC 44, 310; in IRT models 183, 195, 200, 208, 213, 215–16, 230–1; in mixture models 152, 159–60, 168, 175
Aitkin, M. 234
Akaike information criterion *see* AIC
analysis of variance (ANOVA) 95; in modeling of change over time 134, 135
attention control (ATTC) 62

Baneke, J.J. 266
Bauer, D.J. 115
Bayesian analysis 117
Bayesian information criterion *see* BIC
Bentler, P.M. 43
BIC 44, 310; in IRT models 183, 195, 200, 208, 213, 215–16, 230–1; in mixture models 152, 159–60, 168, 175
bifactor model 245–7, 310
BMPAT 237–8, 310
Bock, R.D. 234
Bollen, K.A. 41, 113, 114–15
Bollen–Stine correction 50–1
bootstrap 41
bootstrap likelihood ratio test 152, 159
bootstrap model goodness of fit test; dichotomous IRT models 190, 205, 211; polytomous IRT models 221, 224, 227
bootstrap modified parallel analysis test (BMPAT) 237–8, 310

Cai, L. 234
CFA *see* confirmatory factor analysis

CFI 42, 310
chi-square difference statistic (χ_Δ^2) 43–4, 77–8, 86, 310
chi-square goodness of fit test 15–16, 40–1, 152, 310
chi-square statistic (χ^2) 189
classical test theory (CTT), in R 178–80
classification and regression trees (CART) 124–5
Cohen, J. 101
Cohen's d 101
collinearity 119
commands; entering 1–2; executing 2; key 299–309
comment line indicators 66, 283
communality 18
comparative fit index (CFI) 42, 310
compensatory 2 PL MIRT model 242–5
conditional-covariance-based methods 234
configural invariance (CI) 84, 310
confirmatory factor analysis (CFA) 9, 37–56; EFA vs. 10, 37–8; extension into structural models *see* structural equation modeling; fitting CFA models using lavaan 45–56; model fit assessment 40–5; model parameter estimation 39–40; multiple groups *see* multiple groups confirmatory factor analysis; two- vs. three- vs. four-factor models 53
Cronbach's α 179
CTT *see* classical test theory

data; handling 1–8; missing 5–6; types 6–7
data frame 27, 311
data simulations 279–97; for IRT 289–94; for LCA 295–7; for SEM 280–9
de Ayala, R.J. 216, 218, 238–9

DETECT 234

diagonally weighted least squares (DWLS)
40, 62, 78, 89, 119, 123, 311

dichotomous IRT 180–216; assessing
absolute model fit for Rasch model 189–91;
comparing model fit 213–16; fitting 1 PL
model in R 193–9; fitting 2 PL model
in R 199–207; fitting 3 PL model in R
207–13; fitting Rasch model in R 180–9;
obtaining latent trait estimates for Rasch
model 191–3

differential item functioning (DIF) 247–65,
311; logistic regression (LR) for detecting
255–60; Lord's chi-square test for detecting
262–5; Mantel–Haenzel statistic (MH)
for detecting 250–5; Mokken scaling
265–71, 313; nonparametric IRT modeling
265–71; nonuniform 247–8, 314; Raju's
area method for detecting 260–2, 263;
uniform 247–8

difficulty; item 178, 312;
multidimensional 242

DIMTEST 234

direct effects 66, 70, 71, 75, 77

directionality 61, 74–5

discrimination; item 178, 181, 312;
multidimensional 242

DWLS see diagonally weighted least squares

Ebel's criteria 179

Educational Testing Service (ETS) Δ 250

EFA see exploratory factor analysis

effect sizes 101

eigenvalue greater than 1 criterion see
Kaiser's Little Jiffy

EIS 274–5

endogenous variables 59, 61, 311

exogenous variables 59, 61, 311

expectation maximization (EM)
algorithm 234

expected item score (EIS) 274–5

exploratory factor analysis (EFA) 9–35;
CFA vs. 10, 37–8; factor extraction 13;
factor rotation 13–14, 311; fitting EFA
models using fa 27–32; fitting EFA models
using factanal 17–26; for item response
data 234–7; optimal number of factors
determination 14–17; PCA vs. 33, 34

factor analysis 9, 311 see also confirmatory
factor analysis; exploratory factor analysis

factor extraction 13

factor invariance (FI) 84–5, 311

factor loadings 12, 311

factor rotation 13–14, 311

Ferdous, A.A. 238–9

fit; absolute see absolute fit; relative see
relative fit

function call 18

functions 2–3; alpha 179–80; as.factor 6;
as.numeric 6; difMH 250; f1 285; fa 27;
factanal 27; ggplot 136–8, 148; glm 171;
growth 139; item.exam 178; ltm 200;
mardia 45; na.omit 5; nScree 22; OpenMx
126–7; plotnScree 22; poLCA 155, 156;
poLCA.simdata 295; princomp 33; prune.
semtree 130–1; rasch 182, 292; refit 171;
semtree 126, 127, 130; simIrt 291–2, 293;
systemfit 115–16; unidimTest 237

GCM see growth curve modeling

general factors 245

generalized partial credit model (GPCM)
225–7, 311; comparing with other
models 229–31

graded response model (GRM) 227–9, 311;
comparing with other models 230–1

growth curve modeling (GCM) 134–50, 312;
assessing change over time in multiple
variables simultaneously 145–9; fitting
linear GCMs in R 136–41; fitting nonlinear
GCMs in R 141–3; including covariates in
GCMs 143–5

Hancock, G.R. 101

Hau, K.T. 118

Henry, N.W. 176

Horn, J.L. 16, 237

Hu, L. 43

ICCs see item characteristic curves

IICs see item information curves

indirect effects 66, 70, 71, 75, 77, 81

information indices 44 see also AIC;
BIC; SBIC

instrumental variables (IVs) 114–16

invariance assessment 84; steps in 85–7

IRT see item response theory

item characteristic curves (ICCs) 312;
dichotomous IRT models 184–6, 194–5,
201–2, 209–10; polytomous IRT models
220–2, 223–4, 226, 228–9

item difficulty 178, 312

item discrimination 178, 181, 312

item information 185–7, 312

item information curves (IICs); dichotomous
IRT models 185–7, 194–7, 201–5, 209–12;
polytomous IRT models 221–2, 223–4,
226, 228–9

item location 217

item purification 250
item response theory (IRT) 177–8, 312; assessing local independence 238–41; assessing unidimensionality 233–8; data simulations for 289–94; and factor analysis parameters 177; foundational assumptions 181; kernel smoothing 271–5; nonparametric IRT modeling 265–71 *see also* dichotomous IRT; differential item functioning; multidimensional IRT (MIRT) models; polytomous IRT

Jöreskog, K.G. 113
Judd, C.M. 118

Kaiser's Little Jiffy 15, 22
Kenny, D.A. 118
kernel smoothing 312; IRT 271–5
key R commands 299–309
Kim, D. 238–9
Kline, R.B. 61
KR20 statistic 179–80

language achievement assessment 136–49
latent class analysis (LCA) 152–4, 312 *see also* LCA models
latent class regression models *see* mixture regression models
latent growth curve modeling *see* growth curve modeling
latent means, comparison 95–101
latent variables; endogenous 59, 61, 311; exogenous 59, 61, 311; interactions among 117–24
law school admissions test (LSAT) 242, 245
Lazarsfeld, P.F. 176
LCA 152–4, 312
LCA models 151–69; covariates in 153, 164; data simulation for 295–7; fitting basic LCA in R 154–64; fitting LCA model with covariates in R 164–9; latent class regression *see* mixture regression models; standard 153
libraries 2–3, 312; boot 239–40; catIrt 289–90, 291, 293; difR 249, 256; flexmix 169–75; ggplot 136; KernSmoothIRT 272, 274; lavaan 47, 136, 283, 287, 312; ltm 182, 191, 200, 207, 215, 219, 223, 225, 228, 237, 292, 312; mirt 234, 243; mokken 267, 270; nFactors 22; poLCA 155, 159, 295, 314; psych 20, 27, 45; psychometric 178, 180; Rcmdr 7; semtree 130; sirt 239
likelihood ratio goodness of fit test 152, 215–16, 312

local independence 181, 312; assessing 238–41
logistic regression (LR); for DIF detection 255–60; models 153
Lord, F.M. 214, 262
Lord's chi-square test for DIF detection 262–5
Lo–Rendall–Rubin test 152, 159

McGuire, B. 272
Mantel–Haenzel statistic (MH) for DIF detection 250–5
Mardia's test 45–6, 313
Marsh, H.W. 118
Masters, G.N. 217
mastery achievement orientation (MAO) 62, 87
mastery approach (MAP) trait 11
mastery avoidant (MAV) trait 11
mathematics achievement test data 178
maximum likelihood (ML) 13, 39, 313
Mazza, A. 272
MBRP 124, 125
measurement invariance (MI) 84–5, 313
measurement models 60, 313; fitting in R 62–5
mediator effect 66
Meijer, R.R. 266
metric invariance 84–5
Metropolis–Hastings approach 234
MGCFA *see* multiple groups confirmatory factor analysis
MH chi-square test 254–5
MIMIC model 101–9, 143, 313; path diagram 101, 105; using lavaan 102–9
MIRT models *see* multidimensional IRT (MIRT) models
missing data 5–6
mixture models 151–76, 313 *see also* LCA models
mixture regression models 154, 313; fitting in R 169–75; simple linear 154
model-based recursive partitioning (MBRP) 124, 125
model invariance, assessment *see* invariance assessment
moderation models 117–18
modified parallel analysis 237
Mokken, R.J. 266–7
Mokken scaling 265–70, 313
monotonicity 181, 313
Monte Carlo simulations 279, 313 *see also* data simulation
multidimensional difficulty 242
multidimensional discrimination 242

multidimensional IRT (MIRT) models
241–2, 313; bifactor model 245–7, 310;
compensatory 2 PL 242–5; fitting in
R 241–7
multilevel models 116, 117
multinomial logistic regression model 169
multiple groups confirmatory factor analysis
(MGCFA) 84, 95; using lavaan 87–94
multiple groups SEM 83–5, 313
multiple indicators multiple causes model *see*
MIMIC model
multivariate analysis of variance
(MANOVA) 134

Nering, M.L. 238–9
nonnormed fit index (NNFI) *see*
Tucker–Lewis index
nonrecursive SEM 112–17, 314
non-referent indicators 115
nonuniform DIF 247–8, 314

oblique rotation 14
OCCs 272–4
one-parameter logistic (1PL) model 181,
314; comparing with other models 214–16;
fitting in R 193–9
Optimal Coordinates approach 23
option characteristic curves (OCCs) 272–4
orthogonal rotation 14
other-oriented perfectionism (OTHER) 78

parallel analysis 16, 20–3, 237
partial credit model (PCM) 314; 1PL
222–5; comparing model fit 229–31;
generalized (GPCM) 225–7, 311; Rasch
version 217–22
partial invariance 95, 314
partially mediated models 62, 65, 78
pattern invariance 84–5
PCM *see* partial credit model
perfectionism 60, 81; other-oriented
(OTHER) 78; self-oriented (SOP) 62
performance approach (PAP) trait 11
performance avoidant (PAV) trait 11
polytomous IRT 217–31; comparing model
fit 229–31; generalized partial credit model
(GPCM) 225–7, 311; graded response
model (GRM) 227–9, 311; partial credit
model (PCM) (1PL) 222–5; partial credit
model (PCM) (Rasch) 217–22
principal axis factoring (PAF) 13, 20
principal components analysis (PCA) 33–4;
EFA vs. 33, 34

product indicator method 118–19
pseudo-chance 207, 314
Punzo, A. 272
purpose in life survey 154–69, 267

quasi-maximum likelihood 117

R; Commander 7–8, 314; commands *see*
commands; console 1–2, 3; data *see* data;
functions *see* functions; libraries *see*
libraries; packages 2–3, 4; reading data
into 3–5; scripts 1–2
Raju, N.S. 260
Raju's area method for detecting DIF
260–2, 263
Ramsay, J.O. 271
random number generating seed 285
Rasch model 181, 314; assessing absolute
model fit for 189–91; data simulation for
289–93; fitting in R 180–9; obtaining latent
trait estimates for 191–3
recursive SEM 112, 314
referent indicator variables 113–14
relative efficiency (RE) 214, 230, 314
relative fit 189
repeated measures ANOVA 134
repeated measures MANOVA 134
root mean square error of approximation
(RMSEA) 42, 314
rootograms 172, 173, 174, 314
RStudio 7–8

Stine, R. 41
sample-size-adjusted BIC (SBIC) 44, 315
sample size planning 279
Satorra–Bentler correction 41, 50
SBIC 44, 315
scalability coefficients 266–7
scalar invariance (SI) 85, 315
scale development 270
Scree plot 15, 22–3
self-confirmation bias 61
self-oriented perfectionism (SOP) 62
SEM *see* structural equation modeling
sensitive measurement 266
simple structure (Thurstone's) 13–14, 315
specific factor 245
standardized coefficient, for interaction
term 124
standardized root mean square residual
(SRMR) 43, 315
strict factor invariance (SFI) 85, 315
strong factorial invariance 85

structural equation modeling (SEM); data simulations for 280–9; fitting alternative SEMs 71–81; fitting measurement model in R 62–5; fitting structural model in R 65–71; foundations 59–81; for multiple groups *see* multiple groups SEM; nonrecursive 112–17, 314; recursive 112, 314; substantive theory importance in 60–2
structural equation model trees (SEM Trees) 124–31
structural model 65–6, 315; fitting in R 65–71

test information curves (TICs) 187–8, 196–7, 203–4, 211–12
theta (θ) parameter 177, 218; 1PL distribution of 198–9; 2PL distribution of 206; 3PL distribution of 213
three-parameter logistic (3PL) model 177, 207, 315; comparing with other models 214–16; data simulation for 293–4; fitting in R 207–13
thresholds 218, 315
Thurstone, L.L. 13–14

Thurstone's simple structure 13–14, 315
total information 187–9
t-test 95–6
Tucker–Lewis index (TLI) 42–3, 315
two-parameter logistic (2PL) model 200, 315; comparing with other models 214–16; fitting in R 199–207
two-stage least squares (2SLS) 113–16, 315

unidimensionality 181, 315; assessing 227–32
uniform DIF 247–8

variable centering 119

weak factorial invariance 84–5
weighted least squares (WLS) 39–40, 316
Wen, Z. 118

Yen, W.M. 239
Yen's Q_3 statistic 239, 316
Youth Risk Behavior Survey 218–31
Yuan–Bentler correction 50–1